THE

BORDER WARFARE OF NEW YORK,

DURING THE REVOLUTION;

OR, THE

ANNALS OF TRYON COUNTY.

BY WILLIAM W. CAMPBELL.

"The whole confederacy, except a little more than half of the Oneidas, took up arms against us. They hung like the scythe of death upon the rear of our settlements, and their deeds are inscribed with the scalping-knife and the tomahawk, in characters of blood, on the fields of Wyoming and Cherry Valley, and on the banks of the Mohawk."
DE WITT CLINTON.

NEW YORK:
BAKER & SCRIBNER,
145 Nassau Street, and 36 Park Row.

1849.

Facsimile Reprint

Published 1992 By

HERITAGE BOOKS, INC.
1540E Pointer Ridge Place Bowie, Maryland 20716
(301) 390-7709

ISBN 1-55613-612-9

HON. WILLIAM KENT.

My dear Sir: Eighteen years ago the following "Annals of Tryon County" were dedicated to your illustrious father. He, who was regarded by you with such deep filial affection, and who was the object of veneration to his friends, has recently, after a long sojourn upon the earth, been gathered to his fathers in peace. It is a source of unaffected gratification to me, that I was permitted, when a young man, to form his acquaintance, and from that period down to the close of his life, continued to share somewhat of his notice and his friendship. To you, his son, my early professional instructor and my friend, I now present this new edition of a work, which, though it has but little intrinsic merit, either in its style or arrangement, possesses, perhaps, some interest, from the fact that it was the pioneer history of the border wars of our native State. For me it has a melancholy interest, because all the actors in the Revolutionary drama who were living at the time of its first appearance, in 1831, and from whose lips the personal narratives were gathered, have gone the way of all the living, and are now numbered with the dead. Of the then aged men and women scattered along the valley of the Mohawk and the head-waters of the Susquehanna, with whom it was my good fortune to sit down and listen to the stories of their trials and their triumphs, not one survives.

The materials were, at the time, collected from the manuscripts of the Committee of Safety on the borders, from the correspondence of the principal actors, and from the oral statements of those who survived to my day. While several large volumes have since been written, covering the same ground, it is believed that the Annals, as originally drawn and published by me, contained all the principal events which occurred upon the frontier of New York during the Revolution, and were in all essential particulars correct. When first published, the whole history of the border wars of New York scarcely made up a page in any then existing historical work. As this book was the first, and was prepared from materials in a great degree new, succeeding writers on the same subject drew largely upon it, and, in some instances, made extensive extracts without credit or reference. My first intention was, in presenting a new edition, to revise and alter, but upon reflection I determined to leave the work substantially in its original form. Since its first publication I have at various times examined many additional documents, and prepared articles which throw some new light upon portions of the work, and which tend to confirm its positions and statements. The original text will be left as it was, and these articles, even at the expense of some repetition, will be inserted in the Appendix. Such is the "Memoir of General James Clinton," read before the New York Historical Society in 1837; also, the article on the "Direct agency of the British Government in the employment of the Indians in the

Revolutionary war," read before the same Society in 1845, and the "Centennial Address," delivered at my native town of Cherry Valley, in 1840.

The novelist and the poet have embellished and adorned the annals of our brave and patriotic borderers. My ambition was to rescue from oblivion, materials for the future historian of the Empire State. Like the wandering Arab, who, as he passes, lays a stone upon his father's grave, to mark the place of his sepulture, I bring my contribution, my rough block, in the hope that it may be hewn into shape and polished by others, and form a part of that historic column, upon which our children and their descendants may read the record of the struggles and the patriotism of those ancestors, to whom we and they are and will be indebted for our liberty and our Republic.

I am, respectfully, your friend,

WILLIAM W. CAMPBELL.

NEW YORK, January 1st, 1849.

TO THE

HON. JAMES KENT, LL.D.

LATE CHIEF JUSTICE AND CHANCELLOR OF THE STATE OF NEW YORK,
AND PRESIDENT OF THE NEW YORK HISTORICAL SOCIETY,

THE FOLLOWING PAGES ARE RESPECTFULLY DEDICATED.

"Historia, testis temporum et nuntia veritatis, præclari facinoris famam, posteritatis memoria tradet."

That the evening of your life may be as serene and happy as its meridian has been useful and distinguished, is the sincere wish of

THE AUTHOR.

NEW YORK, 1831

PREFACE TO FIRST EDITION.

In presenting this volume of Annals to the public, I would wish to say a few words as to its origin. It is a right which every reader of a book, purporting to be a record of facts, possesses, and may exercise, to examine its authenticity, and to demand whence the author has drawn his conclusions. In the fall of 1830 a society was formed in the village of Cherry Valley for literary purposes generally, but especially for collecting facts illustrative of the natural and civil history of that section of country. I had been often requested to collect and imbody the events of its civil history, and was again solicited to prosecute this branch of inquiry. I at first contemplated writing only the history of Cherry Valley. Born and reared in that valley, I had, from early life, been in some degree familiar with the incidents which had occurred there. They were interwoven with my earliest impressions; and I entered upon the business of arranging and compiling them with an interest which the subject, perhaps, did not merit. Upon examination, I found its revolutionary history connected with that of the valley of the Mohawk, and thinking I might, from the documents and information which I had obtained, throw some light upon the comparatively imperfect history of that valley, during that interesting period, I dropped the original plan, and adopted the one which I have followed in the subsequent pages. I have, however, dwelt more particularly upon the events which occurred in Cherry Valley; not that they were more important or interesting, but partly from reasons before mentioned, and partly for the reason that an accurate account of the minute transactions of that settlement was immediately within my reach, and upon the authenticity of which I could rely with the greatest confidence.

Some of the written documents were obtained in the office of the Secretary of State, but most of them from the venerable John Frey, one of the chairmen of the Tryon County committee, and who is now standing almost upon the brow of a hundred years—a monument of other days. Several gentlemen, relatives or descendants of those who acted conspicuous parts, have very politely furnished me with original papers. To all of them I would here most sincerely tender my thanks. Some of the accounts, merely traditionary, have been obtained from persons conversant and on intimate terms with the actors; but most of them from those who could say to me, "pars magna fui." Under these circumstances, it is possible there may be errors. I have, however, in all cases, compared the statements where they varied; and I flatter myself that I have generally arrived at the truth. I may be mistaken; but I have written nothing which I do not believe to be true.

WILLIAM W. CAMPBELL.

New York, August 16th, 1831.

CONTENTS.

INTRODUCTION,

CHAPTER IV.

CHAPTER V.

CHAPTER VI.

CHAPTER VII.

CHAPTER VIII.

CHAPTER IX.

CHAPTER X

CHAPTER XI.

APPENDIX.

INTRODUCTION.

New York, at the time of its discovery and settlement by the Europeans, was inhabited by a race of men distinguished, above all the other aborigines of this Continent, for their intelligence and prowess. Five distinct and independent tribes, speaking a language radically the same, and practicing similar customs, had united in forming a confederacy which, for durability and power, was unequalled in Indian history. They were the Mohawks, Oneidas, Onondagas, Cayugas, and Senecas, called the Iroquois by the French, and the Five Nations by the English. In cases of great emergency, each tribe or nation acted separately and independently; but a general council usually assembled at Onondaga, near the centre of their territory, and determined upon peace or war, and all other matters which regarded the interests of the whole. The powers of this council appear to have been not much dissimilar to those of the United States Congress under the old confederation.

Their language, though guttural, was sonorous. Their orators studied euphony in their words and in their arrangement. Their graceful attitudes and gestures, and their flowing sentences, rendered their discourses, if not always eloquent, at least highly impressive. An erect and commanding figure, with a blanket thrown loosely over the shoulder, with his naked arm raised, and addressing in impassioned strains a group of similar persons sitting upon the ground around him, would, to use the illustration of an early historian of this State, give no faint picture of Rome in her early days.*

They were very methodical in their harangues. When in conference with other nations, at the conclusion of every important sentence of the opposite speaker, a sachem gave a small stick to the orator who was to reply, charging him at the same time to remember it. After a short consultation with the others, he was enabled to repeat most of the discourse, which he answered article by article.†

These nations were distinguished for their prowess in war, as well as for their sagacity and eloquence in council. War was their delight. Believing it to be the most honorable employment of men, they infused into their children in early life high ideas of military glory. They carried their arms into Canada, across the Connecticut, to the banks of the Mississippi, and almost to the Gulf of Mexico. Formidable by their numbers and their skill, they excited respect and awe in the most powerful tribes, and exacted tribute and obedience from the weak.

In 1608, the first efficient settlement was made in Canada by Governor Champlain, who founded Que-

---

* Smith's History of New York. † Ibid.

bec. At this time the Five Nations were waging a desperate war with the Hurons and Algonquins, who inhabited a part of that province. Champlain, unfortunately for the colony, entered into an alliance with the latter tribes, and by furnishing them with men and fire-arms, enabled them to gain a temporary ascendency.* The confederates, who had always been victorious, and who considered the Hurons and Algonquins as little better than vassals, could not brook this defeat. They applied to, and courted the friendship of the Dutch, who found their way up the Hudson River, and established themselves at Albany, soon after the settlement of Quebec. From them they obtained arms and munitions, and soon regained the influence and power which they had lost. This opportune arrival and assistance of the Dutch, together with their mild, concilatory manners, endeared them to the Five Nations, who afterward looked up to them for advice and direction in their own affairs, and protected and fought for them with cheerfulness and courage. But the interference of the French aroused the indignation of these haughty warriors; for almost a century they harassed their infant colonies, and visited with a dreadful vengeance both the authors of their disgrace and their descendants. This, if not the iron, was the golden age of the Iroquois. During this period, the hardy German passed up the Mohawk in his light canoe, and penetrated into the remote bounds of their territory, where he exchanged his

* Vide Edinb. Encyclopedia—Art. America.

merchandise and munitions of war for the peltry of the Indians.

In 1664 the province of New York was surrendered to the English by Peter Stuyvesant, the last of the Dutch governors. The English, perceiving the importance of being on friendly terms with the Indians, exerted themselves to preserve that good understanding which had existed between the latter and the Dutch. Conventions were frequently called at Albany, at which the governors met and conferred with them; presents were distributed liberally, and no opportunity was neglected to impress them with ideas of the wealth and power of the English monarch. The French were not idle. Jealous of the growing power and influence of the English colonies, and desirous of monopolizing the Indian trade, they adopted various plans to detach the Iroquois from their alliance with the English. They endeavored to break up the confederacy, that they might conquer the nations in detail. They attacked the English, in hopes that, by gaining some splendid victories over them, they would convince the Indians of the weakness of their allies, and of the strength of their enemies. They sent missionaries among them, more desirous of making allies for France than converts to Christianity; in this they partially succeeded; and in 1671, persuaded the Caughnawagas to remove from their settlements on the Mohawk, and to establish themselves in Canada.

In 1688 the vengeance of the Five Nations was

---

* Memoirs of an American Lady.

again aroused by a stratagem of the Dinondadies, a tribe at war with them, and in alliance with France. The Dinondadies killed several of their ambassadors while going to hold a conference in Canada, and falsely pretended that they had been informed of their journey by the French governor. Incensed at what they considered a great breach of faith, about twelve hundred warriors of the Five Nations landed at Montreal on the 26th July, 1688, and killed about a thousand French—men, women, and children, and carried away twenty-six prisoners, whom they afterward burned alive. The French retaliated for these aggressions by making incursions into the Indian country, and burning their villages.

In 1690 the French made an attack upon Schenectady; took the place by surprise, as it was in the dead of winter, and no danger was apprehended; the whole village was destroyed; about sixty of the inhabitants were killed, and most of the remainder perished, as they fled naked through the snow toward Albany.*

This was the first intimation the colony of New York received that a war was meditated on the part of the French; it was the more perfidious, as negotiations were then pending in Europe for the purpose of settling the claims of the two governments in America. During this war the confederates remained attached to the English, and rendered important services by harassing the frontiers of their enemies. About 1701 a general treaty of peace was made be-

---

* See Appendix—Note A.

tween the French and Five Nations, which put an end to these long and afflicting wars, in which both parties had been sufferers. In the early part of this century, (about 1712,) the Monecons, or Tuscaroras, a tribe of Indians living in the Carolinas, made war upon the inhabitants of those colonies; they were vanquished by the colonists, and forced to abandon their country; they are thought to have been allies of the Five Nations in some of their southern expeditions. From a similarity in their language, the confederates supposed them derived from a common origin; they received them into the confederacy, assigned them a section of their territory to dwell in; after this they were called the Six Nations. The Tuscaroras never possessed the energy and courage of the other confederates. Tradition says that they were obliged to wear a woman's pocket for a tobacco pouch, as a mark of their effeminacy and want of courage.

From the commencement of this century down to 1750, the French missionaries and agents were very successful. That body of men, the French Jesuits, who by their zeal put to shame many men engaged in a better cause, entered upon this field of labor with great ardor. At one time they doffed the clerical habit, and putting on the Indian garb, accompanied the warriors on distant and hazardous expeditions; and at another, they astonished their savage audience with the splendid and imposing rites and ceremonies of the Romish church. They spoke in glowing terms of the resources and magnificence of *le grand Monarque*, as they termed the King of France.

They obtained permission for the French to build forts in their territory; and in short, when the last French war broke out in 1754, the four western tribes went over to the French, and took up the hatchet against the English. This war terminated by the complete subjection of Canada, and the annexing it to the British dominions. The Indians,* however,

---

* In 1774 Governor William Tryon, the royal governor of the province of New York, made a return to the British government, embracing the general condition of the province, its civil history, political and judicial, the general features of the country, rivers, mountains, cities, forts, population, commerce; in short, giving a complete view of the province. This document is among the papers at Albany, obtained by Mr. Brodhead, and ought to be published at length. It was the closing account of the *province* of New York, which was soon thereafter to give place to the *state*.

One of the questions relates to the Indians, and was answered by Gov. Tryon, upon information derived from Sir William Johnson, and the statement may be implicitly relied on. It shows of course the numbers and situation of the Indians at the commencement of the war.

"What number of Indians have you, and how are they inclined?"

"The Indians who formerly possessed Nassau or Long Island, and that part of this province which lies below Albany, are now reduced to a small number, and are in general so scattered and dispersed, and so addicted to wandering, that no certain account can be obtained of them. They are the remnants of the tribes Montocks and others of Long Island, Wappingers of Dutchess County, Esopus, Papagonk, &c. in Ulster County, and a few Skachticokes. These tribes have generally been denominated River Indians, and consist of about *three hundred fighting men.*

"They speak a language radically the same, and are understood by the Delawares, being originally of the same race. Most of these people at present profess Christianity, and as far as in their power adopt our customs. The greater part of them attended the army during the late war, but not with the same *reputation as those who are still deemed hunters.*

witnessing the defeat of the French, had many of them returned, before the close of the war, to the English, by whom they were again received as allies.

"The Mohawks, the first in rank of the Six Nation confederacy, though now much reduced in numbers, originally occupied the country westward from Albany to the German Flats, a space of about ninety miles, and had many towns, but having at different times been prevailed on to dispose of their lands, they have little property left except to the northward, and are reduced to two villages on the Mohawk river, and a few families at Schoharie. The lower Mohawks are in number about one hundred and eighty-five, and the upper, or those of Canajoharie, two hundred and twenty one, making together four hundred and six. This nation hath always been warm in their attachment to the English, and on this account suffered great loss during the late war.

"The nation beyond and to the westward of the Mohawk, is the Oneidas. The villages where they reside, including Onoaughquaga, are just beyond the Indian line or boundary established at Fort Stanwix, in 1768, and their property within that line, except to the northward, has been sold. This nation consists of at least fifteen hundred, and *are firmly attached to the English.*

"The other nations of that confederacy, and who live further beyond the Indian line, are the Onondagas, Cayugas, Senecas and Tuscaroras, and are well *inclined to the British interest.* The whole Six Nations consist of about *two thousand fighting men*, and their number of souls according to their latest returns at least *ten thousand;* the Seneca nation amounting alone to one half that number."

"What is the strength of the neighboring Indians?"

"The Indians north of this province near Montreal, with those living on the river St. Lawrence, near the 45th degree of northern latitude, form a body of about three thousand five hundred. They are in alliance with, and held in great esteem by the rest; are good warriors, and have behaved well since they became allies to the English previous to the reduction of Canada.

"The tribes of Indians within the province of Massachusetts Bay, and the colonies of Connecticut and Rhode Island, &c. are under similar circumstances with those denominated River Indians; and the Stock-

Major General William Johnson* rendered very important services during this war; his complete victory over Baron Dieskau, Sept. 1757, at the head of Lake George, and the capture of Fort Niagara by him, had aided materially in bringing the war to a successful termination. He was created a baronet, and Parliament voted him five thousand pounds sterling; he was also appointed general superintendent of Indian affairs: he had settled upon the Mohawk in 1734, having emigrated there from Ireland, and thus rose to rank and affluence. Stern, determined in purpose, at times even arbitrary, sagacious and

---

bridge Indians, living on the eastern borders of New York, may be considered as within it, as they formerly claimed the lands near Albany, and still hold up some claim in that vicinity. They served as a corps during the late war, and are in number about three hundred.

"Of the Susquehanna tribes many have retired further westward, among which are some not well affected to the British government. They are all dependents and allies of the Six Nations.

"Within the department of Sir William Johnson, His Majesty's Superintendent of Indian affairs, there are twenty-five thousand four hundred and twenty fighting men, and may be about one hundred and thirty thousand Indians in the whole, extending westward to the Mississippi."

It is thus seen that the Indian warriors of the Six Nations were as numerous as the able-bodied men of Tryon County, while the warriors under the superintendence of Sir William Johnson, and afterwards under that of Col. Guy Johnson, were equal nearly to the militia of the whole province. The whole body of warriors could be called out if necessary. Being under the pay of England, and having no domestic labors, and war being their delight, it was evident that it would be a fearful event to the Colonies if the Indians took part in the controversy.

* See Appendix—Note B.

penetrating, but when necessary, urbane and conciliatory in his manners, he was eminently qualified for the station to which he was appointed. No person has ever exerted an equal influence over those unlettered children of the forest. He lived at Johnstown, where he had a beautiful residence, and was surrounded by the Mohawks. The Indians looked up to him as their father, paying the utmost deference to his advice, and consulting him on all occasions. Out of compliment to them, he frequently wore in winter their dress; he received them cordially at his house, where sometimes hundreds of them assembled. So great was the respect they had for him, that though the house contained many valuables, nothing was purloined from it, even in their carousals. Being a widower, he received into his family an Indian maiden, a sister of the celebrated sachem Joseph Thayendanegea, called the Brant.

The influence of Sir William continued until his death, about the commencement of the revolutionary war, when the principal events took place, which I design hereafter to relate.

CHAPTER I.

"Time rolls his ceaseless course. The race of yore,
Who danced our infancy upon their knee,
And told our marvelling boyhood legend's store
Of their strange ventures happ'd by land or sea;
How they are blotted from the things that be!
How few, all weak, and withered of their force,
Wait on the verge of dark eternity,
Like stranded wrecks, the tide returning hoarse,
To sweep them from our sight; Time rolls his ceaseless course."

It is always a pleasing task to rescue from oblivion the names, and to record the deeds, of those individuals, however humble, who were the pioneers of our country, who purchased the wilderness from the savage, and afterward disputed the dominion over it with the wolf and the bear.

The pleasure is increased, and a deep and thrilling interest is awakened, as we trace out those individuals ardently engaged on the side of their country in that revolution which terminated in our entire independence; in the planting of that tree of liberty, whose beautiful foliage and wide-spreading branches have excited universal admiration, and a scion from which may yet be engrafted into all the nations of the east.

This is the object of the following imperfect sketch, which, if it add little to the materials for the future history of our State, may be a source of some pleasure and satisfaction to those connected with the actors themselves; and to the survivors, those venerable relics of other times, a few of whom have come down to us, but who, one by one, are daily dropping into eternity.

In 1738 a patent for 8000 acres of land, lying about ten miles south of the Mohawk River, and fifty-two west from Albany, was granted by George Clark, then lieutenant governor, with the consent of the council of the then province of New York, to John Lindesay, Jacob Roseboom, Lendert Gansevoort, and Sybrant Van Schaick. This patent is situated in the extreme north-eastern part of the now county of Otsego, embracing a part of the town and village of Cherry Valley. The face of the country generally, in this county, is uneven; a great number of valleys run nearly north and south, in which are Otsego and Schuyler Lakes, and through which flow several streams, forming the eastern branch of the Susquehanna. These valleys are bounded on the north by a ridge of table land, in which many of the smaller streams take their rise, and from whose northern declivity flow several unimportant tributaries of the Mohawk; there are indentations or passes at the northern extremities of all these valleys; differing, however, in their elevations and in the distances between the sources of the tributary waters of the two rivers. None of these valleys are very extensive, but the soil is fertile, and the rolling land between them produces all kinds of grain, and furnishes excellent pasturage in great abundance. The valley, through which runs Cherry Valley Creek, is about sixteen miles in length, and varies from one quarter to a mile in breadth; at the village it is 1335 feet, and where it terminates in its pass about a mile north, 1418 feet, above tide water. Chains of highland stretch along both sides of this valley; that on the east may properly be considered a spur of the Catskill. It terminates abruptly about three miles north-east of the village, in Mount Independence, from whose top the land slopes gradually to the north; its summit is more than 2000 feet above tide water, and 1700 above the valley of the Mohawk; from hence a beautiful prospect opens in some directions nearly one hundred miles in extent. The Mohawk valley, with a large portion of the northern part of the State, is spread out as a map; while far in the north-east are dimly seen the tops of the Green Mountains, as they mingle with the horizon.*

Early in the eighteenth century, nearly three thousand German Palatinates emigrated to this country under the patronage of Queen Anne; most of them settled in Pennsylvania; a few made their way, in 1713, from Albany, over the Helleberg, to Schoharie Creek, and under the most discouraging circumstances succeeded in effecting a settlement upon the rich alluvial lands bordering upon that stream. Small colonies from here, and from Albany and Schenectady, established themselves in various places along the Mohawk; and in 1722 had extended as far up as the German Flats, near where stands the village of Herkimer; but all the inhabitants were found in the

* Upon this northern slope, and about three miles from Mount Independence, is built the famous "Pavilion" at Sharon Springs, from the piazza of which the prospect is both beautiful and grand.

neighborhood of these streams; none had ventured out in that unbroken wilderness which lay to the south and west of these settlements.

Mr. Lindesay, having obtained an assignment from the three other patentees to himself and Governor Clark, in 1739 caused the patent to be surveyed and subdivided into lots, and chose for himself the farm afterward successively owned by Mr. John Wells and Judge Hudson, and gave to it the name of Lindesay's Bush. In the following summer he left New York with his family, consisting of his wife, and father-in-law, Mr. Congreve, a lieutenant in the British army, and a few domestics, and settled upon his farm. He was a Scotch gentleman of some fortune and distinction, having held several offices under government, and anticipated much pleasure from a residence in this high and rolling country, whose valleys, and hills, and lakes, would constantly remind him of the wild and romantic scenery of his native land. A luxuriant growth of beach and maple, interspersed with the wild cherry, covered the valley, and extended along up the sides of the hills, whose tops were crowned with clusters of evergreen; elk and deer were found here in great numbers, as were bears, wolves, beavers, and foxes; it was a favorite hunting-ground of the Mohawks, who erected their cabins near some little spring, and hunted their game upon the mountains. Mr. Lindesay, as well as all the early settlers, found it important to cultivate their friendship; he received them into his house, and treated them with such hospitality as circumstances would permit; this kindness was not lost upon the high-minded savages, one of whom gave proof of no ordinary friendship during the first winter after his removal to Lindesay's Bush. Whatever of happiness and independence Mr. Lindesay may have looked forward to, he knew little of the privations of the settlers of a new country, especially such a country as he had selected; his farm was fifteen miles from any settlement, difficult of access from that settlement which was on the Mohawk River, by reason of its elevation above it; and the intervening country was traversed only by an Indian footpath.

In the winter of 1740, the snow fell to a great depth; the paths were filled up; all communication with the settlers upon the Mohawk was stopped; Mr. Lindesay had not made sufficient preparation for such a winter; he had but a scanty supply of provisions; these were almost consumed long before spring; a wretched and lingering death was in prospect for him and his family. At this critical time an Indian came to his house, having travelled upon the snow with snow-shoes; when informed of their situation, he readily undertook to relieve them; he went to the settlements upon the Mohawk, and having procured provisions, returned with them upon his back, and during the remainder of the winter, this faithful child of the forest thus continued to relieve them, and thus preserved the lives of the first inhabitants of our town and county.

In New York, Mr. Lindesay became acquainted with the Rev. Samuel Dunlop, and prevailed upon him to visit his patent, offering him a tract of land of several hundred acres, on condition that he would settle upon it, and would use his influence with his his friends, and persuade them to accompany him. Pleased with the situation, and the generous proprietor of the patent, he accepted of the proposal. He was an Irishman by birth, but had been educated in Edinburgh; had spent several years in the provinces, having travelled over most of those at the south; and at the time of his first acquaintance with Mr. Lindesay, was on a tour through those at the north. He went to Londonderry in New Hampshire, where several of his countrymen were settled, whom he persuaded to remove, and in 1741 David Ramsay, William Gallt, James Campbell, William Dickson, and one or two others, with their families, in all about thirty persons, came and purchased farms, and immediately commenced making improvements upon them. They had emigrated from the north of Ireland several years anterior to their removal here; some of them were originally from Scotland; they were called Scotch Irish—a general name given to the inhabitants of the north of Ireland, many of whom are of Scotch descent; hardy and industrious, inured to toil from their infancy, they were well calculated to sustain the labors necessary in clearing the forest, and fitting it for the abode of civilized man.

The following circumstance gave rise to its name: Mr. Dunlop, engaged in writing some letters, inquired of Mr. Lindesay where he should date them, who proposed the name of a town in Scotland; Mr. Dunlop, pointing to some fine wild cherry-trees, and to the valley, replied, "let us give our place an appropriate name, and call it Cherry Valley," which was readily agreed to; it was for a long time the distinguishing name of a large section of country, south and west. Soon after the arrival of these settlers, measures were taken for the erection of a grist-mill and saw-mill, and a building for a school-house and church. Mr. Dunlop left Ireland under an engagement of marriage with a young lady of that country; and having made the necessary arrangements for his future residence in Cherry Valley, returned to fulfill it. This engagement was conditional; if he did not return in seven years from the time of his departure, it should be optional with her to abide by or put an end to the contract; the time had almost expired; she had heard nothing from him for some time, and supposed him either dead or unfaithful; another offered, was accepted, and the day appointed for the marriage. In the mean time Mr. Dunlop had been driven off the coast of Scotland by a storm: after a detention of several days, he finally made port in Ireland, and hastening on his journey, arrived the day previous; his arrival was as joyful as it was unexpected; he was married, and returned immediately with his wife to Cherry Valley, and entered upon his duties as the first pastor of its little church. A log-house had been erected to the north of Mr. Lindesay's, on the declivity of the little hill upon which his house was situated; where, though possessing little of this world's wealth, they offered up the homage of devout and grateful hearts. Most of the adult inhabitants were members of the church; the clergyman was to receive ten shillings on the hundred acres of land; a mere pittance, by reason of the small number of inhabitants;

but he lived frugally; they made presents to him of the productions of their farms, which, with the avails of his own, afforded him a competent support. In these early days, an excellent state of feeling toward each other prevailed; common danger and common interest united them. In their worship and observances they were very strict. During the ten subsequent years, not more than three or four families had come into the settlement. Among them was Mr. John Wells, grandfather of the late John Wells of New York City. He also was an Irishman, and became a resident in 1743, and in '44 purchased the farm which Mr. Lindesay had selected for himself, and upon which he resided.

Mr. Lindesay was unacquainted with pratical farming, and his property had been expended to little advantage; after struggling several years, he was compelled to abandon his enterprise. The war between France and Great Britain had been, in part, transferred to America, and in 1744 our northern frontier was threatened with an attack by the French and Indians. Reinforcements were ordered to Oswego, and among them, the company of Independent Greens, in which Mr. Congreve was a lieutenant; he resigned his commission in favor of his son-in-law, Mr. Lindesay, who, having spent several years in the service, died in New York, leaving no children. Mr. Wells, a man of amiable disposition, and of great integrity, before there was any officer of justice, was frequently appealed to as the arbiter of any little difference; he was afterwards appointed the first justice of the peace for the town, and one of the judges of Tryon County, which offices he continued to exercise until the time of his death, a little before the breaking out of the Revolution.

Mr. Dunlop, having received a classical education, opened a school for the instruction of boys, who came from the settlements upon the Mohawk, and from Schenectady and Albany. It is worthy of remark, that this was the first grammar-school in the State west of Albany. The boys were received into his house, and constituted a part of his family. The extreme simplicity of the times may be learned from the fact, that they often went into the fields, and there recited their lessons as they followed their instructor about, while engaged in his usual avocations upon his farm; several individuals along the Mohawk, who were afterwards conspicuous in the Revolution, thus received the first rudiments of their education.

The tranquillity which had hitherto prevailed in the settlement was not always to continue; the French by their intrigues had succeeded in alienating the affections of the Indians, who instead of regarding the inhabitants as friends, in many cases looked upon them as intruders. A war colony had been sent out by the Six Nations, which had settled at a place called Oquago, in the now county of Broome, situated on the eastern branch of the Susquehanna. During the Revolution this was a place of general rendezvous for the Six Nations. In the French wars it was composed principally of Mohawks, who remained attached to the English, and who paid their annual visits to Sir William Johnson, to receive their presents. Those who violated the laws were not permitted to share with the others; a few such, fearing to present themselves before Sir William, stayed behind and concerted a plan for destroying this infant settlement. They were to make an attack upon it while the inhabitants were at church on the Sabbath. They were discovered on Sabbath morning, before their arrival at the settlement. The inhabitants, fearing some hostile intention, prepared themselves for defense, taking care to exhibit their arms to the Indians as they approached, who, not wishing to hazard an attack upon them armed, withdrew. But during the last French war, the danger of Indian incursions having become great from the defection of the four western of the Six Nations, and from threatenings of the more distant tribes, a body of eight hundred rangers (so called from their being chiefly employed in ranging the woods) was ordered to be raised for the defense of the county of Tryon, and a company of them, under the command of Capt. M'Kean, stationed at Cherry Valley; some rude fortifications were erected, and during their continuance the settlement was comparatively secure. But previous, and indeed during all the French wars, the inhabitants of this, as of all the other settlements, were frequently called out to repel the French and Indians upon our northern frontier. This service was not only extremely hazardous but burdensome, as they were obliged oftentimes to furnish in addition means of transportation for their own baggage, and also for that of the English. In accordance with the will of the government, they entered upon this service cheerfully. The militia from the northern and western part of the province, lay under Sir William Johnson at Fort Edward, when Fort William Henry was be sieged by the French General Montcalm in 1757. The whole force of General Webb, who was commander at Fort Edward, was about 4000; 3000 were in Fort William Henry under Col. Monro, while the force of Montcalm was little over 8000 French and Indians. The troops of the former were more efficient, and better disciplined than the French and Indians under Montcalm. During the siege and bombardment of Fort William Henry, the provincials at Fort Edward, a distance of only fifteen miles, earnestly demanded to be led to its relief. Gen. Webb after having given permission to Sir William Johnson to lead the men in case they would volunteer, on seeing them all express their willingness and ready to march, broke his promise and ordered them to return to the fort. Indignation was depicted upon every countenance, but indignation and remonstrance were alike unavailing. Fort William Henry, after a vigorous defense by Col. Monro, was surrendered, he having in vain expected that some movement would be made in his favor by Gen. Webb. The terms of surrender were, that the garrison should march out with their arms, but without ammunition, and that a body of the French should guard them to Fort Edward. Montcalm, contrary to stipulation, neglected to send the guard, and thus suffered the Indians to fall upon the garrison, many of whom were barbarously killed, while others stripped of their arms and clothes fled to Fort Edward. Their sufferings deepened that feeling of indignation which the cowardly or treacherous conduct of Webb had created. The interest excited by the subsequent revolution absorbed for a time their thoughts and feelings; but there were individuals in that army under Sir William Johnson, from the little settlement of Cherry Valley, who, when age had furrowed their cheeks and whitened their locks, could scarcely repress their feelings as they recounted the events of that siege.

Col. Monro died soon after very suddenly at Albany, not without suspicions however that unfair means had been used to prevent his preferring a complaint against Gen. Webb to the English government.

During these harassing wars the population of the western part of the province continued to increase. Small settlements had been made in various directions around Cherry Valley. A family of Harpers, who were afterwards distinguished for their courage and ardent attachment to the cause of American liberty, removed from Cherry Valley some years before the Revolution, and established themselves at Harpersfield in the now county of Delaware. The Rev. William Johnstone had succeeded in planting a flourishing little colony on the east side of the Susquehanna, a short distance below the forks of the Unadilla; and several families were scattered through Springfield, Middlefield, then called Newtown-Martin, and Laurens and Otego, called Old England district. The population of Cherry Valley was short of three hundred, and that of the whole county of Tryon but a few thousand, when the Revolution commenced.* This county was taken

* In 1756 the whole population of the province of New York was 96,775. In 1771 it had increased to 168,007; and in 1774 to 182,251.

from Albany County in 1772, and named in honor of William Tryon, then governor of the province. In 1784 it was changed to that of Montgomery. When formed, it embraced all that part of the State lying west of a line running north and south nearly through the centre of the present county of Schoharie. It was divided into five districts, which were again subdivided into smaller districts or precincts. The first, beginning at the east, was the Mohawk district, embracing Fort Hunter, Caughnawaga, Johnstown, and Kingsborough; Canajoharie district, embracing the present town of that name, with all the country south, including Cherry Valley and Harpersfield; Palatine district, north of the river, and including the country known by the same name, with Stone Arabia, &c.; and German Flats and Kingsland districts, being then the most western settlements, and the former now known by the same name. The county buildings were at Johnstown, where, as before mentioned, was the residencc of Sir William Johnson.

In 1771, the population of the county of Albany was 38,829; and as the county of Albany embraced all the northern and western part of the State, reaching from the city of Albany to Niagara, and the eastern part of the county was by far the most populous, it is not probable that the county of Tryon contained more than 10,000 inhabitants. It was estimated in 1774 that the population of the province of New York doubled by natural increase in 20 years. With a population of 182,251, there was estimated a militia force of 32,000; and this was probably a fair estimate of the able-bodied men of New York at the commencement of the Revolution.

CHAPTER II.

Of all the English colonies in North America, none was more loyal than New York; but while her colonial history exhibits her inhabitants professing a warm attachment to the English crown, it presents them also uniformly and zealously maintaining their own inherent rights and privileges. As early as 1691 an act was passed by the colonial Assembly, asserting the grounds of their right of being represented in Assembly; that it was one of the distinguishing liberties of Englishmen, and was not a privilege enjoyed through the grace of the crown; and in 1708 the following resolution, reported by the committee of grievances, was adopted by the Assembly: "Resolved, that the imposing and laying of any monies upon any of her Majesty's subjects of his colony, under any pretence or color whatever, without consent in General Assembly, is a grievance, and a violation of the people's property." From this period down, we find this colony steadily resisting every attempt of her governors to encroach upon her rights, while contributing at the same time freely and largely for their support, and that of the government generally. During the long and harassing French wars, her levies both of men and money, considering her population and resources, were immense. Her territory was the principal scene of action, and she seconded with all her powers the measures adopted by the English to destroy the influence of the French in America: the successful termination of the last of those wars, thus freeing New York from constant alarm and danger; the common privations and sufferings endured by the Provincial and English armies; the numerous connections by marriage formed by the officers of the latter; and the extensive and flourishing commerce of the city, all tended to strengthen the attachment of this province to the mother country.

Still asserting her own exclusive right of taxation, the Stamp Act was opposed in this province with much warmth in 1765, and the first committee of correspondence was chosen; which, communicating with the committees of other provinces, prepared the way for the calling of the Congress which convened in the city of New York the same year. With the repeal of the Stamp Act, the loyalty of the inhabitants again returned; and the aforementioned causes still operating, together with the direct influence supposed to have been exerted by the English ministers, prevented the early adoption by the Assembly of the measures recommended by the Continental Congress of Philadelphia in 1774.

In Tryon County, during the period between the repeal of the Stamp Act and the assembling of Congress in '74, a state of things existed unfavorable to the cause of the Colonies. Sir William Johnson, respected for his talents, and distinguished by the official stations which he had filled with so much credit, had endeared himself, not only to the Indians, who looked up to him as a father, but also to the other inhabitants, who regarded him as the patron of of the County, and who consulted him upon all matters of importance. Drawing towards the close of life, his opinions were those of a sage, and expressed, as they would naturally be, in favor of that government which had so highly honored and enriched him, had a tendency, if not entirely to change, at least to neutralize many individuals, who otherwise would have espoused with warmth the colonial cause. He was supposed, however, to have been actuated more by what he considered his duty to the English government, than governed by his own private opinions. He could but view therefore with regret, those acts of the British Parliament which were goading on the Americans to resistance by force. His sons-in-law, Colonel Guy Johnson, and Colonel Claus, and his son, Sir John Johnson, especially Guy and Sir John, espoused the cause of the crown with great ardor. Possessing large estates and occupying splendid residences along the eastern boundary of the County, they presented a formidable barrier to the transmission and circulation of general intelligence relative to existing differences. If they were not individually possessed of the influence and reputation of Sir William, they made up the deficiency by their zeal and activity. In the early part of the disturbance, they formed sagacious plans to prejudice the Six Nations against the American cause, and also to secure the co-operation in favor of Great Britain of their numerous dependents and friends. Among the latter were John and Walter Butler, who lived near Caughnawaga, a few miles from Johnstown, and Joseph Brant,* all of whom visited with such dreadful massacres the settlements of western Pennsylvania and New York. The inhabitants of Tryon County, friendly to the American cause, were not idle. They, in common with their friends of this and the other provinces, had viewed with alarm and indignation the enactment and operation of the oppressive acts of the English Parliament, and warmly sympathized with the inhabitants of Massachusetts. They hailed with joy the proposition for calling a Continental Congress. A meeting for Palatine district was called the 27th of August, 1774, which was attended by a large number of the inhabitants. It was said by Dr. Franklin, upon his examination before the British House of Commons, in 1766, relative to the operation of the Stamp Act, "that the Germans who inhabit Pennsylvania are more dissatisfied with the duty than the native colonists themselves." The following resolutions, adopted at this meeting, will show what were the feelings and sentiments of their brethren on the Mohawk. They contain the sentiments of the times, and they breathe a spirit highly commendable, and which could hardly have been expected to exist, and existing, must have required some deeision and courage to publish in this then remote and defenseless county, filled too with loyalists and Indians under their control. It will be romembered that it was in June preceding, the Boston Port Bill went into operation, and when the first mea-

* See Appendix—Note C.

sures were adopted by the Assembly of that province for the calling of a General Congress.

"This meeting, looking with concern and heartfelt sorrow on the alarming and calamitous condition which the inhabitants of Boston are in, in consequence of the act of Parliament blocking up the port of Boston, and considering the tendency of the late acts of Parliament, for the purpose of raising a revenue in America, has to the abridging the liberties and privileges of the American colonies, do resolve:

I. That King George the Third is lawful and rightful Lord and Sovereign of Great Britain, and the dominions thereunto belonging; and that, as part of his dominions, we hereby testify, that we will bear true faith and allegiance unto him; and that we will, with our lives and fortunes, support and maintain him upon the throne of his ancestors, and the just dependence of these, his colonies, upon the crown of Great Britain.

II. That we think and consider it as our greatest happiness, to be governed by the laws of Great Britain, and that with cheerfulness we will always pay submission thereunto as far as we consistently can with the security of the constitutional rights and liberties of English subjects, which are so sacred that we cannot permit the same to be violated.

III. That we think it is our undeniable privilege to be taxed only with our own consent, given by ourselves or our representatives. That taxes otherwise laid and exacted are unjust and unconstitutional. That the late acts of Parliament, declarative of their right of laying internal taxes on the American colonies, are obvious encroachments on the rights and liberties of the British subjects in America.

IV. That the act for blocking up the port of Boston is oppressive and arbitrary; injurious in its principles, and particularly oppressive to the inhabitants of Boston, whom we consider brethren suffering in the common cause.

V. That we will unite and join with the different districts of this county, in giving whatever relief it is in our power, to the poor, distressed inhabitants of Boston; and that we will join and unite with our brethren of the rest of this colony, in anything tending to support and defend our rights and liberties.

VI. That we think the sending of delegates from the different colonies to a general continental Congress is a salutary measure, and absolutely necessary at this alarming crisis, and that we entirely approve of the five gentlemen chosen delegates for this colony by our brethren of New York, hereby adopting and choosing the same persons to represent this colony in the Congress.

VII. That we hereby engage faithfully to abide by and adhere to such regulations as shall be made and agreed upon by the said Congress.

VIII. That we consider it necessary that there be appointed a standing committee of this county, to correspond with the committees of New York and Albany, and we do hereby appoint Christopher P. Yates, Isaac Paris, John Frey, and Andrew Fink, who, together with persons to be appointed by the other districts of this county, are to compose a committee of correspondence to convey the sentiments of this county, in a set of resolves, to New York.

IX. It is voted by this meeting, that copies of the proceedings of this day, certified by the chairman, be transmitted to the supervisors of the different districts of this county, and that we recommend it to the inhabitants of the said districts to appoint persons to compose a committee of correspondence."

The Continental Congress which met in Philadelphia in September following, after a session of eight weeks adjourned until May, 1775. Several important and patriotic addresses had been sent forth, well calculated to awaken the people to a knowledge of their rights.

At a court held in Johnstown in the spring of 1775, a declaration was drawn up and circulated by the loyalists of Tryon County, in which they avowed their opposition to the measures adopted by the Congress. Warm altercations and debates ensued, but it was signed by most of the grand jury, and nearly all the magistrates.

This proceeding applied the torch to that train of combustible materials which had been accumulating, and which immediately kindled into a blaze. The minds of men were generally prepared for a decisive step, and meetings were called, and committees appointed in all the districts, and sub-committees in almost every precinct and hamlet in the county.

On the day appointed for the meeting in Cherry Valley, the little church was filled with the inhabitants, of every age. Parents took their children with them, that they might early breathe the air of freedom, and that their first lispings might be in favor of the liberties of their country. Thomas Spencer, a resident in the place, and an Indian interpreter, addressed the meeting in a strain of rude, though impassioned eloquence. The noblest efforts of a Henry or an Otis never wrought more sensibly upon the feelings of the respective congresses which they addressed, than did the harangue of this unlettered patriot upon that little assembly. The article of association was carried round to the different persons, most of whom subscribed it.

These meetings were called early in May, and the following was the article of association: "Whereas the grand jury of this county, and a number of the magistrates, have signed a declaration, declaring their disapprobation of the opposition made by the Colonies to the oppressive and arbitrary acts of Parliament, the purport of which is evidently to entail slavery on America; and as the said declaration may, in some measure, be looked upon as the sense of the County in general, if the same be passed over in silence; we the subscribers, freeholders, and the inhabitants of the said County, inspired with a sincere love for our country, and deeply interested in the common cause, do solemnly declare our fixed attachment and entire approbation of the proceedings of the grand Continental Congress held at Philadelphia last fall, and that we will strictly adhere to, and repose our confidence in the wisdom and integrity of the present Continental Congress; and that we will support the same to the utmost of our power, and that we will religiously and inviolably observe the regulations of that august body."

On the 18th of May the Palatine committee met and wrote a letter to the committee of Albany, which, as it gives a full view of the affairs of the County, is inserted at length.

"We are so peculiarly circumstanced in this county, relating to the present struggle for American liberty, that we cannot longer defer laying the situation of this county before you. The district we represent has been foremost in avowing its attachment to liberty, and approving the method of opposition adopted in America, and are now signing an association similar to what has been signed in other counties in this province, and we hope, in a few days, to have the pleasure to transmit it down for the press. The County being extensive, it takes a considerable time before the people who are favorable to the cause can be got to sign: for we have caused copies of the association to be dispersed in divers parts of the County. This county has, for a series of years, been ruled by one family, the different branches of which are still strenuous in dissuading people from coming into congressional measures, and even have, last week, at a numerous meeting of the Mohawk district, appeared with all their dependents armed to oppose the people considering of their grievances: their number being so large, and the people unarmed, struck terror into most of them, and they dispersed. We are informed that Johnson Hall is fortifying by placing a parcel of swivel guns round the same; and that Colonel Johnson has had parts of his regiment of militia under arms yesterday, no doubt with a design to prevent the friends of liberty from publishing their attachment to the cause to the world. Besides which, we are told that about 150 Highlanders (Roman Catholics) in and about Johnstown, are armed, and ready to march upon the like occasion. We have been informed that Colonel Johnson has stopped two New Englanders and searched them, being, we suppose, suspicious that they came to solicit aid from us or the Indians, whom we dread most, there being a current report through the County, that they are to be made use of in keeping us in awe.

"We recommend it strongly and seriously to you to take it in your consideration whether any powder and ammunition ought to be permitted to be sent up this way, unless it is done under the inspection of the committee, and consigned to the committee here, and for such particular shopkeepers as we in our next shall acquaint you of. We are determined to suffer none in our district to sell any, but such as we approve of, and sign the association. When any thing particular comes to our knowledge relating to the Indians, (whom we shall watch,) or any other thing interesting, we shall take the earliest opportunity in communicating the same to you. And as we are a young county, remote from the metropolis, we beg you will give us all the intelligence in your power. We shall not be able to send down any deputies to the Provincial Congress, as we cannot possibly obtain the sense of the County soon enough to make it worth our while to send any, but be assured we are not the less attached to American liberty. For we are determined, although few in number, to let the world see who are, and who are not such; and to wipe off the indelible disgrace brought on us by the declaration signed by our grand jury and some of our magistrates; who in general are considered by the majority of the County as enemies to their country. In a word, gentlemen, it is our fixed resolution to support and carry into execution every thing recommended by the Continental Congress, *and to be free or die.*"

This same committee met on the 21st of May, when the following letters were laid before them. The first, being a letter from some of the Mohawk Indians to the Oneidas, had been found in the road, where it was supposed to have been lost by some Indian.

Translated into English, it was as follows: "Written at Guy Johnson's, May, 1775. This is your letter, you great ones or Sachems. Guy Johnson says he will be glad if you get this intelligence, you Oneidas, how it goes with him now, and he is now more certain concerning the intention of the Boston people. Guy Johnson is in great fear of being taken prisoner by the Bostonians. We Mohawks are obliged to watch him constantly. Therefore we send you this intelligence that you shall know it, and Guy Johnson assures himself, and depends upon your coming to his assistance, and that you will without fail be of that opinion. He believes not that you will assent to let him suffer. We therofore expect you in a couple of days' time. So much at present. We send but so far as to you Oneidas, but afterward perhaps to all the other nations. We conclude and expect that you will have concern about our ruler, Guy Johnson, because we are all united." This letter was signed by Joseph Brant, secretary to Guy Johnson, and four other chiefs.

The following letter was from Guy Johnson to the magistrates, and others of the upper districts, dated Guy Park, May 20th, 1775. "Gentlemen, I have lately had repeated accounts that a body of New Englanders, or others, were to come and seize and carry away my person, and attack our family, under color of malicious insinuations, that I intended to set the Indians upon the people. Men of sense and character know that my office is of the highest importance to promote peace among the Six Nations, and prevent their entering into any such disputes. This I effected last year, when they were much vexed about the attack made upon the Shawnese, and I last winter appointed them to meet me this month to receive the answer of the Virginians. All men must allow, that if the Indians find their council-fire disturbed, and their superintendent insulted, *they will take a dreadful revenge.* It is therefore the duty of all people to prevent this, and to satisfy any who may have been imposed on, that their suspicions, and the allegations they have collected against me, are false, and inconsistent with my character and office. I recommend this to you as highly necessary at this time, as my regard for the interest of the County and self-preservation has obliged me to fortify my house, and keep men armed for my defense, till these idle and malicious reports are removed."

The committee, taking these letters into consideration, adopted unanimously the following resolutions:

"I. That it is the opinion of this committee that the Indians who signed the letter never would have presumed to write or send the same, if they had not been countenanced.

II. That as we have unanimously adopted the proceedings of the grand Continental Congress, and mean virtuously to support the same, so we feel and commiserate the sufferings of our brethren in the Massachusetts Bay, and the other colonies in America, and that we mean never to submit to any arbitrary and oppressive acts of any power under heaven, or to any illegal and unwarrantable action of any man or set of men.

III. That as the whole Continent has approved of the actions and proceeding of the Massachusetts Bay, and other of the provinces of New England, we do adopt and approve of the same. Wherefore we must and do consider that any fortification or armed force raised to be made use of against them, is evidently designed to overawe and make us submit.

IV. That Col. Johnson's conduct in raising fortifications round his house, keeping a number of Indians and armed men constantly about him, and stopping and searching travellers upon the King's highway, and stopping our communication with Albany, is very alarming to this county, and is highly arbitrary, illegal, oppressive and unwarrantable; and confirms us in our fears, that his design is to keep us in awe, and oblige us to submit to a state of slavery.

V. That as we abhor a state of slavery, we do join and unite together under all the ties of religion, honor, justice, and a love for our country, never to become slaves, and to defend our freedom with our lives and fortunes."

The following letter was at the same time written, and sent by express to the committee of Albany.

"Upon the alarming news that expresses were gone to call down the upper nations of Indians to Col. Johnson's, we caused ourselves to be convened this day, to take the state of this County into our consideration; upon which we have determined to order the inhabitants of this district to provide themselves with sufficient arms and ammunition, and to be ready at a moment's warning. We are sorry to acquaint you that all communication with your county is entirely stopped by Col. Johnson, who has five hundred men to guard his house, which he has fortified, under pretense that he is afraid of a visit of the New England men, as will appear by a copy of a letter we intercepted this morning. We have not 50 pounds of powder in our district, and it will be impossible for you to help us to any till the communication is opened, not a man being suffered to pass, without being searched. To-morrow is to be a meeting of Canajoharie district, when we expect they will adopt Congressional measures very heartily, and we purpose to have a meeting of the committees of both districts, and propose the question, whether we will not open the communication by force; if which question is determined in the affirmative, we shall despatch another express to you, acquainting you with the day, when we hope you will be on your way up with some ammunition. We have just sent off an express to the German Flats and Kingsland districts, desiring them to unite with us and give us their assistance; which districts, or at least a great majority of them, we are credibly informed, are very hearty in the present struggle for American liberty. We are, gentlemen, perhaps in a worse situation than any part of America is at present. We have an open enemy before our faces, and treacherous friends at our backs, for which reason we hope you will take our case into your immediate consideration, and give us an answer by the bearers, who go express by the way of Schoharie, as we dare not trust them any other way. They have orders to wait for an answer. We have reason to think that a great many of the Indians are not satisfied with Col. Johnson's conduct, for which reason we have thought it would not be improper to send a couple of men, well acquainted with the Indian language, to dissuade them from coming down. And we think it would be of service to us if you could send two also, who are able to make the Indians sensible of the present dispute with the mother country and us. We have the pleasure to acquaint you, that we are very unanimous in our district, as well as in Canajoharie, and we are determined by no means to submit to the oppressive acts of Parliament, much less to Col. Johnson's arbitrary conduct."

On the 22d of May, the mayor, aldermen, and commonalty of the city of Albany, to whom a letter similar to the one addressed to the magistrates of Tryon County had been sent by Guy Johnson, returned the following answer. "We this day received yours without date, directed to the magistrates and committee of Albany and Schenectady, and to the mayor, corporation, &c. of Albany, wherein you write, that you have received repeated accounts that either the New Englanders, or some persons in or about this city, or the town of Schenectady, are coming up to a considerable number to seize and imprison you, on a ridiculous and malicious report, that you intend to make the Indians destroy the inhabitants, or to that effect, and that you, in consequence thereof, have been put to the great trouble and expense of fortifying your house, and keeping a large body of men for the defense of your person, &c. You proceed and say, that the absurdity of this apprehension may easily be seen by men of sense, but that as many credulous and ignorant persons may be led astray, and inclined to believe it, &c., it is become the duty of all those who have authority or influence to disabuse the public, and prevent consequences *which you foresee with very great concern.* We are very sorry to learn from you that any groundless reports should have arisen, and be propagated to your prejudice, considering your character, station, and the large property you have in the county. And we trust that you are so well acquainted with the nature and duties of your office, that you will pursue the dictates of an honest heart, and study the interest, peace and welfare of your county. In which case, we presume you need not be apprehensive of any injury in your person or property; neither can we learn or conceive that there either is, or has been, any intention of taking you captive, or offering you any indignity whatever, either by the New England people, or any of the inhabitants of this city, or any one else; and we have but too much reason to think that these groundless reports have been raised and industriously propagated, in your own phraseology, by some busy people in your county, to rouse up the Indians from their peaceful habitations, and take up arms against such of our American brethren as are engaged on the part of America in the unhappy contest between Great Britain and her colonies.

"As it appears from your letter, that you consider the station wherein you are placed, as superintendent of Indian affairs, to be of the highest importance to the public, we hope that you will use all possible means in your power to restore peace and tranquillity among the Indians, and assure them, that the report propagated prejudicial to you or to them is totally groundless of any just foundation, and that nothing will afford His Majesty's subjects in general a greater satisfaction, than to be and continue with them on the strictest terms of peace and friendship."

A letter was also written by the Albany committee to Guy Johnson, of the same purport; also one to the Tryon County committee, informing them that they had no ammunition for them, and advising, as the most prudent course, not to attempt to open by force the communication between the two counties. This proposition was abandoned. Four members were, however, sent to Albany, who were directed to obtain all the information possible relative to the situation of the country, and also to procure a quantity of powder and lead, for the payment for which the committee themselves became responsible. In consequence of some threats of Guy Johnson, the following resolution was unanimously adopted:

"That, whereas, the persons of some of the members of this committee have been threatened with imprisonment on account of their being concerned in our just opposition, in which case we do associate and unite together, that to the utmost of our power we will do our endeavors by force, or otherwise, to rescue them from imprisonment, unless such person or persons are confined by a legal process, issued upon a legal ground, and executed in a legal manner."

Secrecy as to all proceedings, except those which were to be published, was enjoined upon all the members. Resolutions were adopted, by which they bound themselves to have no connection or dealing with those who had not signed the association. The owners of slaves were directed not to suffer them to go from home, unless with a certificate that they were employed in their master's business. They assumed the exercise of legislative, executive, and judicial powers. The members scattered over the County as sub-committees, and aided by the Whigs, who entered upon the measures proposed by the committee with great zeal, were generally enabled to bring their plans to a successful termination.

On the 25th of May, the Indian council which had been called met at Guy Park. Delegates from Albany and Tryon counties were present. The Mohawks alone appear to have been represented in it. Little Abraham, chief of the Mohawks, *speaker*, said: "He was glad to meet them and to hear the reports concerning taking Guy Johnson, their superintendent, were false. That the Indians do not wish to have a quarrel with the inhabitants. That during Sir William Johnson's lifetime, and since, we have been peaceably disposed. That the Indians are alarmed on account of the reports that our powder was stopped. We get our things from superintendent. If we lived as you do, it would not be so great a loss. If our ammunition is stopped we shall distrust you. We are pleased to hear you say, you will communicate freely, and we will at all times listen to what you say in presence of our superintendent."

The committee, after consulting, replied: "That they were glad to hear them confirm the old friendship of their forefathers—that the reports were false—whenever they had any business they would apply at their council-fires in presence of their superintendent."

The speaker of the Mohawks replied: "The Indians are glad that you are not surprised we cannot spare Col. Johnson. The love we have for the memory of Sir William Johnson, and the obligations the whole Six Nations are under to him, must make us regard and protect every branch of his family. That we will explain these things to all the Indians, and hope you will do the same to your people." The council broke up with apparent good feeling on all sides, which it was hoped and expected would continue.

On the 2d day of June, 1775, a meeting of the committee was held, at which the members from the Mohawk district were for the first time present, having been kept away by the Johnsons. The whole county was now represented, and as this was the first united meeting, it may be interesting to some to give the names of this body of men, who had so often professed their willingness to peril their lives and property in defense of the liberties of their country. (From Palatine district,) Christopher P. Yates, John Frey, Andrew Fink, Andrew Reeber, Peter Waggoner, Daniel McDougal, Jacob Klock, George Ecker, Jr., Harmanus Van Slyck, Christopher W. Fox, Anthony Van Veghten—(Canajoharie district,) Nicholas Herkimer, Ebenezer Cox, William Seeber, John Moore, Samuel Campbell, Samuel Clyde, Thomas Henry, John Pickard—(Kingsland and German Flats district,) Edward Wall, William Petry, John Petry, Augustine Hess, Frederick Orendorf, George Wentz, Michael Ittig, Frederick Fox, George Herkimer, Duncan McDougal, Frederick Helmer, John Frink—(Mohawk district,) John Morlett, John Bliven, Abraham Van Horne, Adam Fonda, Frederick Fisher, Sampson Simmons, William Schuyler, Volkert Veeder, James McMaster, Daniel Lane—42. Christopher P. Yates was chosen chairman of this body. He had been chairman of the Palatine committee, and had drafted most of the foregoing letters and spirited resolutions. The following letter was written to Guy Johnson at this meeting:

"According to the example of the counties in this and the neighboring colonies, the people of the district we represent have met in a peaceable manner to consider of the present dispute with the mother country and the colonies, signed a general association, and appointed us a committee to meet in order to consult the common safety of our rights and liberties, which are infringed in a most enormous manner, by enforcing opppressive and unconstitutional acts of the British Parliament, by an armed force in the Massachusetts Bay.

"Was it any longer a doubt that we are oppressed by the mother country, and that it is the avowed design of the ministers to enslave us, we might perhaps be induced to use argument, to point out in what particulars we conceive that it is the birthright of English subjects to be exempted from all taxes, except those which are laid on them by their representatives, and think we have a right, not only by the laws and constitution of England to meet for the purpose we have done. Which meeting, we probably would have postponed a while, had there been the least kind of probability that the petition of the General Assembly would have been noticed more than the united petition of almost the whole continent of America, by their delegates in Congress. Which, so far from being any ways complied with, was treated with superlative contempt by the ministry, and fresh oppressions were, and are, daily heaped upon us. Upon which principles, principles which are undeniable, we have been appointed to consult methods to contribute what little lies in our power to save our devoted country from ruin and devastation; which, with the assistance of Divine Providence, it is our fixed and determined resolution to do; and if called upon we shall be foremost in sharing the toil and danger of the field. We consider New England suffering in the common cause, and commiserate their distressed situation; and we should be wanting in our duty to our country, and to ourselves, if we were any longer backward in announcing our determination to the world.

"We know that some of the members of this committee have been charged with compelling people to come into the measures which we have adopted, and with drinking treasonable toasts. But as we are convinced that these reports are false and malicious, spread by our enemies with the sole intent to lessen us in the esteem of the world, and as we are conscious of being guilty of no crime, and of having barely done our duty, we are entirely unconcerned as to anything that is said of us, or can be done with us. We should, however, be careless of our character, did we not wish to detect the despicable wretch who could be so base as to charge us with things which we never have entertained the most distant thoughts of. We are not ignorant of the very great importance of your office, as superintendent of the Indians, and therefore it is no more our duty, than inclination, to protect you in the discharge of the duty of your proper province; and we meet you with pleasure in behalf of ourselves and our constituents, to thank you for meeting the Indians in the upper parts of the County, which may be the means of easing the people of the remainder of their fears on this account, and prevent the Indians committing irregularities on their way down to Guy Park. And we beg of you to use your endeavors with the Indians to dissuade them from interfering in the dispute with the mother country and the colonies. We cannot think that, as you and your family possess very large estates in this County, you are unfavorable to American freedom, although you may differ with us in the mode of obtaining a redress of grievances. Permit us further to observe, that we cannot pass over in silence the interruption which the people of the Mohawk district met in their meeting; which, we are informed, was conducted in a peaceable manner; and the inhuman treatment of a man whose only crime was being faithful to his employers, and refusing to give an account of the receipt of certain papers, to persons who had not the least color of right to demand anything of that kind. We assure you, that we are much concerned about it, as two important rights of English subjects are thereby infringed, to wit, a right to meet and to obtain all the intelligence in their power."

Dissatisfied with the council which had been held at his house, yet professing to be desirous to promote peace between the Indians and the inhabitants, Guy Johnson had called another council to meet in the western part of the County. Under pretense of meeting the Indians in this council, he had removed with his family and retinue from Guy Park to the house of Mr. Thomson in Cosby's Manor, a little above the German Flats, where he was waited upon by Edward Wall and Gen. Nicholas Herkimer, with the letter of which the foregoing is a part. To this letter he returned the following answer:

"Cosby's Manor, June 6th, 1775. I have received the paper signed Chris. P. Yates, chairman on behalf of the district therein mentioned, which I am now to answer; and shall do it briefly, in the order you have stated matters. As to the letter from some Indians to the Oneidas, I really knew nothing of it till I heard such a thing had been by some means obtained from an Indian messenger; and from what I have heard of its contents, I can't see anything material in it, or that could justify such idle apprehensions; but I must observe that these fears among the people were talked of long before, and were, I fear, propagated by some malicious persons for a bad purpose.

"As to your political sentiments, on which you enter in the next paragraph, I have no occasion to enter on them or the merits of the cause. I desire to enjoy liberty of conscience and the exercise of my own judgment, and that all others should have the same privilege; but with regard to your saying you might have postponed the affair, if there had been the least kind of probability that the petition of the General Assembly would have been noticed, more than that of the delegates, I must, as a true friend to the country, in which I have a large interest, say that the present dispute is viewed in different lights, according to the education and principles of the parties affected, and that however reasonable it may appear to a considerable number of honest men here, that the petition of the delegates should merit attention, it is not viewed in the same light in a country which admits of no authority that is not constitutionally established; and I persuade myself you have that reverence for His Majesty, that you will pay due regard to the royal assurance given in his speech to Parliament, that whenever the American grievances should be laid before him by their constitutional assemblies, they should be fully attended to. I have heard that compulsory steps were taken to induce some persons to come into your measures, and treasonable toasts drank; but I am happy to hear you disavow them.

"I am glad to find my calling a congress on the frontiers gives satisfaction; this was principally my design, though I cannot sufficiently express my surprise at those who have, either through malice or ignorance, misconstrued my intentions, and supposed me capable of setting the Indians on the peaceable inhabitants of this county. The interest our family has in this county, and my own, is considerable; and they have been its best benefactors; and malicious charges, therefore, to their prejudice, are highly injurious, and ought to be totally suppressed.

"The office I hold is greatly for the benefit and protection of this country, and on my frequent meetings with the Indians depends their peace and security; I therefore cannot but be astonished to find the endeavors made use of to obstruct me in my duties, and the weakness of some people in withholding many things from me, which are indispensably necessary for rendering the Indians contented; and I am willing to hope that you, gentlemen, will duly consider this and discountenance the same.

"You have been much misinformed as to the origin of the reports which obliged me to fortify my house, and stand on my defense. I had it, gentlemen, from undoubted authority from Albany, and since confirmed by letters from one of the committee at Philadelphia, that a large body of men were to make me prisoner. As the effect this must have on the Indians might have been of dangerous consequences to you, (a circumstance not thought of,) I was obliged at great expense to take these measures. But the many reports of my stopping travellers were false in every particular, and the only instance of detaining anybody was in the case of two New England men, which I explained fully to those of your body who brought your letter, and wherein I acted strictly agreeable to law, and as a magistrate should have done.

"I am very sorry that such idle and injurious reports meet with any encouragement. I rely on you, gentlemen, to exert yourselves in discountenancing them, and am happy in this opportunity of assuring the people of a county I regard, that they have nothing to apprehend from my endeavors, but I shall always be glad to promote their true interests."

During this correspondence, the fears not only of the inhabitants of western New-York, but of all the northern provinces, were excited. They had suffered too much from Indian warfare, to be indifferent to the course which should be adopted by the Six Nations. The Provincial Congress of Massachusetts had this subject under consideration on the 13th of June, and sent a circular to the Provincial Congress of New York. The conclusion is as follows:—"We also have had the disagreeable account of methods taken to fill the minds of the Indian tribes adjacent to these colonies with sentiments very injurious to us. Particularly we have been informed that Col. Guy Johnson has taken great pains with the Six Nations, in order to bring them into a belief that it is designed by the Colonies to fall upon them, and cut them off. We have therefore desired the honorable Continental Congress that they would with all convenient speed use their influence in guarding against the evil intended by this malevolent misrepresentation, and we desire you to join with us in such application."

A letter was immediately written by the New York Congress to Johnson, disclaiming, as had often been done by the committee, any and every intention to injure him or the Indians. (He had removed with his retinue to Fort Stanwix, and thence on to Ontario, where he met 1340 Indian warriors in council.) Pretending unjust interference in the former council, he was sure at this place, so far removed from the settlements of the whites, of exerting to the best advantage that influence which he derived from British gold, and the merited reputation of his father-in-law. From this place, under date of the 8th of July, he wrote an answer to P. V. B. Livingston, Esq., the President of the Congress, in which he complained bitterly of the malcontents and those who disturb regular governments. This letter is a very loyal one, and concludes thus:—"I should be much obliged by your promises of discountenancing any attempt against myself, did they not appear to be made on condition of compliance with continental or provincial congresses, or even committees, formed or to be formed, many of whose resolves may neither consist with my conscience, duty, or loyalty. I trust I shall always manifest more humanity than to promote the destruction of the innocent inhabitants of a colony, to which I have been always warmly attached; a declaration that must appear perfectly suitable to the character of a man of honor and principle, who can on no account neglect those duties that are consistent therewith, however they may diffe·

from sentiments now adopted in so many parts of America."

To the last, Col. Johnson persisted in allegations which had no foundation—allegations which, if true, present the people of Massachusetts and New York warring against their own important interests—a charge which their conduct at this time, and during the war, was far from warranting. They had the desired effect upon the Indians. Having by these and other means secured for the English the attachment of the Indians, Col. Johnson went from Ontario to Oswego, and thence to Montreal, where he took up his residence. During the war he continued to act as agent, distributing to the Indians liberal rewards for their deeds of cruelty, and, by promises, stimulating them to future exertions. It required no uncommon sagacity to penetrate his motives, though he had professed his attachment to this province so warmly and frequently in his letters, and pretended to shudder at the thought of employing the savages against its "innocent inhabitants."

The committee entertained suspicions of his ultimate designs, too well founded, when they saw him moving up the Mohawk with his family, and accompanied by a large number of dependents. The unarmed state of the inhabitants would not, however, warrant any attempt to check his movements. Besides, such a step, though recommended by some, would not have been considered justifiable by a majority of the Whigs, as Johnson had not yet committed any act of hostility.

Few of the Mohawks returned to their native homes

upon the banks of that river which bears their name. The graves of their ancestors were abandoned. Their council-fires were extinguished. Every movement indicated the gathering of that storm so much dreaded, and which afterward burst with such desolating effects upon the inhabitants of this defenseless frontier. Those inhabitants had the satisfaction of reflecting that it was a calamity which they had not called down upon themselves, but which they had labored with all their powers to avert. They had proffered to their red brethren the calumet of peace, though in vain. That the Indians, and especially the Mohawks, should have remained attached to the English government is by no means strange; for they had been furnished by that government with the necessaries of life, and with arms and other munitions, both for the chase and for war; and the chain of their friendship had been brightened by constant use for more than an hundred years. We find therefore not so much to censure in the conduct of the Indians themselves, as in that of the British ministers, who reccommended the plan of employing them in the war, and in that of their agents, who carried that plan into effect. It has rendered infamous the names of men who might otherwise have been ranked among the great and good of our country, and it has imprinted a dark spot upon the pages of English history. This was pretended at the time to be a retaliatory measure, and was justified on that ground. But no plan for employing the Indians is believed to have been recommended or adopted, by either the continental or any of the provincial congresses. If such a course was ever mentioned, it was probably by private, unauthorized persons. It would have argued an extreme of weakness to have provoked, by setting the example, the employment of such a foe in a war which was to be carried on in their own territory, and where, if acts of cruelty were committed, their own wives and children must necessarily be the sufferers.*

The Rev. Samuel Kirkland, missionary to the Oneidas, was requested to use his influence with that tribe, and endeavor to persuade them to remain neutral during the war. Several conferences were held with them. On the 28th of June, the Oneidas and Tuscaroras assembled at the German Flats, where they were met by the inhabitants of that district, and the delegates from Albany. The inhabitants of the Flats delivered to them the following speech:

"*Brothers!* We are glad to have you here to return you thanks. We should have been much pleased to have spoken with you at the appointed place; that is, by your superintendent, where of late you kept your council-fire; but since his removing so far from us, we do not think it wrong or imprudent to communicate our sentiments of peace to you here. It is at this place, brothers, it has often been done, and here again we renew it, and brighten the old chain of peace and brotherly love.

"*Brothers!* We cannot see the cause of your late council-fire, or superintendent going away from among

---

* See Appendix, M. Since this volume was written, the author has had access to the documents procured in England by the agent of the State, J. Romeyn Brodhead, Esq., and they fully confirm the views originally expressed, and the reader who is interested in the subject will find it discussed in the Appendix.

us. We did him no harm, and you well know that none of us ever did, and you may depend on it, there was no such thing meant against him. He told our people he was going up to Thompson's (Cosby's Manor) to hold a council-fire with our brothers the Five Nations there. We helped him to provisions to support you there, and every thing we had that he wanted. But he is gone away from among us, and told some of our people, that he would come back with company which would not please us; which, if true, it is certain his intentions are bad, and he may depend that whatever force he may or can bring, we regard not.

"*Brothers!* Our present meeting does not arise from any unfriendly thoughts we entertain of you, or from any fear of ourselves. It is purely on account of the old friendship which has so long been kept up between us, that friendship we want to maintain. It is that friendship which will be an equal benefit to us. It is as much wanted on your side as ours.

"*Brothers!* We cannot too much express our satisfaction of your conduct toward us by your late proceedings with the superintendent, at the carrying place, for which we are also obliged to you, and do not doubt but that your conduct will be blessed with greater benefits than any other of those who will hurry themselves into mischief; which can never be of any other benefit to them, but sorrow for the innocent blood that may be shed on an occasion wherewith they have no concern.

"We look to you, particularly, to be men of more understanding than others, by the benefits you have received in learning; wherefore we confide and trust the more freely in you, that you can communicate to the other tribes and nations, the error they want to lead you in, and cannot doubt but your wisdom and influence with the other nations will be attended with that happy success which will hereafter be a blessing to you and your posterity.

"*Brothers!* What we have said is supposed to be sufficient to convince you that our meaning is for our joint peace and friendship; in which we hope that we and our children may continue to the end of time."

Most of the Oneidas agreed to remain neutral; a few joined the English. When Gen. Schuyler had command of the northern army, they asked permission to take up the hatchet. But he always dissuaded them. It shows not only the consistency but the amiableness of character of that man, so much esteemed by his contemporaries. Some of the Oneidas rendered very important services by traversing the country, and notifying the inhabitants of approaching danger. Others, contrary to advice, joined in the war. The latter were a small part of the tribe. Among them was Skenando,* distinguished along the border by the appellation of the "white man's friend."

* See Appendix—Note D.

CHAPTER III.

The removal of Guy Johnson to Canada excited no surprise; but while hovering upon the frontier, reports were circulated which caused considerable alarm. It was said that he intended to attack Little Falls, with eight or nine hundred Indians, and to proceed thence down the river, and ravage the whole county below. Measures were taken to make a vigorous resistance, in case the report should prove true. The militia were ordered to arm, and to be ready to march on the first notice, and expresses were sent for assistance to Albany and Schenectady. Whether the rumor was unfounded, or whether the invasion was contemplated, but was abandoned in consequence of the preparations made to resist him, is not known. Col. Johnson withdrew, as before stated, without committing any acts of hostility.

The committee, freed from immediate danger in that direction, turned their attention to the internal regulation of the county. They determined civil causes—officered and organized the militia—arrested and tried suspicious persons, some of whom they fined, and others they imprisoned—ordered that no person should come into or go out of the county without a pass from some acknowledged public body, either a congress or a committee; and, in short, exercised such powers as the exigencies of the times demanded, and which were necessary to secure tranquillity within, and guard against danger from without.

Though these committees generally exercised powers which were not delegated to them when first appointed, their regulations were submitted to, and their resolves obeyed cheerfully by their constituents, who perceived the necessity of concentrating as much power as possible in that body. The discordant and disorganizing materials thrown together by such strifes require the control of a strong arm. The rash are to be checked, the vicious are to be punished, and the irresolute and wavering encouraged and confirmed. The exposed situation of Tryon County, with the great number of open and avowed enemies, furnished an additional reason why the committee should exercise an almost absolute authority.

Brant and the Butlers had accompanied Guy Johnson, but the loyalists were still numerous in the county. They found a willing and active leader in Sir John Johnson, whose house now became their principal place of rendezvous.

They strove to weaken the confidence of the people in the committee. At one time they called meetings in some of the districts, and chose new committees. At another, they ridiculed their proceedings. Sometimes they asserted that their acts were illegal, and at other times that they were tyrannical. Under such circumstances, and with the feelings which such strifes are apt to engender, it is not singular that the proceedings of the committee against those men were characterized by considerable severity. It is worthy of remark, however, that no sacrifice was required of their constituents, which they themselves were unwilling to make; no dangers to be encountered which they were unwilling to share. Several of the committee were killed in battle, and there were few of those who escaped with their lives, who did not sustain a total loss of property during the subsequent Indian ravages.

Christopher P. Yates, the first chairman, went a volunteer to Ticonderoga, and into Canada with Gen. Montgomery. During the latter part of the summer of 1775, he raised a company of rangers, and in the following summer was commissioned a major. He was succeeded by Nicholas Herkimer, afterwards brigadier general of the militia, and he by Isaac Paris.

The following extract is from a letter of the State Committee of Safety, under date of December, 1775, signed by John M'Kesson, clerk of the Provincial Congress. "I was directed by this Congress to assure you of the high esteem and respect they have for your vigilant, noble-spirited county committee." The following was from Gen. Schuyler in the summer of '76: "The propriety of your conduct, and your generous exertions in the cause of your country, entitle you to the thanks of every one of its friends—please to accept of mine most sincerely."

Among the loyalists of Tryon County was Alexander White, sheriff of the county. He had assisted in his official capacity, in dispersing the people assembled in the Mohawk district to appoint a committee, and had uttered violent threats against them. The committee refused to acknowledge him as such officer, and procured the election of John Frey in his place. They wrote a letter to the Provincial Congress soliciting their interference in procuring a commission for Mr. Frey.

In a subsequent letter they say, " We must further hear that Gov. Tryon shall have granted again a commission to the great villain, Alexander White, for high sheriff in our county ; but we shall never suffer any exercise of such office in our county, by the said White." He left the county soon after, but returned the following summer; was arrested and confined, though afterward suffered to go at large upon parole.

The following is from a letter of the committee to Provincial Congress of New York, Sept. 7, 1775. " There is a great number of proved enemies against our association and regulations thereof, proceeding in and about Johnstown and Kingsborough, under the direction and order of Sir John Johnson, being Highlanders, amounting to 200 men, according to intelligence. We are daily scandalized by them, provoked and threatened, and we must surely expect a havoc of them upon our families if we should be required and called elsewhere for the defense of our country's cause. The people on our side are not willing that the committee should proceed so indulgently any longer. We have great suspicions, and are almost assured that Sir John has a continual correspondence with Col. Guy Johnson and his party."

It was afterward ascertained that such a correspondence was carried on through the Indians, who conveyed letters in the heads of their tomahawks and in the ornaments worn about their persons. The Indians also brought powder across from Canada.

On the 26th of October the committee wrote to Sir John the following letter: "Tryon County Committee Chamber, Oct. 26th, 1775. Honorable Sir: As we find particular reason to be convinced of your opinion in the questions hereafter expressed, we request you that you'll oblige us with your sentiments thereupon in a few lines by our messengers the bearers hereof, Messrs. Ebenezer Cox, James M'Master, and John J. Clock, members of our committee. We wish to know whether you will allow the inhabitants of Johnstown and Kingsborough to form themselves into companies, according to the regulations of our Continental Congress, for the defense of our country's cause; and whether your honor would be ready himself to give his personal assistance to the same purpose; also, whether you pretend a prerogative to our county court-house and gaol, and would hinder or interrupt the committee making use of the same to our want and service in the common cause.

"We do not doubt you will comply with our reasonable request, and thereby oblige," &c.

To this letter Sir John replied, "That as to embodying his tenants, he never did or should forbid them; but they might save themselves further trouble, as he knew his tenants would not consent. Concerning himself, sooner than lift his hand against his king, or sign any association, he would suffer his head to be cut off. As to the court-house and gaol, he would not deny the use of it for the purpose for which it was built, but that they were his property until he should be refunded seven hundred pounds. He further said he had been informed that two-thirds of Canajoharie and German Flats people had been forced to sign the association." The deputies replied, that his authority spared the truth, for it appeared of itself ridiculous that one-third should have forced two-thirds to sign.

The Provincial Congress, to whom a letter containing the proceedings of the committee had been sent, returned an answer as follows: "Dec. 9th. The Congress have this day entered into the consideration of your letter of the 28th of October, and are of opinion that your application to Sir John Johnson, requesting an answer from him whether he would allow his tenants to form themselves into companies and associate with their brethren of your county according to the resolves of the Continental Congress, for the defense of our liberties, was improper with respect to him, and too condescending on your part, as it was a matter that came properly within your province; and to which we doubt not but you are competent, as you have a line of conduct prescribed to you by Congress. With respect to your second question, whether he would take any active part in the controversy at present existing between Great Britain and her colonies, we conceive it to be very proper, and thank you for your information on that head.

"As to the third question, we conceive that he has no claim nor title to the court-house or gaol in your county, as we are credibly told that his father, Sir William Johnson, did in his lifetime convey the same to two gentlemen, in trust for the use of your county. However, as an attempt to use the same for the purpose of confining persons inimical to our country, may be productive of bad consequences, we beg leave to recommend to you, to procure some other place which may answer the end of a gaol. And give you our advice not to molest Sir John as long as he shall continue inactive, and not impede the measures necessary to be carried into execution from being completed." This advice was followed, and a private house was procured for that purpose, while some of the prisoners were sent to Albany and Hartford.

The fears of the people were again excited, during the subsequent winter, by preparations made by Sir John for the erection of a fortification around Johnson Hall. The number of armed dependents which he retained around him, gave credit to a report that, when the fortification should be completed, it would be garrisoned by three hundred Indians in addition to his own men, and that from thence they would sally out and ravage the surrounding country.

Gen. Schuyler had been informed of the movements of Sir John, and in Jan. 1776, in the dead of winter, together with Gen. Ten Broeck, and Col. Varick, and a few others, with a small detachment of soldiers, came into Tryon County. General Herkimer ordered out all the militia. They were paraded on the ice on the Mohawk River. The place of meeting was Major Fonda's, a few miles from Johnson Hall. Major Fonda was sent a messenger to Sir John. An answer was returned, and a correspondence carried on which was continued two or three days. The precise nature of it is not known. It resulted in Sir John surrendering himself a prisoner, and disarming his dependents and tenants. He was sent down to Fishkill, where he was liberated upon his parole. This surrender removed the fears of the inhabitants during the remainder of the winter. In the following May, however, Sir John, regardless of his promises, broke his parole, and, accompanied by a large number of his tenants, went north from Johnstown, by the way of Sacondaga, to Montreal. Sir William Johnson would have frowned with indignation upon this unmanly and disgraceful conduct of his son. The Provincial Congress of New York immediately wrote a letter to Gen. Washington: "We apprehend no doubt can exist, whether the affair of Sir John Johnson is within your immediate cognizance. He held a commission as brigadier general of the militia, and it is said another commission as major general. That he hath shamefully broken his parole is evident, but whether it would be more proper to have him returned or exchanged is entirely in your excellency's prudence." It is believed that neither the one nor the other was ever done. He left much valuable property, which was confiscated by Congress, and sold under the direction of the committee. During the war he commanded a regiment of refugees, known in the predatory border warfare of this province by the name of "Johnson's Greens."

The first delegates to the Provincial Congress were John Marlatt and John Moore. Afterward, William Wills, Benj. Newkirk, Volkert Veeder, and William Harper were appointed. The two latter were for a long time members of the State Committee of Safety. A new county committee was this spring elected, of which John Frey, Esq. was chosen chairman. At a meeting in May, it was unanimously resolved to instruct the delegates from this county in the Provincial Congress to vote for the entire independence of the Colonies.

The Declaration of Independence of the 4th of July following was hailed by them with joy, and they were willing to maintain it "with their lives and fortunes."

Tryon County, during the summer, was comparatively tranquil and secure. Scouts were sent out upon the borders, who with the continental troops kept at a distance the few detached parties of Indians and Tories. The following winter the Indians collected in considerable numbers at Oquago on the Susquehanna. Col. John Harper, of Harpersfield, was sent by the Provincial Congress with a letter to them, to ascertain their feelings toward the country and their intentions. Col. Harper having given private orders to the captains of his regiment of militia to hold themselves in readiness in case their services should be required, went to Oquago accompanied by one Indian and one white man. He arrived there the 27th of February. He soon ascertained that the report of a contemplated invasion was untrue. He caused an ox to be roasted, and invited the Indians to the entertainment thus provided. The letter was received in a friendly manner, and the Indians expressed their sorrow on account of the troubles of the country, and declared that they would take no active part against it.

Joseph Brant, having had some disagreement with Guy Johnson, came to Oquago after the visit of Col.

Harper. In June following, 1777, he went up to Unadilla with a party of seventy or eighty Indians, and sent for the officers of the militia company and the Rev. Mr. Johnstone. Brant informed them that the Indians were in want of provisions. That if they could not get them by consent they must by force; that their agreement with the king was very strong, and that they were not such villains as to break their covenant with him; that they were natural warriors, and could not bear to be threatened by Gen. Schuyler. They were informed that the Mohawks were confined, (that is, probably the few who remained behind,) and had not liberty to pass and repass as formerly. That they were determined to be free, as they were a free people, and desired to have their friends removed from the Mohawk River, lest, if the western Indians should come down, their friends might suffer with the rest, as they would pay no respect to persons. The inhabitants let them have provisions. After staying two days they returned, taking with them cattle, sheep, &c. The inhabitants friendly to the country immediately removed their families and effects to places of greater security.

Information having been given, Gen. Herkimer in July marched to Unadilla with 380 militia. He was met here by Brant at the head of 130 warriors. Brant complained of the same grievances as above set forth. To the question whether he would remain at peace if these things were rectified, he replied: "The Indians were in concert with the king, as their fathers and grandfathers had been. That the king's belts were yet lodged with them, and they could not falsify their pledge. That Gen. Herkimer and the rest had joined the Boston people against their king. That Boston people were resolute, but the king would humble them. That Mr. Schuyler, or General, or what you please to call him, was very smart on the Indians at the treaty at German Flats; but was not at the same time able to afford them the smallest article of clothing. That the Indians had formerly made war on the white people all united; and now they were divided, the Indians were not frightened."

After Brant had declared his determination to espouse the cause of the king, Col. Cox said, if such was his resolution the matter was ended. Brant turned and spoke to his warriors, who shouted and ran to their camp about a mile distant, when, seizing their arms, they fired a number of guns, and raised the Indian war-whoop. They returned immediately, when Gen. Herkimer addressing Brant, told him he had not come to fight. Brant motioned his followers to remain in their places. Then, assuming a threatening attitude, he said, if their purpose was war, he was ready for them. He then proposed that Mr. Stewart, the missionary among the Mohawks, (who was supposed friendly to the English,) and the wife of Col. Butler should be permitted to pass from the lower to the upper Mohawk castle.

Gen. Herkimer assented, but demanded that the Tories and deserters should be given up to him. This was refused by Brant, who after some farther remarks, added that he would go to Oswego, and hold a treaty with Col. Butler. This singular conference was singularly terminated. It was early in July, and the sun shone forth without a cloud to obscure it, and as its rays gilded the tops of the forest trees, or were reflected from the waters of the Susquehanna, imparted a rich tint to the wild scenery with which they were surrounded. The echo of the war-whoop had scarcely died away before the heavens became black, and a violent storm of hail and rain obliged each party to withdraw and seek the nearest shelter. Men less superstitious than many of the unlettered yeomen who, leaning upon their arms, were witnesses of the events of this day, could not have failed in after times to have looked back upon them, if not as an omen, at least as an emblem of those dreadful massacres with which these Indians and their associates afterward visited the inhabitants of this unfortunate frontier.

Gen. Herkimer appears to have been unwilling to urge matters to extreme, though he had sufficient power to have defeated the Indians. He no doubt entertained hopes that some amicable arrangement would eventually be made with them.

This is believed to have been the last conference held with any of the Six Nations, except the Oneidas, in which an effort was made to prevent the Indians engaging in the war. In the remarks of Brant will be found what was no doubt one of the principal reasons of the Indians joining the English, and which liberal gifts on our part might probably have prevented. As before remarked, they had been accustomed to receive most of their clothing and other necessaries from the English agents and superintendent. And now, when they received from the Americans little save professions of friendship, they were led to conclude that they were either poor or penurious, and therefore continued an alliance coupled with more immediate and substantial benefits. Col. Guy Johnson is said to have addressed the Indians at one of their councils as follows: "Are they (the Americans) able to give you any thing more than a piece of bread and a glass of rum? Are you willing to go with them, and suffer them to make horses and oxen of you, to put you into wheelbarrows, and to bring us all into slavery?"

CHAPTER IV.

THE campaign of 1777 had long been a favorite one with the British ministers, and during the previous winter great preparations had been made for its successful prosecution. Should Sir Henry Clinton and Gen. Burgoyne, with the southern and northern armies, succeed in uniting at Albany, the province of New York, cut off from all communication with the eastern provinces, must necessarily submit, and the way would be prepared for the speedy subjugation of all the others. Gen. Burgoyne, who had superseded Gen. Carleton, left Canada with 7500 well disciplined troops, and a large train of artillery, and accompanied by a numerous body of Canadians and Indians. On the 3d of July he arrived before Ticonderoga,*

* The following is Gov. Tryon's account of the forts in the province of New York in 1774:

"The city of New York, the metropolis, is protected by a fort and a range of batteries at the entrance of the East River or harbor, in good order, and capable of mounting about one hundred pieces of ordnance. Albany and Schenectady are defended by forts, and both places encircled by large pickets or stockades. with blockhouses at proper distances from each other, but which, since the peace, have been suffered to go to decay, and are now totally out of repair.

"The western forts are Fort Stanwix, and the forts at Oswego and Niagara; the two former are dismantled—a few men only kept at Os wego. Niagara is occupied by a garrison of the King's troops.

which was garrisoned by 3000 continental soldiers and militia under Gen. St. Clair. Finding themselves unable to maintain the fortress against a force so much superior, the Americans, on the night of the 5th, withdrew and retreated toward Fort Edward. The English immediately took possession of Ticonderoga, with a large quantity of provisions and military stores. The Americans were pursued and overtaken, and in several actions suffered severely. This fortress was an important one, and its surrender was as unfortunate as it was unexpected. Besides, Gen. Schuyler, who had the command of the American army, numbered little rising of 4000 men after all the troops of St. Clair were united with his own at Fort Edward; an army which, under equal circumstances, could present no barrier to the progress of the victorious army of Burgoyne. A general alarm spread throughout the country, and especially through New York. This alarm was increased in Tryon County, when, on the 15th of July, Thomas, one of the principal Oneida sachems, who had just returned from Canada, where he had been present at an Indian council held at the Indian castle of Cassassenny, gave the following account:

"Col. Claus invited strongly the Indians to join him in his expedition to Fort Schuyler, mentioning

---

"The northern forts are Fort Edward, which is abandoned. A few men only are kept at the works at the south end of Lake George to facilitate the transportation to the next forts, which are Ticonderoga and Crown Point. These are both garrisoned by His Majesty's troops, but since the fire only a small guard is kept there, the principal part of the garrison being withdrawn and posted at Ticonderoga."

the number of his white men, and saying, that he has sent already a number of Indians with the army to Ticonderoga, and he is sure that Ticonderoga will be rendered to them and Claus. Repeated again thus: Ticonderoga is mine. This is true, you may depend on it, and not one gun shall be fired.

"The same is true with Fort Schuyler; I am sure, said Col. Claus, that when I come toward that fort, and the commanding officer there shall see me, he shall also not fire one shot, and render the fort to me." The sachem, after relating this speech, added: "Now, brothers, this which I related to you is the real truth, and I tell you further, for notice, that Sir John Johnson, with his family, and Col. Claus, with his family, are now in Oswego, with 700 Indians, and their number of white men are 400 regulars and about 600 Tories, lying yet on an island on this side of Oswegatchie; therefore now is your time, brothers, to awake and not to sleep longer; or, on the contrary, it shall go with Fort Schuyler as it went already with Ticonderoga. Col. Butler is, as I heard, to arrive yesterday (being the 14th) from Niagara at Oswego, with his party, not knowing how strong in number, and shall immediately keep a council there with the Five Nations, (which are already called,) and offer the hatchet to them to join him and strike the Americans.

"*Brothers!* I therefore desire you to be spirited, and to encourage one another to march on in assistance of Fort Schuyler. Come up and show yourselves as men, to defend and save your country, before it is too late. Despatch yourselves to clear the brush about the fort, and send a party to cut trees in the Wood Creek to stop up the same.

"*Brothers!* If you don't come soon without delay to assist this place, we cannot stay much longer on your side; for if you leave this fort without succor, and the enemy shall get possession thereof, we shall suffer like you in your settlements, and shall be destroyed with you. We are suspicious that your enemies have engaged the Indians, and endeavor daily yet to strike and fight against you; and Gen. Schuyler refuses always that we shall take up arms in the country's behalf.

"*Brothers!* I can assure you that as soon as Butler's speech at Oswego shall be over, they intend to march down the country immediately, till to Albany. You may judge yourselves; if you don't try to resist we will be obliged to join them or fly from our castles, as we cannot hinder them alone. We, the good friends of the country, are of opinion that if more force appears at Fort Schuyler the enemy will not move from Oswego to invade these frontiers; you may depend on it we are willing to help you if you will do some efforts too."

In the spring of 1776, Colonels Van Schaick and Dayton were sent into Tryon County with detachments of continental soldiers, and were stationed at Johnstown and German Flats. Col. Dayton, stationed at the latter place, was ordered by Gen. Schuyler, in June of this year, to take post and erect a fortification at Fort Stanwix. The militia of the county were called out to assist him. This fort occupied a part of the site of the present village of Rome, in

Oneida County, situated at the head of navigation of the Mohawk, and at the carrying-place between that river and Wood Creek, from whence the boats passed to Oswego; it was a post of great importance to the western part of New York. The French, with their usual sagacity, when endeavoring to monopolize the Indian trade, had erected a fortification at this place. At the commencement of the war it appears to have gone to decay; a few families had settled there, forming the extreme western outpost of civilization, save the forts of Oswego and Niagara. The fort erected by Col. Dayton was called Fort Schuyler, in honor of Gen. Schuyler. It is designated by that name in most of the letters and official communications of the officers, including Gen. Schuyler himself. It has been confounded by some with Fort Schuyler, which was built in the French wars, near where Utica now stands, and named in honor of Col. Schuyler, the uncle of Gen. Schuyler. At the time of the Revolution there was no fort at the latter place. There was a clear field, which still retained the name of Fort Schuyler, as did the settlement west that of Fort Stanwix.

The last of April, 1777, Col. Gansevoort, with the 3d regiment of the New York line of State troops, was ordered to Fort Schuyler. The fort was still unfinished, and the early part of the summer was spent in advancing the works. It was not even completed when afterward invested. The duties of the troops in consequence were extremely arduous.

The information as above given by the Oneida sachem occasioned some alarm. It developes part of the original plan of the campaign. The forces destined against this fort were under the command of Gen. Barry St. Leger. Should he succeed in taking Fort Schuyler, he was to pass down the Mohawk valley to Johnstown, and to fortify himself there. From this place he could easily make a diversion in favor of Burgoyne, or aid in cutting off the retreat of the American army, as circumstances should render necessary. The rich Mohawk country would at the same time furnish provisions for his own and the other invading armies.

Secret information of their movements had been industriously circulated among all the disaffected inhabitants of Tryon County. Insinuations of an alarming nature were thrown out, and not without effect. The Indians, it was said, would ravage the whole intervening country. Many who had not before acted decidedly, now espoused the cause of the mother country, and in small parties stole away and went to the enemy.

A few days before the communication of the sachem was made, the committee had ordered out 200 militia to aid in garrisoning Fort Schuyler. A part only obeyed; on the 15th they ordered two companies of continental troops, stationed at different places in the county under their direction, to repair to the fort. They made various excuses, that they had been sent out as scouts, and were unfit for garrison duty, and refused to comply with the orders; they afterward complied. Under these circumstances, on the 17th of July, Brig. Gen. Nicholas Herkimer published the following proclamation:

"Whereas, it appears certain that the enemy, of about 2000 strong, Christians and savages, are arrived at Oswego with the intention to invade our frontiers, I think it proper and most necessary for the defense of our country, and it shall be ordered by me as soon as the enemy approaches, that every male person, being in health, from 16 to 60 years of age, in this our county, shall, as in duty bound, repair immediately, with arms and accoutrements, to the place to be appointed in my orders, and will then march to oppose the enemy with vigor, as true patriots, for the just defense of their country. And those that are above 60 years, or really unwell and incapable to march, shall then assemble, also armed, at the respective places where women and children will be gathered together, in order for defense against the enemy, if attacked, as much as lies in their power. But concerning the disaffected, and who will not directly obey such orders, they shall be taken along with their arms, secured under guard, to join the main body. And as such an invasion regards every friend to the country in general, but of this county in particular, to show his zeal and well-affected spirit in actual defense of the same, all the members of the committee, as well as all those who, by former commissions or otherwise, have been exempted from any other military duty, are requested to repair also, when called, to such place as shall be appointed, and join to repulse our foes. Not doubting that the Almighty Power, upon our humble prayers and sincere trust in him, will then graciously succor our arms in battle, for our just cause, and victory cannot fail on our side."

On the 30th of July, the committee received the following letter from Thomas Spencer, dated Oneida, July 29th.

"At a meeting of the chiefs, they tell me that there is but four days remaining of the time set for the king's troops to come to Fort Schuyler, and they think it likely they will be here sooner. The chiefs desire the commanding officers at Fort Schuyler not to make a Ticonderoga of it; but they hope you will be courageous. They desire Gen. Schuyler may have this with speed, and send a good army here; there is nothing to do at New York; we think there is men to be spared; we expect the road is stopped to the inhabitants by a party through the woods; we shall be surrounded as soon as they come. This may be our last advice, as these soldiers are part of those that are to hold a treaty. Send this to the committee; as soon as they receive it let the militia rise up and come to Fort Schuyler. To-morrow we are a-going to the Three Rivers to the treaty. We expect to meet the warriors, and when we come there and declare we are for peace, we expect to be used with indifference and sent away. Let all the troops that come to Fort Schuyler take care on their march, as there is a party of Indians to stop the road below the Fort, about 80 or 100. We hear they are to bring their cannon up Fish Creek. We hear there is 1000 going to meet the enemy. We advise not—the army is too large for so few men to defend the fort—we send a belt of 8 rows to confirm the truth of what we say." Spencer added—"It looks likely to me the troops are near; hope all friends to liberty, and that love their families, will not be backward, but exert themselves, as one resolute blow would secure the friendship of the Six Nations, and almost free this part of the country from the incursions of the enemy."

About the time of the receipt of this letter several batteaux, guarded by one or two companies of batteauxmen, arrived from Schenectady with stores destined for Fort Schuyler. When the letter was laid before the committee, a question arose whether the militia should be ordered out immediately, or whether they should wait the arrival of troops who would undoubtedly be sent by Gen. Schuyler. The necessity of guarding more effectually the batteaux was urged. The former course was adopted, and means were taken for assembling as many of the militia as possible. Their own firesides were to be invaded; the time for exertion had come—a time which they ought to have anticipated, and for which, from the ample notice they had received, they ought to have made the best possible preparations. They were determined, however, to atone for their neglect. The fears excited by the previous losses had considerably subsided, and Gen. Herkimer soon found himself at the head of 800 men; most of the committee were among the number, as officers or volunteers. Little order was observed on their march, and those precautions so necessary to guard against surprise were too much neglected. This was the less excusable, as they had been apprised of the ambuscade of the Indians. Spencer, who had joined the troops, insisted on keeping out flanking parties. In this he was seconded by several of the officers. Gen. Herkimer himself was of this opinion; but in consequence of some remarks made by some of the inferior officers, imputing cowardice to him, he directed them to advance with all possible dispatch. If any excuse can be offered, it must arise from the fact, that they had learned that the fort was invested, and were fearful it might be surrendered before their arrival. The distance most of the troops marched, was between fifty and sixty miles, through woods and over miseral le roads. Flanking parties, travelling through woods, and crossing streams and marshes, would nece sarily retard the progress of the main body, should they only keep pace with them.

Gen. St. Leger left Oswego, about the time before mentioned, for Fort Schuyler, with about 1700 men. On the 28th of July he sent forward Lieut. Bird, with 60 or 70 men, to reconnoitre and to ascertain the situation of the fort. Under date of July 31st, St. Leger wrote to him the following letter:

"I have received yours of the 30th. If they are strongly posted, risk nothing, as by both parties (yours and Hare's) joined, an investiture may be easily made till my arrival, which will be sometime to-morrow, with my artillery, the 34th and King's regiment, with the Hessian riflemen, and the whole corps of Indians. The rest of the army is led by Sir John, and will be up the day afterward.

Yours, very faithfully,

BARRY ST. LEGER,

Brig. General.

On the 2d of August, Lieut. Bird wrote to Gen. St. Leger, and the following is the conclusion: "Twelve Massesaugers came up two or three hours after my departure. These, with the scout of fifteen, I had the honor to mention to you in my last, are sufficient to invest Fort Stanwix, if you honor me so far as not to order to the contrary."

Under the same date St. Leger returned the following answer:

"I this instant received your letter containing the account of your operations since you were detached, which I with great pleasure tell you have been sensible and spirited; your resolution of investing Fort Stanwix is perfectly right; and to enable you to do it with greater effect, I have detached Joseph (Brant) and his corps of Indians to reinforce you. You will observe that I will have nothing but an investiture made, and in case the enemy, observing the discretion and judgment with which it is made, should offer to capitulate, you are to tell them that you are sure I am well disposed to listen to them; this is not to take any honor out of a young soldier's hands, but by the presence of the troops to prevent the barbarity and carnage which will ever obtain where Indians make so superior a part of a detachment; I shall move from hence at eleven o'clock, and be early in the afternoon at the entrance of the creek.

I am, sir, your most obt. and humble ser't,

BARRY ST. LEGER.

Nine Mile Point, Aug. 2, 1777.

On the 3d of August, Gen. St. Leger arrived before

the fort; he soon found that the garrison had no disposition to surrender. Col. Gansevoort had anticipated his approach, and with his brave soldiers were determined to defend their post to the last. Soon after St. Leger published the following proclamation:

"By Barry St. Leger, commander in chief of a chosen body of troops from the grand army, as well as an extensive corps of Indian allies from all the Nations, &c. &c.

"The forces intrusted to my command are designed to act in concert, and upon a common principle with the numerous armies and fleets which already display, in every quarter of America, the power, the justice, and when properly sought, the mercy of the king. The cause in which the British armies are thus exerted, applies to the most affecting interests of the human heart; and the military servants of the crown, at first called forth for the sole purpose of restoring the rights of the constitution, now combine with love of their country and duty to their sovereign, the other extensive incitements which spring from a due sense of the general privileges of mankind. To the eyes and ears of the temperate part of the public, and to the hearts of suffering thousands in the provinces, be the melancholy appeal, whether the present unnatural rebellion has not been made a foundation for the completest system of tyranny, that ever God in his displeasure suffered for a time to be exercised over a froward and stubborn generation.

"Arbitrary imprisonment, confiscation of property, persecution and torture unprecedented in the inquisitions of the Romish Church, are among the palpable enormities that verify the affirmation. These are inflicted by assemblies and committees, who dare to profess themselves friends to liberty, upon the most quiet subjects, without distinction of age or sex, for the sole crime, often for the sole suspicion, of having adhered in principle to the government under which they were born, and to which, by every tie divine and human, they owe allegiance. To consummate these shocking proceedings, the profanation of religion is added to the most profligate prostitution of common reason; the consciences of men are set at naught, and multitudes are compelled not only to bear arms, but also to swear subjection to an usurpation they abhor.

"Animated by these considerations; at the head of troops in the full powers of health, discipline, and valor; determined to strike where necessary, and anxious to spare where possible, I, by these presents, invite and exhort all persons in all places where the progress of this army may point, and by the blessing of God I will extend it far, to maintain such a conduct as may justify me in protecting their lands, habitations, and families. The intention of this address is to hold forth security and not depredation to the country.

"To those, whose spirit and principle may induce to partake the glorious task of redeeming their countrymen from dungeons, and re-establishing the blessings of legal government, I offer encouragement and employment, and upon the first intelligence of their associations, I will find means to assist their undertakings. The domestic, the industrious, the infirm, and even the timid inhabitants, I am desirous to protect, provided they remain quietly at their houses—that they do not suffer their bridges or roads to be broken up, nor by any other acts, directly or indirectly, endeavor to obstruct the operations of the king's troops, or supply or assist those of the enemy. Every species of provisions brought to my camp will be paid for at an eqiutable rate, and in solid coin.

"If, notwithstanding these endeavors, and sincere inclinations to effect them, the frenzy of hostility should remain, I trust I shall stand acquitted in the eyes of God and men, in denouncing and executing the vengeance of the state against the wilful outcasts. The messengers of justice and of wrath await them in the field, and devastation, famine, and every concomitant horror, that a reluctant, but indispensable prosecution of military duty must occasion, will bar the way to their return.

(*Signed*) BARRY ST. LEGER.

By order of the Commander in Chief,

WILL. OSB. HAMILTON, *Secretary.*

How well the threats and promises set forth in the foregoing letters and proclamation were fulfilled, will appear in the sequel.

Learning that Gen. Herkimer was approaching to the relief of the garrison, and not being disposed to receive him in his camp, St. Leger detached a body of Indians and Tories under Brant and Col. Butler to watch his approach, and to intercept, if possible, his march. The surrounding country afforded every facility for the practice of the Indian mode of warfare. In the deep recesses of its forests they were secure from observation, and to them they could retreat in case they were defeated. Finding that the militia approached in a very careless manner, Butler determined to attack them by surprise. He selected a place well fitted for such an attack. A few miles from the fort there was a deep ravine, sweeping toward the east in a semicircular form, and having a northern and southern direction. The bottom of this ravine was marshy, and the road along which the militia were marching crossed it by means of a log causeway. The ground thus partly enclosed by the ravine was elevated and level. Along the road, on each side on this height of land, Butler disposed his men.

About ten o'clock on the morning of the 6th of August, the Tryon County militia arrived at this place without any suspicions of danger. The dark foliage of the forest trees, with a thick growth of underbrush, entirely concealed the enemy from their view. The advanced guard, with about two-thirds of the whole force, had gained the elevated ground; the baggage wagons had descended into the ravine—Col. Fisher's regiment was still on the east side—when the Indians arose, and with a dreadful yell poured a destructive fire upon them. The advanced guard was entirely cut off. Those who survived the first fire were immediately cut down with the tomahawk. The horror of the scene was increased by the personal appearance of the savages, who were almost naked, and painted in a most hideous manner. They ran down each side, keeping up a constant fire, and united at the causeway; thus dividing the militia into two bodies. The rear regiment, after a feeble resistance, fled in confusion, and were pursued by the Indians. They suffered more severely than they would have done had they stood their ground, or advanced to the support of the main body in front.

The latter course would have been attended with great loss, but might probably have been effected. The forward division had no alternative but to fight. Facing out in every direction, they sought shelter behind the trees and returned the fire of the enemy with spirit. In the beginning of the battle the Indians, whenever they saw that a gun was fired from behind a tree, rushed up and tomahawked the person thus firing before he had time to reload his gun.* To counteract this, two men were ordered to station themselves behind one tree, the one reserving his fire until the Indian ran up. In this way the Indians were made to suffer severely in return. The fighting had continued for some time, and the Indians had begun to give way, when Major Watts, a brother-in-law of Sir John Johnson, brought up a reinforcement, consisting of a detachment of Johnson's Greens. The blood of the Germans boiled with indignation at the sight of these men. Many of the Greens were personally known to them. They had fled their country, and were now

* "Again. Let me recall, gentlemen, to your recollection, that bloody field in which Herkimer fell. There was found the Indian and the white man born on the banks of the Mohawk, their left hand clenched in each other's hair, the right grasping in a gripe of death the knife plunged in each other's bosom; thus they lay frowning."—*Gouverneur Morris's Address before the New York Historical Society.*

returned in arms to subdue it. Their presence under any circumstances would have kindled up the resentment of these militia; but coming up as they now did, in aid of a retreating foe, called into exercise the most bitter feelings of hostility. They fired upon them as they advanced, and then, rushing from behind their covers, attacked them with their bayonets, and those who had none, with the butt end of their muskets—"rage supplies arms." This contest was maintained, hand to hand, for nearly half an hour. The Greens made a manful resistance, but were finally obliged to give way before the dreadful fury of their assailants, with the loss of thirty killed upon the spot where they first entered. Major Watts was wounded and taken prisoner, though afterward left upon the field.

In this assault Col. Cox is said to have been killed; possessing an athletic frame, with a daring spirit, he mingled in the thickest of the fight. His voice could be distinctly heard, as he cheeered on his men, or isssued his orders, amid the clashing of arms and the yells of the contending savages.

About one o'clock Adam Helmer, who had been sent by Gen. Herkimer with a letter to Col. Gansevoort, announcing his approach, arrived at the fort. At 2 o'clock, Lieut. Col. Willet, with two hundred and and seven men, sallied from the fort for the purpose of making a diversion in favor of Gen. Herkimer, and attacked the camp of the enemy. This engagement lasted about an hour, when the enemy were driven off with considerable loss. Col. Willet having thrown out flanking parties, and ascertained that the retreat was not feigned, ordered his men to take as much of the spoil as they could remove, and to destroy the remainder. On their return to the fort, above the landing, and near where the old French fort stood, a party of 200 regular troops appeared, and prepared to give battle. A smart fire of musketry, aided by the cannon from the fort, soon obliged them to retreat, when Willet returned into the fort with his spoil, and without the loss of a single man. A part of that spoil was placed upon the walls of the fortress, where it waved in triumph in sight of the vanquished enemy.

This timely and well-conducted sally was attended with complete success. A shower of rain had already caused the enemy to slacken their fire, when finding by their reports that their camp was attacked and taken, they withdrew and left the militia in possession of the field.

Few battles have been fought at a greater disadvantage than was that of Oriskany, on the part of the Americans. After recovering from the confusion of the first attack, they found themselves without ammunition, save that in their cartouch-boxes. Their baggage wagons were in possession of the enemy. The weather was warm, and, surrounded by the enemy, they could get no water. In this state they defended themselves against a far superior force for five or six hours. The severe remarks which have been made upon the militia engaged in this battle, are certainly not warranted. They had been imprudent, but they were brave, and, in this kind of fight, skillful.

The Americans lost in killed nearly 200, and about as many wounded and prisoners; they carried off beween 40 and 50 of their wounded. They encamped the first night upon the ground where old Fort Schuyler was built.

Among the wounded was Gen. Herkimer. Early in the action his leg was fractured by a musket ball. The leg was amputated a few days after, but in consequence of the unfavorable state of the weather, and want of skill in the surgeons, mortification ensued, and occasioned his death. On receiving his wound, his horse having been killed, he directed his saddle to be placed upon a little hillock of earth and rested himself upon it. Being advised to choose a place where he would be less exposed, he replied: "I will face the enemy." Surrounded by a few men, he continued to issue his orders with firmness. In this situation, and in the heat of the battle, he very deliberately took from his pocket his tinder-box and lit his pipe, which he smoked with great composure. He was certainly to blame for not using greater caution on his march, but the coolness and intrepidity which he exhibited when he found himself ambuscaded, aided materially in restoring order and in inspiring his men with courage. His loss was deeply lamented by his friends and by the inhabitants of Tryon County. The Continental Congress, in October following, directed that a monument should be erected to his memory, of the value of five hundred dollars.

In a letter accompanying the resolution, the Congress say: "Every mark of distinction shown to the memory of such illustrious men as offer up their lives for the liberty and happiness of this country, reflects real honor on those who pay the grateful tribute; and by holding up to others the prospect of fame and immortality, will animate them to tread in the same path.

Governor George Clinton, who forwarded the letter and resolution to the Tryon County committee added:

"Enclosed you have a copy of a letter and resolves of Congress for erecting a monument to the memory of your late gallant General. While with you I lament the causes, I am impressed with a due sense of the great and justly merited honor the continent has, in this instance, paid to the memory of that brave man." We regret to state that no monument has ever been erected to his memory in pursuance of that or any other resolve.*

---

* The scenes with which this sturdy old patriot was connected, were of thrilling and romantic interest. His interview with Brant, at Unadilla; his conduct on the bloody field of Oriskany, and his subsequent death, were all characteristic, and would form a fine subject for the poet or the painter. Henry R. Schoolcraft, Esq., to whom the country is so much indebted for his researches in Indian history, thus describes the closing scenes:

"The wounded General himself was thus carried by his affectionate soldiery to his own house, below the Little Falls, with his leg badly shattered and bandaged. Ten days after the battle, amputation became necessary. The operation was unskillfully performed by a French surgeon in Arnold's detachment, who could not succeed in effectually staunching the blood, and he thus fell a victim to professional ignorance. But he preserved, on his dying bed, the same calmness and composure which had marked his conduct on the field. As he saw that his dissolution must shortly ensue from the continued bleeding and the bad state of his wound, he called for his family Bible, and having gathered his domestic circle around him, he read aloud, in a clear voice, the thirty-ninth psalm—'O Lord, rebuke me not in thy wrath, neither chasten me in thy hot displeasure; for thine arrows stick fast in me, and thy hand presseth me sore.' The entire psalm is one of singular appropriateness; and the acquaintance with the sacred volume

Tryon County suffered dreadfully in this battle; Col. Cox, Majors Eisinlord, Klepsattle, and Van Slyck were killed, as was also Thomas Spencer, the Indian interpreter.

John Frey, major of brigade, with Col. Bellenger, were taken prisoners. Most of the inferior officers were either killed or taken. The county was filled with mourning. The enemy sustained a severe loss likewise. The Indians, according to their own statements, lost in killed nearly 100 warriors. More than 30 of the Seneca tribe alone were killed. The loss of the regulars and Tories is not known, but in the contest with Herkimer and Willet must have been nearly or quite a hundred.

The following extracts are from a statement made

---

which its selection evinces, proves that if, in the field, he was an undaunted soldier, he was not less, on the threshold of another world, a trustful Christian. Other generals have fallen in the arms of victory, but Nicholas Herkimer may be said to have fallen in the arms of his MAKER. Congress passed a resolution, and appropriated money to erect a monument to his memory—an act of justice yet unperformed; but his name has long been inscribed in the hearts of his countrymen as one of the noble patriots to whom we owe our national independence."—*Proceedings of the N. Y. Historical Society.*"

Two or three years ago, upon the memorial of the New York Historical Society, a bill was reported by the Committee on Revolutionary Claims, in the House of Representatives of the United States, making a liberal appropriation for the erection of a monument to Herkimer. But it was swallowed up in the great gulf of "unfinished business;" the bill was never reached on the calendar. The remains of General Herkimer lie buried in the hillside, near his former residence, at a point overloking, to a great extent, the valley of the Mohawk. But there is no monument to attract the attention of the teeming millions who throng that great travelled thoroughfare. A small rough and unby the State Council of Safety, on the 15th of August, to the delegates of the province in General Congress:

"If it is not inconsistent with the general interest, we would most earnestly wish for one or two regiments of riflemen, who would be very useful in our woody country, and whose very name would serve to intimidate the savages. Would the circumstances admit of our drawing our whole force to a point, and were the passes to the southward secured by a sufficient number of troops, exclusive of our militia, we should not have thought it necessary to call in any aid from the neighboring States; but at present, attacked on every side, we stand in need of more assistance than we have, from present appearances, reason to hope for."

The same report thus alludes to the late transaction in Tryon County:

---

hewn head-stone, without figure or letter of any description, alone marks the place of his sepulture.

It is a matter of some historical interest, that the siege of Fort Schuyler and battle of Oriskany, was the *first subject* of congratulation in the *first message* of the *first Governor* of the *State* of New York.

"At present, by the kind interposition of Providence, the cloud which hung over us seems in a great measure dispelled, and we have reason to expect a happy issue to this campaign. *The good conduct and bravery of the garrison of Fort Schuyler, seconded by the intrepidity of the late gallant General Herkimer and the militia of Tryon County, have entirely frustrated the designs of the enemy upon that part of the State."—Extract from Message of Gov. George Clinton, Sept.* 10, 1777.

And, singular as it may seem, the subject of a monument to General Herkimer, formed the *last* recommendation in the *last* message of De Witt Clinton, the illustrious nephew of the first Governor:

"At the last meeting of the Legislature, I recommended a monumental erection in honor of General Herkimer, and to which I beg leave to refer you."—*Gov. Clinton's Message, Jan.* 1*st*, 1828.

"By the papers enclosed you will find that our troops and militia have behaved with becoming spirit in Tryon County; but as it is out of our power to support them, we fear that that county must fall into the hands of the enemy; in which case, by means of the Indians, who will then be wholly in their power, they may ravage all that part of this State which lies to the westward of Hudson's River, as well as the frontiers of New Jersey and Pennsylvania."

After reviewing the general state of the province, and remarking that in many places the disaffected had gained the ascendency, and compelled the Whigs to side with them, they added, with true Spartan spirit: "We are resolved, if we do fall, to fall as becomes brave men."

But to return to Fort Schuyler: St. Leger, availing himself of this disastrous battle, endeavored by strong representations of Indian cruelty to obtain immediate possession of the fort. Major Frey, who was wounded, and Col. Bellenger, both prisoners, threatened probably with the treatment which some others received, on the evening of the battle wrote to Col. Gansevoort the following letter:

"9 *o'clock, P. M.—Camp before Fort Stanwix,*
6*th August*, 1777.

"SIR,

"It is with concern we are to acquaint you that this was the fatal day in which the succors, which were intended for your relief, have been attacked and defeated with great loss of numbers of killed, wounded, and taken prisoners. Our regard for your safety and lives, and our sincere advice to you is, if you will avoid inevitable ruin and destruction, to surrender the fort you pretend to defend against a formidable body of troops and a good train of artillery, which we are witnesses of; when at the same time you have no farther support or relief to expect. We are sorry to inform you that most of the principal officers are killed, to wit, Gen. Herkimer, Colonels Cox, Seeber, Isaac Paris, Captain Graves, and many others, too tedious to mention. The British army from Canada being now perhaps before Albany, the possession of which place of course includes the conquest of the Mohawk River and this fort."

The following endorsement is on the back of this letter: "Gen. St. Leger, on the day of the date of this letter; made a verbal summons of the fort by his adjutant general and Colonel Butler, and who then handed this letter; when Colonel Gansevoort refused any answer to a verbal summons, unless made by Gen. St. Leger himself, but at the mouth of his cannon"—a written summons was the result. This demand was repeated on the 8th, when the adjutant general and Col. Butler were led blindfolded into the presence of the gallant commanders, Gansevoort and Willet. To the promises and threats of Butler they replied, that it would only be another Fort William Henry scene, and that they would not surrender it, and especially upon a verbal summons.

On the 9th, St. Leger wrote Col. Gansevoort the following letter:

"Sir,

"Agreeably to your wishes, I have the honor to give you, on paper, the message of yesterday; though I cannot conceive, explicit and humane as it was, how it could admit of more than one construction. After the defeat of the reinforcement, and the fate of all your principal leaders, on which naturally you built your hopes, and having the strongest reason, from verbal intelligence, and the matter contained in the letters that fell into my hands, and knowing thoroughly the situation of Gen. Burgoyne's army, to be confident that you are without resource; in my fears and tenderness for your personal safety from the hands of the Indians, enraged for the loss of some of their principal and most favorite leaders, I called to council the chiefs of all the nations, and after having used every method that humanity could suggest, to soften their minds, and lead them patiently to bear their own losses, by reflecting on the irretrievable misfortune of their enemy, I at last labored the point my humanity wished for; which the chiefs assured me of the next morning, after a consultation with each nation that evening, at their fire-places. Their answer, in its fullest extent, they insisted should be carried by Col. Butler; which he has given you in the most categorical manner. You are well acquainted that Indians never send messages without accompanying them with menaces on non-compliance, that a civilized enemy would never think of doing. You may rest assured, therefore, that no insult was meant to be offered to your situation by the king's servants in the message they peremptorily demanded to be carried by Col. Butler; I am now to repeat what has been told you by my adjutant general. That provided you deliver up your garrison, with everything as it stood at the moment the first message was sent, your people shall be treated with every attention that a humane and generous enemy can give.

I have the honor to be, Sir,

Your most obedient and humble servant,

BARRY ST. LEGER,

Brigadier General of his Majesty's Forces.

Camp before Fort Stanwix, Aug. 9th, 1777.

"P. S. I expect an immediate answer, as the Indians are extremely impatient; and if this proposal is rejected, I am afraid it will be attended with very fatal consequences, not only to you and your garrison, but the whole country down the Mohawk River; such consequences as would be very repugnant to my sentiments of humanity, but after this entirely out of my power to prevent."

Colonel Gansevoort returned the following laconic answer:

"SIR,

"In answer to your letter of this day's date, I have only to say that it is my determined resolution, with the forces under my command, to defend this fort, at every hazard, to the last extremity, in behalf of the United American States, who have placed me here to defend it against all their enemies.

I have the honor to be, Sir,

Your most obt. and humble ser't,

PETER GANSEVOORT,

Col. commanding Fort Stanwix.

St. Leger threw up several redoubts, but his artillery was not sufficient to make any impression upon the fort. "The siege continued until the 22d of August, 1777, when St. Leger had advanced to within one hundred and fifty yards of the fort. Ignorant of the fate of Colonel Willet, his second in command, who, with Lieutenant Stockwell, had undertaken a hazardous enterprise to procure relief for the garrison; his provisions daily exhausting; some of his officers, anxious to accept the proffered protection of St. Leger from the fury of the savages by making a timely surrender; all communication with the fort cut off by the besiegers, and having no certain prospect of relief; Gansevoort, who knew not how to yield when he was guarding his country's honor and safety, had adopted the desperate resolution, in case no reinforcement should arrive before his provisions were reduced to a few days' supply (after distributing them among his men) to head the brave remnant of his garrison, and fight his way at night through the enemy, or perish in the attempt. Those who knew him best, knew how well he dared to execute his resolves."*

Col. Willet and Lieut. Stockwell left the fort by night, and, having eluded the enemy, passed down the Mohawk country for the purpose of again assembling the militia for its relief. It is one among the many instances of personal courage which were exhibited upon this frontier, by that intrepid soldier, Col. Willet. So successful was he in all his movements, that the Indians, believing him to be possessed

* American Biographical Dictionary.

of supernatural powers, gave to him the name of "the Devil."

Gen. Schuyler, who from the beginning had felt a great anxiety as to the event of this siege, knowing how disastrous it would be, should the fort be taken, on the news of the defeat of Gen. Herkimer dispatched Gens. Learned and Arnold, with a brigade of men, to its relief. Under date of August 10th, Albany, he wrote Col. Gansevoort the following letter:

"Dear Colonel—A body of troops left this yesterday, and others are following, to raise the siege of Fort Schuyler. Everybody here believes you will defend it to the last; and I strictly enjoin you so to do.

"Gen. Burgoyne is at Fort Edward—our army at Stillwater—great reinforcements coming from the eastward, and we trust all will be well, and that the enemy will be repulsed."

Gen. Arnold, with about 900 light troops, leaving behind all the heavy baggage, advanced some distance before Gen. Learned, and on the 22d of August addressed the following letter to Col. Gansevoort, dated at German Flats:

"Dear Colonel—I wrote you the 19th, that I should be with you in a few days; since which your express is arrived, and informs me you are in high spirits, and no apprehensions at present. I have been retarded by the badness of the roads, waiting for some baggage and ammunition wagons, and for the militia, who did not at first turn out with that spirit I expected; they are now joining me in great numbers; a few days will relieve you ; be under no kind of apprehension ; I know the strength of the enemy, and how to deal with them. Enclosed are several letters and papers, which will announce to you a signal victory gained by Gen. Stark over the enemy ; you will accept my congratulatory compliments on the occasion. Howe, with the shattered remnant of his army, are now on shipboard. The last date was the 4th August; he was in the Gulf Stream, becalmed. Burgoyne, I hear this minute, is retreating to Ty. I make no doubt our army, which is near fifteen thousand, will cut off his retreat.

"Adieu, and believe me to be, dear colonel, yours sincerely,

B. ARNOLD."

From this place, a few days before, Gen. Arnold sent forward Hanyost Schuyler, a refugee, to the camp of St. Leger. He had given him his liberty, on condition that he would announce his approach, and make an exaggerated statement of his forces. He retained his brother as an hostage.

In the camp of St. Leger all was confusion. The Indians, disappointed in obtaining plunder, and enraged on account of their losses, could scarcely be restrained. They supposed that in the action they had fired across and killed each other. The confusion was greatly increased by the arrival of Schuyler. On being questioned as to the number of troops approaching, he answered—he knew not, but they were as numerous as the leaves upon the forest trees. The Indians refused to remain any longer. All the arts of their leaders were unavailing. On the 22d of August, St. Leger retired in great confusion, leaving his camp with a great part of his baggage. The Indians plundered from their friends in the retreat, and, it is said, raised a shout that the Americans were coming, and then amused themselves in witnessing the terror it occasioned. St. Leger has been accused by his subaltern officers of a want of energy. He is said to have been in a state of intoxication during most of the time his forces lay before the fort.

Thus ended the siege of Fort Schuyler, and a campaign which, at the commencement, threatened the valley of the Mohawk with conquest and devastation.

On the 24th of August, Gen. Arnold arrived, to the great joy of the garrison.

The fury and cruelty of the Indians and Tories may be learned from the following affidavit, the original of which is now in the office of the Secretary of State.. The high standing of Dr. Younglove, who died a few years since in the city of Hudson, is a sufficient voucher for its truth. The compiler has seen several persons to whom the same facts were communicated by him in his lifetime.

"Moses Younglove,* surgeon of General Herkimer's brigade of militia, deposeth and saith, that being in the battle of said militia, above Oriskany, on the 6th of August last, toward the close of said battle he surrendered himself a prisoner to a savage, who immediately gave him up to a sergeant of Sir John Johnson's regiment; soon after which, a lieutenant in

* See Appendix—Note E.

the Indian department came up, in company with several other Tories, when said Mr. Grinnis by name, drew his tomahawk at this deponent, and with deal of persuasion was hardly prevailed on to spare his life. He then plundered him of his watch, buckles, spurs, &c., and other Tories following his example, stripped him almost naked, with a great many threats, while they were stripping and massacreing prisoners on every side. That this deponent, on being brought before Mr. Butler, senior, who demanded of him what he was fighting for; to which this deponent answered, 'he fought for the liberty that God and nature gave him, and to defend himself and dearest connections from the massacre of savages.' To which Butler replied, 'you are a damned impudent rebel;' and so saying, immediately turned to the savages, encouraging them to kill him, and if they did not, the deponent and the other prisoners should be hanged on a gallows then preparing. That several prisoners were then taken forward towards the enemy's head-quarters, with frequent scenes of horror and massacre, in which Tories were active as well as savages; and in particular, one Davis, formerly known in Tryon County, on the Mohawk River. That Lieut. Singleton, of Sir John Johnson's regiment, being wounded, entreated the savages to kill the prisoners; which they accordingly did, as nigh as this deponent can judge, about six or seven.

"That Isaac Paris, Esq., was also taken the same road without receiving from them any remarkable insult except stripping, until some Tories came up, who kicked and abused him, after which the savages, thinking him a notable offender, murdered him barbarously. That those of the prisoners who were delivered up to the provost guards, were kept without victuals for many days, and had neither clothes, blankets, shelter nor fire, while the guards were ordered not to use any violence in protecting the prisoners from the savages, who came every day in large companies with knives, feeling of the prisoners, to know who were fattest. That they dragged one of the prisoners out of the guard with the most lamentable cries; tortured him for a long time, and this deponent was informed by both Tories and Indians, that they ate him, as appears they did another on an island in Lake Ontario, by bones found there nearly picked, just after they had crossed the lake with the prisoners. That the prisoners who were not delivered up, were murdered in considerable numbers from day to day round the camp, some of them so nigh that their shrieks were heard. That Capt. Martin, of the batteaux-men, was delivered to the Indians at Oswego, on pretense of his having kept back some useful intelligence. That this deponent during his imprisonment, and his fellows, were kept almost starved for provisions, and what they drew were of the worst kind, such as spoiled flour, biscuit full of maggots and mouldy, and no soap allowed, or other method of keeping clean, and were insulted, struck, &c., without mercy by the guards, without any provocation given. That this deponent was informed by several sergeants orderly on Gen. St. Leger, that twenty dollars were offered in general orders for every American scalp.

Moses Younglove.

John Barclay, *Chairman of Albany Committee.*"

Col. Gansevoort, in a letter under date of July 29th, confirms the statement, that St. Leger had offered twenty dollars for every American scalp. Small parties of Indians were then lurking around. A few days before, he adds, a firing was heard in the woods about five hundred yards from the fort. On sallying out, it was found that the Indians had fired upon three young girls who were engaged picking berries. Two of them were killed and scalped, and the third made her escape, wounded by two balls shot through her shoulder. The foregoing statements need no comment. The men who employed such instruments, and who stimulated them by promises and rewards, have received the just execration of an indignant people. I shall leave it to the reader to compare their conduct with their professions.

The retreat of St. Leger, with the success of the American arms at Bennington, restored hope and animation. Tryon County, smiling through her tears, obeyed with alacrity the call to reinforce Gen. Gates in the month of September following. Her militia mounted on horseback, some without saddles, others without bridles, sallied forth. If as uncouth in appearance, they were equally as zealous as the Knight of La Mancha. Large reinforcements of eastern militia having come on, the Tryon County militia were directed to return home before the surrender. The splendid victory over Burgoyne at Saratoga, with the surrender of his whole army, produced feelings of joy in the bosom of the Americans as deep and pervading as had been those of their despondency. Counting upon that success, many a hope was entertained, and many a prayer put up, that a speedy termination would be put to the unhappy war in which they were engaged.

It is not our province to inquire into the policy or propriety of the change of commanders of the northern army. Gen. Schuyler* was always a favorite with the inhabitants of New York. Those few survivors, who have come down to us, the relics of his day, still cherish his name in grateful remembrance. Tryon County owed much to his vigilance and attention. He rejoiced with her when she rejoiced, and wept with her when she wept. Alive to her exposed situation, he was always ready to afford relief, so far as it could be done consistently. The following is the conclusion of one of his letters to the committee on this subject, under date of July the 4th, 1777.

"I entreat you to keep up the spirits of the people; encourage them to step forth with alacrity whenever they may be called upon, and our enemies will be baffled in their attempts; and do not suppose that the United States of America will not afford you protection. I am sure I have always been ready and willing to afford every protection in my power, and hitherto it has been effectual, for no mischief worth mentioning has as yet been perpetrated in any part of your county, and you may depend upon it that upon no necessary occasion will you be left without proper support. May God keep you in his protection, is the sincere wish of, gentlemen,

Your friend and humble servant,

PHILIP SCHUYLER."

---

* See Appendix—Note G.

The Baroness De Reidesel, whose husband acted a conspicuous part under Burgoyne, bears the following testimony to his character, which I trust I shall be excused for inserting. After the surrender of Burgoyne, she was invited by Gen. Schuyler to spend some time in his family; Gen. Burgoyne was also a guest.

"Some days after this we arrived at Albany, where we so often wished ourselves; but we did not enter it as we expected we should, victors; we were received by the good Gen. Schuyler, his wife and daughters, not as enemies, but kind friends, and they treated us with the most marked attention and politeness, as they did Gen. Burgoyne, who had caused Gen. Schuyler's beautifully finished house to be burnt. In fact, they behaved like persons of exalted minds, who determined to bury all recollections of their own injuries in the contemplation of our misfortunes." Gen. Burgoyne was struck with Gen. Schuyler's generosity, and said to him, "You show me great kindness, although I have done you much injury." "That was the fate of war," replied the brave man; "let us say no more about it."

CHAPTER V.

" Sad was the year; by proud oppression driven,
When transatlantic Liberty arose;
Not in the sunshine and the smile of heaven,
But wrapt in whirlwinds and begirt with woes;
Amidst the strife of fratricidal foes
Her bright star was the light of burning plain
Her baptism is the weight of blood that flows
From kindred hearts—the blood of British veins;
And famine tracks her steps and pestilential pains."

It has been mentioned in a preceding chapter, that the inhabitants of Cherry Valley signed the association early in the summer of 1775. Their committee met with the committee of the county, and were connected with the transactions of that summer. It was stated in the account which has been given of the early settlement of Cherry Valley, that its inhabitants were very strict in their observances. The following letter was written by the committee, and is in confirmation of that statement:

Cherry Valley, June 9th, 1775.

" Sirs,

" We received yours of yesterday, relative to the meeting of the committee on Sunday, which surprised us not a little, inasmuch as it seems not to be on any alarming circumstance; which, if it was, we should readily attend. But as that does not appear to us to be the case, we think it is very improper; for unless the necessity of the committee sitting superexceed the duties to be performed in attending the public worship of God, we think it ought to be put off till another day; and therefore we conclude not to give our attendance at this time, unless you adjourn the sitting of the committee till Monday morning; and in that case, we will give our attendance as early as you please. But otherwise, we do not allow ourselves to be cut short of attending on the public worship; except the case be so necessitous as to exceed sacrifice. We conclude with wishing success to the common cause, and subscribe ourselves the free-born sons of liberty.

John Moore.
Samuel Clyde.
Samuel Campbell.

"If you proceed to sit on the Sabbath, please to read this letter to the committee, which we think will sufficiently assign our reasons for not attending."

This letter was sent to the county committee.

During the early part of the summer of 1776, Capt. Robert M'Kean of Cherry Valley raised a company of rangers, who were stationed at that place. As this settlement was the principal one to the south of the Mohawk, it was much exposed to incursions of the Indians in that direction. The Indians had their paths from Oquago along up the main streams flowing into the eastern branch of the Susquehanna. From thence they passed through the low indentations to the Mohawk. One of these passes was through Cherry Valley. Every movement of the Indians about Oquago was calculated, therefore, to excite their fears. Orders having been given for the removal of Capt. M'Kean's company, the following letter was written to the committee, in the name of the inhabitants, by the Rev. Mr. Dunlop, under date of June 3d, 1776.

"Sirs,

"We, the inhabitants of Cherry Valley, being assembled yesterday at a public town-meeting, and among other things taking the present critical situation of affairs into consideration, looked upon ourselves, and the neighborhood around us, Springfield and Newtown-Martin, as a frontier, lying very open and unguarded, and very much exposed to the enemy, in case an Indian war should break out, or any party of the enemy should take it into their heads to come down upon us; and that it would be absolutely necessary to have a party of men stationed here among us, in order to keep a sharp look-out, and to scout all around our frontiers; lest at any time we be taken by surprise. And therefore, have appointed me to write to you, to lay this matter warmly before the committee, and earnestly to impress them with the absolute necessity of the thing, and to beg of them, that if Capt. M'Kean and his company be removed from this place, that they would be pleased to send some others in his stead; that we may not lie altogether naked and exposed to the assaults of the enemy."

The committee not being able to comply with this

request, on the 1st of July several of the inhabitants drew up and signed the following petition:

"To the honorable members of the Provincial Congress of New York—

"The humble petition of the inhabitants of Cherry Valley, Newtown-Martin, and Springfield, in the county of Tryon, humbly showeth:

"That we, the aforesaid inhabitants, from the most authentic intelligence we have received from our missionaries and Indian friends, learn that we are in imminent danger of being cut off by the savages, our enemies, whom we understand are bribed by Sir John Johnson and Col. Butler to execute the same.

"Know also, honorable gentlemen, that the spirit of our inhabitants has been such for the American cause, that out of the small and scattered bounds of Cherry Valley and Newtown-Martin, no less than thirty-three has turned out for immediate service, and good of their country, and thereby left us in a defenseless condition.

"We therefore, your humble petitioners, humbly pray you would forthwith take this, our deplorable and distressed state and condition, under your immediate consideration, and meditate some speedy relief for us, before it be too late; especially, as the inhabitants of the Old England district, and Unadilla, are daily flying in to our settlement, so that we shall immediately, in all appearance, become an open, defenseless, and unguarded frontier, and very much exposed to the insnlts of theenemy, especially scalping parties; and are at present without either ammunition or men, any way sufficient to defend ourselves; and unless you, gentlemen, that can help us, will help us, by sending ammunition to the inhabitants, and a sufficient number of men, such as you may think proper, to guard our frontiers, we must expect to fall victims to the rage and fury of our merciless enemies. And, therefore, must once more beg you may take this our deplorable circumstances under your consideration, and send us immediate relief, and your petitioners shall ever pray."

This petition was signed by Samuel Dunlop, Samuel Campbell, James Scott, Robert Wells, James Richey, James Moore, Samuel Clyde. Their request was now granted, and a company of rangers under Capt. Winn was ordered here.

Those persons who had held commissions, or who were exempt from military duty in consequence of being above 60 years of age, formed themselves into a company to protect themselves and families. The spirit of disaffection found its way into this settlement, and several went to the enemy during the campaign of 1777. No fortification had yet been erected. Brant, during the summer of 1777, had collected a considerable number of warriors at Oquago. His visit to Unadilla, as before stated, excited the fears of the inhabitants, and they deemed it necessary that some more efficient steps should be taken, to prepare for a defense, in case they should be attacked. The house of Col. Samuel Campbell, being the largest, and situated on elevated ground, was selected as the best place for a fortification. A rude embankment of logs and earth was thrown up, enclosing the house and two large barns. The inhabitants of the surrounding country assembled there, carrying with them such of their effects as were most valuable. The doors were doubled, strong window-shutters were provided, and the whole rendered bullet proof. Two small block-houses were erected within the enclosure. Military law was enforced, and no person was suffered to come into, or leave the settlement, without permission. They remained in this situation during most of the summer, and in the fall returned to their respective habitations. They obeyed the call of Gen. Herkimer, but, being detained, did not arrive until after the action. Lieut. Col. Campbell, and Major, afterward Col. Clyde, were the only persons from Cherry Valley in the battle of Oriskany. They were next in command to Col. Cox, and at the close of that unfortunate contest led off the remains of his brave regiment.

In the spring of 1778, when Gen. La Fayette was at Johnstown, Col. Campbell and Mr. Wilson waited upon him, and represented the exposed situation of Cherry Valley. After examining its location on a map which they furnished him, he directed a fort to be built there. It was considered an object of great importance to keep the inhabitants of the frontiers at their homes, as by moving in they would necessarily create great confusion, and would expose to sudden inroads of the enemy places of great importance. For this reason, small forts were erected, and military posts were maintained along the frontier, wherever it was found practicable.

A fort was subsequently erected, in pursuance of the directions of Gen. La Fayette. Early in the spring, the inhabitants returned to their old quarters, where they remained until it was completed. Many of the inhabitants of Unadilla and other towns came in. As all the exercises and sports were of a military nature, the younger boys, in imitation of their elders, formed themselves into a company. Those who were acquainted with military evolutions, instructed them. Armed with wooden guns, they paraded with all the pride of soldiers. It was a fine pleasant morning, toward the latter part of May, that these minature soldiers sallied out, and paraded upon the green east of the house. That morning, Brant, having come up from Oquago with a party of his men, had posted them upon the hill about a mile farther east; and concealed by the thick woods which covered it, was looking down upon the little fortification. His intention, as afterwards explained by a Tory who accompanied him, was to make an attack the following night, and either to kill, or carry away prisoners, some of the principal persons, and especially the committee. This sagacious warrior was deceived when he saw this little company of boys. Looking down from an elevation, and the view being obstructed by the trees, he supposed them to be men. Turning round to his followers he remarked—" Col. Campbell has got his house well guarded, I perceive." During the day, he ascertained that the inhabitants were in garrison, but that no militia or soldiers from abroad were there. Wishing to gain definite information, as to the force, and the preparations for defense, he moved his party to a place near the main road leading to the Mohawk River, about two miles to the north. Here he lay in wait behind a large rock.

A short distance from this, the road wound along near the top of a ledge of rocks, forming a precipice a hundred and fifty feet high. It was shaded by evergreens, and was dark even at mid-day. Its wildness was increased by the dashing of a small stream which fell over this precipice, called by the Indians the falls of the Tekaharawa. That day, Lieut. Wormwood came up from the Mohawk River, and informed the garrison that Col. Klock would arrive the next day, with a part of his regiment of militia. It was almost night when he started to return, accompanied by Peter Sitz, the bearer of some dispatches. Throwing down his portmanteau, he mounted his horse, saying he should not need it until his return on the morrow, with his company. The fine personal appearance of this young officer, who was clad in a rich suit of ash-colored velvet, attracted much attention during his stay; and many persons remained at the door, looking at the horsemen until they were hid by the hill over which they passed. The clattering of hoofs had scarcely died away upon the ear, when the report of a volley of musketry was heard. Soon after, Wormwood's horse returned; the saddle was covered with blood, which excited fears as to his fate but too well founded. A party went out that evening, but could make no discoveries. The next morning the body was found behind the rock before mentioned. They had arrived near the rock, when they were hailed, and ordered to stop. Disregarding the order, they put spurs to their horses, and endeavored to pass. The Indians immediately fired; Wormwood was wounded, and fell from his horse, when Brant, rushing out, tomahawked him with his own hand. They had been personal friends before the war, and Brant is said to have lamented his death; at the time he supposed him to be a continental officer. Sitz's horse was killed, and he himself taken prisoner. The dispatches which he carried were double. He had presence of mind to destroy the paper containing the true account of the garrison, and to give Brant the other. Brant retired without doing any other injury. The next day, Col. Klock arrived, and the father of Wormwood, who had been immediately apprised of the death of his son. He was a wealthy man, living in Palatine district, and this was his only son. His feelings, as he bent over the dead and mutilated body, were excruciating; and when, in the agony of his soul, he cried out, "Brant, cruel, cruel Brant!" tears started in many an eye which scarcely knew how to weep.

On account of their exposure to sudden attacks of scalping parties, the inhabitants joined together and went round over the different farms; some stood as sentinels, while others labored. This course was not peculiar to this place; it was adopted along the whole frontier. William M'Kown, then a lad of about fourteen years of age, related the following interview, which he had this summer with Brant. Contrary to custom, he was sent out alone, to cure some hay. While engaged in raking, he heard some one walking behind him, and turning round, perceived an Indian very near him. He raised his rake to defend himself, when the Indian, addressing him in English, said, "Do not be afraid, young man, I shall not hurt you." He then inquired where Mr. Foster (a Tory) lived. Having directed him, M'Kown inquired if he knew him; to which the Indian replied, "I am partially acquainted with him, having once seen him at the Halfway Creek" (meaning Bowman's Creek, half-way between Cherry Valley and the Mohawk River.) The Indian then inquired of M'Kown his name. "You are a son of Mr. M'Kown, who lives in the northeast part of the town, I suppose; I know your father very well; he lives neighbor to Capt. M'Kean. I know M'Kean very well, and a fine fellow he is, too." This free, familiar conversation induced M'Kown to inquire of the Indian his name. After a moment's hesitation, he answered, "My name is Brant." "What! Captain Brant?" "No, I am a cousin of his." An arch smile played over his dark features, as he gave this reply; then turning, he directed his course toward Foster's. It was Joseph Brant himself, who afterward gave the same account. M'Kown immediately informed the garrison, and a party went directly to Foster's; but he was not there, and Foster denied having seen him.

In June of this summer, Brant came up with a party, and burned Springfield, carrying away several prisoners. He collected together the women and children into one house, and there left them uninjured—an example which was not always followed by his allies. About the same time, it was reported that he was fortifying at Unadilla, and that great numbers of Indians and Tories were collecting around him. A reward was offered to any person or persons who would gain any satisfactory information relative to his proceedings there. Capt. M'Kean, who was at this time in Cherry Valley, offered to go as a volunteer, provided he should be accompanied by five others. The complement was soon made up. They arrived the first night at the house of a Mr. Sleeper, a Quaker, who lived in the town of Laurens, a distance of some twenty-five miles from Cherry Valley. Sleeper informed them that Brant had been at his house that day with fifty men, and would return there that night. He advised them to leave, as they would be killed or taken in the event of his return. M'Kean looked round upon the house with the eye of a soldier; observing that it was built strong, and of logs, he remarked—" your house, friend Sleeper, shall be my fort to-night; I have with me five good marksmen, and I am not myself deficient in that qualification of a soldier." Sleeper remonstrated, saying, " he wished to remain neutral; that he would be involved in difficulty, and in the end would lose his property, probably his life." M'Kean finally withdrew, and took possession of a vacant house a mile or two distant. It was on this, or another scout a short time afterward, that M'Kean wrote a letter to Brant, and fastening it in a stick, placed the stick in an Indian path. He blamed him for his predatory warfare, and challenged him to meet him, either in single combat, or with an equal number of men, adding, that if he would come to Cherry Valley, and have a fair fight, they would change him from a *Brant into a Goose*. He received this challenge, as appears by a letter written soon after to Parcifer Carr, a Tory, living in Edmeston. The following is an exact transcript of it:

" *Tunadilla, July* 9, 1778.

" Sir,

" I understand by the Indians that was at your house last week, that one Smith lives near with you, has little more corn to spare. I should be much obliged to you, if you would be so kind as to try to get as much corn as Smith can spare; he has sent me five skipples already, of which I am much obliged to him, and will see him paid, and would be very glad if you could spare one or two your men to join us, especially Elias. I would be glad to see him, and I wish you could sent me as many guns you have, as I know you have no use for them, if you any; as I mean now to fight the cruel rebels as well as I can: whatever you will able to sent'd me, you must sent'd by the bearer.

I am your sincere friend and humble ser't,

To Mr. Carr. Joseph Brant.

" P. S. I heard that Cherry Valley people is very bold, and intended to make nothing of us; they call us wild geese, but I know the contrary.

" Jos. B."

M'Kean returned along the Susquehanna River, having succeeded in taking two prisoners. He was pursued by the Indians, and narrowly escaped being taken. When he returned to Cherry Valley, Capt. Ballard had arrived with a detachment of 100 men, being a part of Col. Alden's continental regiment. Col. Alden arrived a day or two after with the remainder of the regiment. Stockades had been placed around the church by the militia and rangers.

Col. Alden immediately took possession of his little fortress. This was an eastern regiment, and few of the officers or soldiers were conversant with the Indian mode of fighting. Col. Gansevoort solicited this post when Col. Alden was ordered here; at the head of the brave regiment he commanded at Fort Schuyler, he would doubtless have given the enemy a different reception on the 11th of November following.

It was in July of this year, that Col. John Butler and Brant, at the head of 800 Indians and rangers, made an incursion into the beautiful valley of Wyoming, and ravaged and laid waste its flourishing settlements. A great number of the inhabitants were killed, and the most wanton acts of barbarity were committed.* The destruction of Wyoming produced a thrill through all the States, and especially along the frontiers similarly exposed. Butler returned to Niagara, and Brant to his stations about Unadilla and Oquago. Brant continued about the branches of the Susquehanna until fall. Early in October, Mr. Dean, the Indian interpreter and agent, wrote Major Robert Cochrane commanding at Fort Schuyler, the following letter:

"As the Seneca chief, called the *Great Tree*, who was all the summer past with General Washington, returned through Oneida, he gave our friends there the most solemn assurances, that upon his arrival in his country he would exert his utmost influence to dispose his tribe to peace and friendship with the United States, and that should his attempts prove un-

---

* See Appendix—Note H.

successful he would immediately leave his nation and join the Oneidas with his friends and adherents. A long time having elapsed without hearing from the Great Tree, the Oneidas, a few days since, despatched a runner to him, desiring an account of his success. The express returned yesterday with the following intelligence, which the sachems immediately forwarded to me by three of their warriors, namely: that upon his arrival in the Seneca country he found that whole people in arms, and the two villages, Kanadaseago and Jennessee, where he was, croweded with their warriors, who were all collected from the remote settlements. That upon the Great Tree's first arrival, appearances seemed to promise him success, but that a rumor being circulated that the Americans were about to invade them, they had all flown to arms. The Great Tree was there, and determined to chastise the enemy that dared presume to think of penetrating their country.

"That they are to be joined by all the Indians as far as the Onondagas, a small party of which tribe has gone to meet them, and likewise by those of the several settlements upon the branches of the Susquehanna. That the Senecas were to march the 8th, and the others the 9th instant. That the whole party were to rendezvous at Kanakals, a place situated on that branch of the Susquehanna called Tioga branch, and from thence were to proceed against the frontiers of Pennsylvania or the Jerseys; our Oneida friends rely on the authenticity of the above intelligence, and beg that it may not be neglected."

On the 6th of November the following letter was sent from Fort Schuyler to Col. Alden:

"Sir,

"We were just now informed by an Oneida Indian, that yesterday an Onondaga Indian arrived at their castle, from one of the branches of the Susquehanna, called the Tioga. That he was present at a great meeting of Indians and Tories at that place, and their result was, to attack Cherry Valley, and that young Butler was to head the Tories. I send you this information that you may be on your guard."

To this letter Col. Alden returned the following answer:

"*Cherry Valley, Nov. 8th,* 1778.

"Sir,

"Received yours of the 6th inst. by express, informing me of the intelligence you obtained by one of the Oneida Indians of a large body of the enemy who were collected on the Susquehanna, and were destined to attack this place. I am much obliged to you for your information, and am,

Sir, your very humble serv't,

Ichabod Alden.

"P. S. Gen. Hand is now here; arrived at this place the day before yesterday; will return soon to Albany."

Capt. Walter Butler, son of Col. John Butler, who went to Canada in 1775 with Guy Johnson, returned early in this summer to Tryon County, where he was taken prisoner and confined in Albany gaol. Being sick, or pretending to be so, he was removed to a private house in the city, and a sentinel was placed over him.

In conjunction with the family, who were secretly disaffected, he succeeded in intoxicating the sentinel. A horse was provided for him, and he escaped and went to Niagara and joined his father. He here procured from him the command of a part of his regiment, called "Butler Rangers," together with permission to employ the forces under Brant. Although it was late in the season, he determined to make an incursion into the county, to avenge the wrongs which he supposed himself to have suffered by his imprisonment.* On his way he met Brant, who was returning to winter quarters at Niagara. Brant was displeased in being thus placed under Walter Butler, but was finally prevailed on to return with him. Their united forces were five hundred Indians and two hundred Rangers.

The inhabitants, many of whom had left in the summer, in consequence of the repeated attacks of the Indians upon the frontiers, had now returned to their homes, thinking the season so far advanced that no danger need be apprehended. On the information above being given to Col. Alden, they requested permission to remove into the fort, or at least to deposit their most valuable property there. Both requests were denied by Col. Alden. He replied, that it would be a temptation to his soldiers to plunder; that the report was probably unfounded ; that it was only an Indian story, and that he would keep out scouts, who would apprise them in season to secure themselves in case of real danger. Scouts were accordingly sent

* It was through his agency, doubtless, that the Senecas were roused up, as detailed in the letter of Mr. Dean.

out to traverse the country in every direction. The scout sent down the Susquehanna kindled up a fire on the night of the 9th, and all very foolishly lay down to sleep. The fire was discovered by the enemy, and a little before daylight on the morning of the 10th they were all surrounded and taken.

On the night of the 10th the enemy encamped on the top of a hill thickly covered with evergreens, about a mile southwest from the fort. On the morning of the 11th the enemy moved from his encampment toward the fort. They had learned from the scout which they had taken, that the officers of the garrison lodged in different private houses out of the fort; their forces were so disposed that a party should surround every house in which an officer lodged nearly at the same time, while the main body would attack the fort. During the night the snow fell several inches. In the morning it turned to rain, and the atmosphere was thick and hazy. The whole settlement thought themselves secure. The assurances of Col. Alden had in a considerable degree quieted their fears. Everything favored the approach of the enemy undiscovered. Col. Alden and Lieut. Col. Stacia, with a small guard, lodged at Mr. Wells's. A Mr. Hamble was coming up that morning from his house, several miles below, on horseback; when a short distance from Mr. Wells's house he was fired upon and wounded by the Indians. He rode in great haste to inform Col. Alden of their approach, and then hastened to the fort. Still incredulous, and believing them to be only a straggling party, he ordered the guard to be called in. The delay of a few minutes gave the Indians time to arrive. The Rangers had stopped to examine their firelocks, the powder in which had been wet with the rain. The Indians, improving this opportunity, rushed by. The advance body was composed principally of Senecas, at that time the wildest and most ferocious of the Six Nations. Col. Alden made his escape from the house, and was pursued down the hill toward the fort by an Indian; when challenged to surrender, he peremptorily refused so to do; several times he turned round and snapped his pistol at the Indian; the latter, after pursuing some distance, threw his tomahawk and struck him on the head, and then rushing up, scalped him. He thus "was one of the first victims of this most criminal neglect of duty." Lieut. Col. Stacia was taken prisoner. The guard were all killed or taken.

The Senecas, who first arrived at the house, with some Tories, commenced an indiscriminate massacre of the family, and before the Rangers arrived had barbarously murdered them all, including Robert Wells, his mother and wife, and four children, his brother and sister, John and Jane, with three domestics. Of this interesting and excellent family not one escaped, except the late John Wells of New York city. His father had left him in Schenectady the previous summer with an aunt, that he might attend the grammar school there. He might almost have exclaimed with Logan, that not a drop of his blood ran in the veins of any human being; or, as it has been beautifully expressed by an eminent English poet —

They "left of all my tribe
Nor man, nor child, nor thing of living birth.
No! not the dog, that watched my household hearth.
Escaped—that 'morn' of blood upon our plains
All perished! I alone am left on earth!
To whom nor relative nor blood remains,
No! not a kindred drop that runs in human veins."

A Tory boasted that he killed Mr. Wells while at prayer. The melancholy fate of Jane Wells deserves a more particular notice. She was a young lady, not distinguished for her personal beauty, but endeared to her friends by her amiable disposition, and her Christian charities; one "in whom the friendless found a friend," and to whom the poor would always say, "God speed thee." She fled from the house to a pile of wood near by, behind which she endeavored to screen herself. Here she was pursued by an Indian, who, as he approached, deliberately wiped his bloody knife upon his leggins, and then placed it in its sheath; then drawing his tomahawk, he seized her by the arm; she possessed some knowledge of the Indian language, and remonstrated, and supplicated, though in vain. Peter Smith, a Tory, who had formerly been a domestic in Mr. Wells's family, now interposed, saying she was his sister, and desiring him to spare her life. He shook his tomahawk at him in defiance, and then, turning round, with one blow smote her to the earth. John Wells, Esq., at this time deceased, and the father of Robert Wells, had been one of the judges of the courts of Tryon County; in that capacity, and as one of the justices of the quorum, he had been on intimate terms with Sir William Johnson and family, who frequently visited at his house, and also with Col. John Butler, likewise a judge. The family were not active either for or against the country ; they wished to remain neutral, so far as they could, in such turbulent times ; they always performed military duty, when called out to defend the country. Col. John Butler, in a conversation relative to them, remarked : "I would have gone miles on my hands and knees to have saved that family, and why my son did not do it God only knows."

Another party of Indians surrounded the house of the Rev. Samuel Dunlop, whom we have frequently had occasion to mention as the pioneer in education in western New York. His wife was immediately killed. The old gentleman and his daughter were preserved by Little Aaron, a chief of the Oquago branch of the Mohawks. Mrs. Wells was also a daughter of Mr. Dunlop; Little Aaron led him out from the house, tottering with age, and stood beside him to protect him. An Indian passing by pulled his hat from his head, and ran away with it; the chief pursued him, and regained it ; on his return, another Indian had carried away his wig ; the rain was falling upon his bare head, while his whole system shook like an aspen, under the combined influence of age, fear, and cold. He was released a few days after ; but the shock was too violent ; he died about a year after: his death was hastened by his misfortunes, though he could have borne up but a few years longer under the increasing infirmities of old age.

A Mr. Mitchell, who was in his field, beheld a party of Indians approaching ; he could not gain his house, and was obliged to flee to the woods. Here he evaded pursuit and escaped. A melancholy spectacle presented itself on his return; it was the corpses of his wife and four children. His house had been plundered and set on fire. He extinguished the fire, and by examination found life still existing in one of his children, a little girl ten or twelve years of age. He raised her up and placed her in the door, and was bending over her when he saw another party approaching. He had barely time to hide himself behind a log fence near by, before they were at the house. From this hiding-place he beheld an infamous Tory, by the name of Newbury, extinguish the little spark of life which remained in his child, with a single blow of his hatchet. The next day, without a single human being to assist him, he carried the remains of his family down to the fort on a sled, and there the soldiers aided him in depositing them in a common grave. Retributive justice sometimes follows close upon the heels of crime. This Tory was arrested as a spy, the following summer, by order of Gen. James Clinton, when he lay with his army at Canajoharie, on the Mohawk River. Mr. Mitchell was called to prove this act. He was found guilty by a court martial, and with a companion suffered an ignominious death.*

---

* *Extract from a letter from Gen. James to Mrs. Clinton, dated July 6th,* 1779.

"I have nothing further to acquaint you of, except that we apprehended a certain Lieut. Henry Hare, and a Sergt. Newbury, both of Col. Butler's regiment, who confessed that they left the Seneca country with sixty-three Indians and two white men, which divided

The party which surrounded the house of Col. Campbell, took Mrs. Campbell and four children prisoners. Mr. Campbell was absent from home, but hastened there on the first alarm, which was a cannon fired at the fort. He arrived only in time to witness the destruction of his property, and not even to learn the fate of his family; their lives were spared, but spared for a long and dreadful captivity.

Many others were killed; some few escaped to the Mohawk River, and the remainder were made prisoners. Thirty-two of the inhabitants, principally women and children, were killed, and sixteen continental soldiers. The terror of the scene was increased by the conflagration of all the houses and out-houses in the settlement; the barns were many of them filled with hay and grain. He who fled to the mountains, saw as he looked back the destruction of his home, and of that little all which he had labored for years to accumulate.

When the enemy approached on the morning of the 11th, Mrs. Clyde, the wife of Col. Clyde, collecting together her children, fled into the woods. During

---

themselves in three parties; one party was to attack Schoharie, another party Cherry Valley and the Mohawk River, and the other party to skulk about Fort Schuyler and the upper part of the Mohawk River, to take prisoners or scalps. I had them tried by a general court-martial for spies, who sentenced them both to be hanged, which was done accordingly at Canajoharie, to the satisfaction of all the inhabitants of that place that were friends to their country, as they were known to be very active in almost all the murders that were committed on these frontiers. They were inhabitants of Tryon County, had each a wife and several children, who came to see them and beg their lives."

that day and the following night, she lay with her children, one of whom was an infant, gathered around her, and concealed under a large log. As we have before mentioned, it was a cold, rainy day, and the storm continued through the night. She could hear the yells of the savages as they triumphed in their work of death; several of them passed near where she lay, and one so near, that the butt of his gun trailed upon the log which covered her. At the intercession of her husband, who was in the fort, a party sallied out the following morning, and, at the risk of their lives, brought her and her children into the fort; they were drenched with the rain, and stiffened with the cold; but they all survived. Mrs. Clyde, at the time of her flight, had missed her eldest daughter, about ten years of age, and supposed she had gained the fort; when she arrived at the fort on the morning of the 12th, this daughter appeared in the neighboring field. When she saw the sentinels, who had wrapped themselves in blankets, she supposed them to be the Indians, and again fled to the woods; she was followed and brought back to the anxious mother. When fleeing from the house she had separated from the rest of the family, and had lain concealed alone, until her appearance in the field. The sufferings of such a child in such a night, thinly clad, alone in the woods, must have been of the most excruciating nature.

Some generous acts were performed by Brant, which, in justice to him, ought to be mentioned. On the day of the massacre, he inquired of some of the prisoners where his friend, Capt. M'Kean, was. They informed him that he had probably gone to the

Mohawk River with his family. "He sent me a challenge once," said Brant; "I have now come to accept it. He is a fine soldier thus to retreat." They answered, "Capt. M'Kean would not turn his back upon an enemy, when there was any probability of success." "I know it; he is a brave man, and I would have given more to have taken him than any other man in Cherry Valley, but I would not have hurt a hair of his head."

In a house which he entered, he found a woman engaged in her usual business. "Are you thus engaged, while all your neighbors are murdered around you?" said Brant. "We are king's people," she replied. "That plea will not avail you to-day. They have murdered Mr. Wells's family, who were as dear to me as my own." "There is one Joseph Brant; if he is with the Indians he will save us." "I am Joseph Brant; but I have not the command, and I know not that I can save you; but I will do what is in my power." While speaking, several Senecas were observed approaching the house. "Get into bed and feign yourself sick," said Brant, hastily. When the Senecas came in, he told them there were no persons there, but a sick woman and her children, and besought them to leave the house; which, after a short conversation, they accordingly did. As soon as they were out of sight, Brant went to the end of the house, and gave a long shrill yell; soon after, a small band of Mohawks were seen crossing the adjoining field with great speed. As they came up, he addressed them—"Where is your paint? here, put my mark upon this woman and her children." As soon as it was done, he added, "You are now probably safe." It may be observed here, that this was a general custom; each tribe had its mark, by which they and their prisoners were designated; most of the other prisoners were thus marked. It was an evidence that they were taken, or claimed by some particular tribe, or individual; and woe to that person upon whom no captor had put his mark!

Brant, jealous of his character, always said, that in the councils he had urged the Indians to be humane, and not to injure the women and children. Where he had the exclusive command, this was in some degree effected. Col. Butler alleged, that Brant secretly incited the Indians in this massacre, in order to stigmatize his son, who had superseded him in command. Others said that he was humane, in order to contrast his own conduct with that of Walter Butler. Brant stoutly denied both charges, and appealed to his conduct in Springfield and other places.

Whatever may have been the motives and conduct of Brant, it will not wipe away the stain from the character of Walter Butler. The night previous to the massacre, some of his Rangers, who were acquainted in Cherry Valley, requested permission to go secretly into the settlement, and apprise his and their friends of their approach, that they might escape the fury of the Indians. This he peremptorily refused, saying, that there were so many families connected, that the one would inform the others, and all would escape. He thus sacrificed his friends, for the sake of punishing his enemies.

Several attacks were made during the day upon

the fort, but without success. The Indians were poor troops when a fortress was to be taken; besides, the enemy had no artillery. They rushed up and fought with considerable courage, but were driven back without much loss on either side. Col. Alden's regiment numbered between two and three hundred men —a number not great enough to make a successful sortie against the enemy, with a force more than double their own.

The principal part of the enemy, with the prisoners, between thirty and forty, including several of the officers of the garrison, encamped the first night in the valley about two miles south of the fort. To the prisoners it was a night of wretchedness, never to be forgotten. A large fire was kindled, around which they were collected, with no shelter, not even in most cases an outer garment, to protect them from the storm. There might be seen the old and infirm, and the middle-aged of both sexes, and "shivering childhood, houseless but for a mother's arms, couchless but for a mother's breast." Around them at a short distance on every side, gleamed the watch-fires of the savages, who were engaged in examining and distributing their plunder, and whose countenances wore a still more fiend-like aspect, as seen indistinctly, through a hazy November atmosphere. Close by their eneampment, if such it might be called, the land rose abruptly into a high hill, thickly studded with dark frowning hemlocks. A lurid glare of light from the watch-fires below played upon their tops, contrasting strongly their dark foliage with the naked branches of the other forest trees, and rendering still more appalling the whoop of some straggling Indian, as it broke the silence of the thicket beneath. Along up the valley they caught occasional glimpses of the ruins of their dwellings, as some sudden gust of wind, or falling timber, awoke into new life the decaying flame. An uncertain fate awaited them. If they augured from the scenes which they had that day witnessed, it was death. Their minds were filled with fearful forebodings—a secret fear which one dare not whisper to his fellow, that they might be reserved as the victims for a more deliberate and dreadful torture.

The morning broke upon a sleepless group; they did not, they could not close their eyes in sleep; they were early divided into small companies, and placed under different parties of the enemy, and in this manner commenced their journey down the Cherry Valley Creek.

On the morning of the second day the prisoners were called together, and it was decided to send back the women and children, a decision which kindled up hope and life anew in their bosoms. This was accordingly done; but Mrs. Campbell and her four children, and Mrs. Moore and her children, whose husbands had been active partisans, were retained. It was at the same time told to them, that they must accompany their captors to the land of the Senecas.

The first day of their journey, Mrs. Cannon, the mother of Mrs. Campbell, being unable to travel, on account of her age, was killed by her side, and the same Indian drove her along with his uplifted and bloody hatchet, threatening her with the same fate if she should be unable to proceed on the journey with the speed which he required. She carried in her arms a child aged eighteen months. The following day she was placed under the care of an Indian advanced in life, and who, during the remainder of the journey, was very humane.

They passed down the Susquehanna to its junction with the Tioga, thence up the Tioga to near its source, and thence across to the head of Seneca Lake, and along down the eastern border of the lake to the Indian castle and village of Kanadaseago, a few miles from the present flourishing and beautiful village of Geneva. The whole distance was between two and three hundred miles. Here they arrived about the last of November. Here all their children were taken from them, not even excepting the infant, and given to different families and tribes of Indians. We shall have occasion to continue somewhat of their history in a future chapter.

The day following the massacre—that is, the 12th—a party of Indians returned, and prowled about for a short time. That day, two hundred militia arrived from the Mohawk River, and the straggling parties of Indians dispersed. The mangled remains of those who had been killed were brought in, and received as decent an interment as circumstances would permit. The most wanton acts of cruelty had been committed, but the detail is too horrible, and I will not pursue it further. The whole settlement exhibited an aspect of entire and complete desolation. The cocks crew from the tops of the forest trees, and the dogs howled through the fields and woods. The inhabitants who escaped, with the prisoners who were set at liberty, abandoned the settlement. The garrison was kept until the following summer, when the fort was also abandoned, and the regiment joined the troops of Gen. James Clinton,* when on their way to join the army of Gen. Sullivan.

---

* Gen. James Clinton was the father of De Witt Clinton, and the reader will find a sketch of his life, with a brief outline of the Clinton family, in Appendix, being a lecture read by the author before the New York Historical Society.

CHAPTER VI.

"But go and rouse your warriors."

The atrocities of which the Indians were guilty at Wyoming, and along the frontiers of New York, drew the attention of the Congress and commander-in-chief to the situation of that section of country. Major Gen. Sullivan was ordered to march into the Indian territory, to lay waste their settlements and destroy their grain; thus visiting upon them some of the inconveniences and hardships attendant upon their mode of warfare. The western and southern parts of New York were the places of his destination.

On the first of May, 1779, the 2d and 4th New York regiments left their camp near the Hudson, and, passing through Warwarsing, arrived upon the Delaware the 9th. They crossed the Delaware, and passed down the west side to Easton, at which place their stores were collected. From thence they marched toward Wyoming, where they arrived the 17th of June. The delay was occasioned by the great labor required to open a road through woods and over an almost impassable swamp, extending many miles. Gen. Sullivan arrived with the main army on the 24th. On the 31st of July, the army left Wyoming for the

Indian settlements. The stores and artillery were conveyed up the Susquehanna in 150 boats. "The boats formed a beautiful appearance as they moved in order from their moorings, and as they passed the fort received a grand salute, which was returned by the loud cheers of the boatmen. The whole scene formed a military display surpassing any which had ever been exhibited at Wyoming, and was well calculated to form a powerful impression upon the minds of those lurking parties of savages, which still continued to range upon the mountains, from which all their movements were visible for many miles." On the 11th they arrived at Tioga, and encamped in the forks of the river. On the 12th a detachment was sent forward to Chemung, twelve miles distant, where they were attacked by a body of Indians, and lost seven men killed and wounded. The next day, having burned the town, they returned to Tioga. About a mile and a quarter above the junction of the Tioga and Susquehanna, these rivers approach each other to within a stone's throw. Here a fort was built, called Fort Sullivan, while the army lay on what might almost be called the island below.

In this situation, Gen. Sullivan awaited the arrival of Gen. James Clinton. This officer, with the 1st and 3d New York regiments, passed up the Mohawk to Canajoharie, where he arrived early in the Spring. An expedition was sent out from here by Gen. Clinton against the Onondaga Indians. The detachment consisted of six companies of New York troops, one of Pennsylvania, one of Massachusetts, and one of rifles, amounting in the whole to five hundred and four, rank and file. Col. Van Schaick of the 1st regiment of the New York line had the command, and was accompanied by Lieut. Col. Willet and Major Cochran, of the 3d regiment. They rendezvoused at Fort Schuyler, and from thence began their march. The whole settlement of the Onondagas, consisting of about fifty houses, and a large quantity of grain, were destroyed. They took 37 prisoners, and killed between 20 and 30 warriors. About one hundred muskets were taken. On their return, they met a small party of Indians, who fired on them, but were soon driven back by the corps of riflemen under Lieut. Evans. They returned to Fort Schuyler in five days and a half from the time of their march from thence; the whole distance going and returning was one hundred and eighty miles.

Gen. Clinton commenced opening a road from Canajoharie to the head of Otsego Lake, distant about 20 miles, and one of the principal sources of the eastern branch of the Susquehanna. This was effected with great labor; his boats were carried across on wagons. It was midsummer before General Clinton found himself, with his army and baggage, at the head of the lake, upon which he had launched his boats. This is a beautiful little lake, about nine miles long, and varies in breadth from one to three miles. Its elevation is 1193 feet, and it is almost surrounded by high land. The water is deep and clear, which is said to be the meaning of its Indian name. The scenery from many points is very picturesque and wild:

> "Tall rocks and tufted knolls their face
> Could on the dark blue mirror trace."

And it has not been unaptly compared to the romantic lakes for which Scotland is so much celebrated. At this time, save in one or two places, no mark of civilization was visible; and though

> "Each boatman, bending to his oar,
> With measured sweep the burthen bore,"

they could not but gaze at times with delight upon the natural beauties which surrounded them.

The outlet of this lake is narrow. Gen. Clinton, having passed his boats through, caused a dam to be thrown across. The lake was raised several feet. A party was sent forward to clear the river of drift-wood. When ready to move, the dam was broken up, and the boats glided swiftly down with the current.*

The few scattered inhabitants along the river below fled, not being able to account for the rapid rise of the river. At Tioga the water flowed back, up the western branch.

On the 22d day of August this division arrived at Tioga, and joined the main army. The whole force now under Gen. Sullivan consisted of Generals Hand, Clinton, Maxwell, and Poor's brigades of infantry, Proctor's artillery, and a corps of riflemen; in all between four and five thousand men.

---

* The word "Otsego" is said by some to be formed from the Indian term of salutation, "O Sago;" and a large rock is shown at the south end of this lake, near which, it is said, in early times, the Indians met in council, and when that term was frequently used. By others, it is said to mean "clear, deep water;" which is at least a very appropriate meaning. At the south end of this lake is situated the beautiful and flourishing village of Cooperstown, over whose early history so much interest has been thrown by Mr. Cooper, in his tale of the Pioneers.

On the 26th, this army, formidable indeed, if the numbers of the enemy be considered, moved from Tioga, up the river of that name, in excellent order. Their progress was necessarily slow, and every precaution was taken to guard against surprise. Large flanking parties were kept out on each side, and a corps of light troops was thrown forward.

On the 28th they destroyed the settlements and grain at Chemung, twelve miles distant from Tioga, and on the morning of the 29th, about 10 o'clock, fell in with the enemy near Newtown, and a short distance from the mouth of Butler's Creek. They were under the Butlers and Brant, and were in number about six hundred Indians and two hundred Tories. After some reconnoitering and skirmishing, the enemy retreated behind their breastwork, and made a spirited resistance. They were soon driven from their position by the artillery. In the mean time Generals Clinton and Poor's brigades filed off to the right, and Gen. Hand's light troops to the left, to gain the enemy's rear, where the land was high. Had this been effected, the enemy could not have escaped; but the movement is said to have been discovered by Brant, who ordered an immediate retreat. Nine Indians were left dead upon the field; their wounded they carried off. The Americans lost in killed three; thirty-four were wounded, among whom were Major Titcomb, Capt. Clayes, and Lieut. M'Colley, the latter of whom died of his wounds. Two prisoners were taken, who gave information as to the force of the enemy.

This was the only stand made by the Indians.

When it was first announced that an army was marching into their country, the Indians laughed at their supposed folly, believing it impossible for a regular army to traverse the wilderness such a distance, and to drive them from their fastnesses.

The following is extracted from the manuscript Journal of an officer.

"*Aug*. 29th. This night encamped on the field of action.

30th. Remained on the ground; large detachments sent off this morning to destroy the corn, beans, &c. about this place, which was not half destroyed. This evening sent off our wounded, heavy artillery, and wagons in boats down the river to Tioga; these boats brought forward such stores as could not be loaded on pack-horses. This day put on half allowance.

31st. Decamped at 8 o'clock; marched over mountainous ground until we arrived at the forks of Newtown; there entered on a low bottom; crossed the Cayuga branch, and encamped on a pine plain—much good land about Newtown. Here we left the Tioga branch to our left.

Sept. 1st. Decamped early in the morning; after marching about three miles, entered a swamp eight or nine miles across; roads very bad, and no pasture here. The army made a forced march, and arrived that night at dark in Catherine's Town. The cattle and most part of the pack-horses, together with our brigade (Clinton's) lay that night in the swamp, without pack or baggage. From this town the enemy seemed to have made a very precipitate retreat.

2d. About 3 o'clock came up with the army at the town, and encamped.

3d. Destroyed it, together with the corn, beans, &c., and decamped at 8 o'clock in the morning; after marching three miles, fell in on the east side of the Seneca Lake. This lake runs north and south, about thirty-six miles in length, and between two and three miles across. At 2 o'clock passed Apple-tree Town, situated on the banks of the lake. This day marched eleven miles over high, though level ground, timbered chiefly with white oak, and encamped in the woods.

4th. Marched twelve miles from last encampment; passed several narrow defiles, and encamped in the woods beside the lake. This day and yesterday passed several corn-fields and scattering houses, which we destroyed as we passed along. The Cayuga Lake runs the same direction with this lake, and is about ten or twelve miles distant—land tolerably good.

5th. Decamped in the morning, and about 12 o'clock arrived at Kandaia, a fine town, lying about half a mile from the lake; here we found a great plenty of apple-trees; it evidently appears to be an old inhabited town; their houses are large and elegant; some beutifully painted; their tombs likewise, especially of their chief warriors, are beautifully painted boxes, which they build over the grave, of planks hewn out of timber.

6th. Decamped at noon, and marched about three miles, when we encamped on the edge of the lake. Land timbered with white and black oak, and very good, the ground naturally descending with an easy descent towards the lake.

7th. This day passed the north end or outlet of the lake, which is very narrow, and marched through a narrow defile about one mile in length; the lake on our left, and a morass through which no one could pass on our right. Arrived at sundown at the north-west corner of the lake, where we destroyed a town and some corn, and proceeded on to Kanadaseago, the capital of the Senecas, where we arrived at 8 o'clock at night. This town lies on a level spot of ground, about one mile and a half north from the lake, and consisted of about sixty houses, and great plenty of apple and peach trees. The enemy, in their retreat from this place, left a white child, about four years old, and some horses and cows, &c.

8th. The army employed this day in destroying the corn, beans, &c. at this place, of which there was a great quantity. The riflemen were detached this morning to destroy Kashanguash, about eight miles south. This morning a captain and 50 men detached to the garrison at Tioga with all the sick and lame, and such others as could not proceed with us to Chennessee.

9th. Marched nine miles.

10th. Decamped early in the morning, and about 2 o'clock fell in with a small lake on our left, at the outlet of which lies the town of Kanandagua, consisting of upwards of twenty houses, which we set fire to and decamped. This town, from the appearance of the buildings, seems to have been inhabited by white people; some houses have very neat chimneys, which the Indians have not, but build a fire in the centre, around which they gather.

11th. Decamped this morning earlier than usual, to reach the next settlement, Hanneyaye, where we arrived in season and encamped. The country from Kanadaseago, excepting this day, is exceedingly level, and soil very good. This day crossed several mountains, between which lie fine rich valleys. This town lies at the head of a small lake, in a fine rich valley, consisting of 13 or 14 good houses, and neatly built. Here we likewise found a great quantity of corn, beans, &c.

12th. Decamped this morning at 11 o'clock; detained by a heavy rain; marched over a rough country; passed another small lake, called *Konyoughejough*, and arrived within two miles of Adjuton, and encamped in the woods. The sick, lame, and some stores were left with a detachment under the command of Capt. Cummings, who took post in one of the blockhouses.

13th. Decamped this morning at 5 o'clock; marched to the town, where we were employed in destroying the corn, &c. until noon; from this place Lieutenant Boyd, of the rifle corps, was detached with fifteen or twenty men to reconnoitre the next town, seven miles distant. Killed and scalped two Indians in the town. On his return, found his retreat cut off, and surrounded by five or six hundred savages; defended himself until his men were all cut off but himself and one more, when he surrendered; whom we afterward found in Chennessee castle, tortured in a most cruel manner." He was the first prisoner taken by the enemy, although they had used all their arts to obtain one, in order to learn the number and destination of the army. One of the party under Lieut. Boyd was

Hanyerry, an Oneida Indian, who had distinguished himself in the Oriskany battle; he exhibited great courage, and being an excellent marksman, did great execution. His conduct had not passed unnoticed by the hostile Indians, and now, when in their power, he was literally hewn to pieces by them. Lieutenant Boyd was taken before Col. Butler, and being examined, was, according to Col. Butler's statement, sent forward with a guard to Niagara, when, passing through Genesee village, an old Indian rushed out and tomahawked him.

"The same day, 13th, encamped that night at *Gathtsegwarohare*, where we found the enemy paraded before the town, and seemed determined to fight us. Clinton's brigade filed off to the right to gain the enemy's rear, which could not be effected; but they retreated in a very precipitate manner.

14th. This morning the whole army paraded at gun-firing, which was half-past three in the morning; lay on our arms until sunrise, expecting an attack from the enemy. At 6 o'clock detached large parties to destroy the corn about this place. At 10 the army passed a branch of the Chennessee River, and entered on the Chennessee Flats." These flats extended along the borders of the Genesee River, about twenty miles in length, and four in breadth, with a rich soil, producing grass near ten feet high. Scarcely a tree was to be seen over the whole extent. Modern curiosity and enterprise had not then rendered familiar the mighty valleys and prairies of the West; and officers and soldiers gazed alike with surprise and admiration upon this garden of our State. The army, as it emerged from the woods, and as company after company filed off and formed upon the plain, presented a highly animating and imposing spectacle. "This river in a high freshet overflows most part of this extensive plain, as appears from several large trunks of trees scattered on the same. After fording the river, raised a considerable hill, timbered chiefly with white oak, and entered on another flat, on which stands the capital of the Chennessee, consisting of upwards of one hundred and twenty houses, and vast quantities of corn, beans, pumpkins, potatoes, &c. Encamped this evening around the town.

15th. This morning the whole army paraded at 6 o'clock, to destroy the corn, &c. about this place, which could be done no other way but by gathering the corn in the houses, and setting fire to them. Here we likewise found a great quantity of corn gathered in houses by the savages. At 3 o'clock in the afternoon we completed the destruction of this place; recrossed the Chennessee River, and encamped on the flats about half a mile north of Gathtsegwarohare. This morning a woman taken prisoner at Wyoming last year, came in to us at the Chennessee castle.

16th. This morning, after destroying the corn, &c. on the southeast corner of the flats, recrossed the branch of the Chennessee River on logs; this river is about one dozen paces wide, with very high banks, and the current hardly perceivable. At ten o'clock passed the last-mentioned town lying on the banks of this branch, and encamped this night at Adjuton.

17th. Decamped early in the morning, and arrived in good season at Hanneyaye, where we encamped this night; found our stores, &c. as we left them.

18th. Decamped, and left Hanneyaye with great difficulty; the horses left at this post having strayed so far from the village, and could not be found; consequently many packs would have been left on the ground, had not those officers entitled to ride dismounted, of whom Gen. Sullivan was one. This day met three Oneida Indians with dispatches for Gen. Sullivan. They informed us the city of New York was laid in ashes, and evacuated. Arrived at Kanandagua some time before night; passed the outlet of the Lake, and encamped about one mile from the outlet. This town lies about a fourth of a mile from a small lake, I suppose of the same name.

19th. Decamped this morning early, proceeded on our way to Kanadaseago, where we encamped a little before sunset.

20th. Remained encamped until 2 o'clock, when we decamped and passed the outlet of the Seneca Lake, and encamped about one mile from the outlet. This morning detached Col. Butler, (Col. Zebulon Butler, of Wyoming,) with the rifle corps and five hundred men, to Cayuga Lake to destroy the settlements there. Col. Gansevoort detached at the same time with one hundred men to Fort Schuyler.

21st. Decamped in the morning, passed Kandaia, and encamped about two miles above. This morning detached Lieut. Col. Dearborn, with two hundred men, to destroy the corn and settlements along the south side of Cayuga Lake.

22d. Decamped early in the morning, passed several defiles, and encamped within seven miles of Catherine's Town.

23d. Decamped and marched about four miles

southeast cf Catherine's Town, at the edge of the swamp, and encamped.

24th. Passed the swamp, so much dreaded for its badness, without any difficulty, and arrived at the forks of Newtown, where Capt. Reid, with a detachment of two hundred men, had thrown up a breastwork to guard some stores and cattle brought forward from Tioga for the army in case of necessity. Saluted by thirteen rounds of cannon from the breastwork on our arrival, which number we returned from our artillery.

25th. This morning the small arms of the whole army were discharged; at 5 o'clock the whole were drawn up in one line, with a field-piece on the right of each brigade, to fire a feu-de-joie; first, thirteen rounds of cannon; second, a running fire of musketry from right to left, which was repeated twice; five oxen were killed on this joyous occasion—one delivered to each brigade, and one to the artillery and staff.

This was done in consequence of Spain declaring war against Great Britain.

26th. Remained encamped. Col. Dearborn's detachment arrived.

27th. Encamped.

28th. Col. Butler with his detachment arrived, having destroyed a vast quantity of corn, beans, apple-trees, &c. on the east side of the Cayuga Lake, and burnt three towns, among which was the capital of the Cayuga tribe. This day Colonels Cortland and Dayton detached with large detachments to destroy corn; the former taking his route up the Tioga branch, to which place he was detached the day before, and destroyed large fields of corn; and the latter taking his route downwards, and destroyed such as the army left undestroyed in going up.

29th. Decamped this morning at 8 o'clock; passed the Cayuga branch, and encamped at Old Chemung, three miles below New Chemung. This day forded the Tioga twice.

30th. Decamped this morning, 7 o'clock; arrived at Fort Sullivan about 1 o'clock; saluted from the fort by thirteen cannon, which number was returned from our artillery; after which we passed the fort and encamped on our old ground in the forks of the river."

On the 3d of October the fort was demolished, and the army returned by the way of Wyoming to Easton, where it arrived the 15th. The whole distance from Easton to the Genesee castle, by the route of the army, was two hundred and eighty miles. The loss of men sustained in this expedition, considering the fatigue and exposure, was very inconsiderable—not more than forty in the whole were killed or died from sickness. It is noted in the journal, that on the 20th of September, Col. Gansevoort was detached with a party of one hundred men to Fort Schuyler. The following were Gen. Sullivan's instructions to him:

"Sir,

"You are to take command of a chosen party, draughted from the army, and proceed by the shortest route to the Mohawk castle, destroy it, and capture, if possible, all the Indians that may be there. The upper castle being inhabited by the Onheskas, you are to spare, and treat them as friends. Such necessary marks of civility and attention you will show them as may engage a continuance of their friendship, and give evidence of our pacific disposition towards them.

"Whatever prisoners may fall into your hands, you are to proceed with to Albany, and collect the baggage of the several regiments from which your party were draughted, and proceed with all possible expedition to head-quarters. You are by no means to leave any of the prisoners at Albany, unless particularly directed by Gen. Washington or Congress.

"As your route will be through the Oneida country, you are to take particular care that your men do not offer the inhabitants the least insult; and if by accident any damage should be done, you are to make reparation, for which I shall stand accountable. From your zeal, activity, and prudence, I trust every precaution will be taken to execute these orders to the advantage and honor of the United States."

The following is Col. Gansevoort's account of the manner in which he had executed his commission.

"Agreeable to my orders, I proceeded by the shortest route to the lower Mohawk castle, passing through the Tuscarora and Oneida castles, where every mark of hospitality and friendship was shown the party. I had the pleasure to find, that not the least damage nor insult was offered any of the inhabitants.

"On the 25th, I arrived at Fort Schuyler, where, refreshing my party, I proceeded down the river, and on the 29th effectually surprised the lower Mohawk castle, making prisoners of every Indian inhabitant. They then occupied but four houses. I was preparing, agreeable to my orders, to destroy them, but was interrupted by the inhabitants of the frontiers, who have been lately driven from their settlements by the savages, praying that they might have liberty to enter into the Mohawks' houses, whilst they could procure other habitations; and well knowing those persons to have lately lost their all, humanity tempted me in this particular to act in some degree contrary to orders, although I could not but be confident of your approbation; especially when you are informed that this castle is in the heart of our settlements, and abounding with every necessary; so that it is remarked, that these Indians live much better than most of the Mohawk River farmers. Their houses were very well furnished with all necessary household utensils, great plenty of grain, several horses, cows, and wagons; of all which I have an inventory, leaving them in the care of Major Newkirk, of that place, who distributed the refugees in the several houses. Such being the situation, I did not allow the party to plunder at all. The prisoners arrived at Albany, on the 2d inst., and were closely secured in the fort."

These prisoners, it is believed, were set at liberty, and restored to their possessions, as would follow from the facts stated in the letter of Gen. Schuyler, President of the Board of Commissioners for Indian affairs.

"Dear Sir,

"Having perused Gen. Sullivan's orders to you respecting the Indians of the lower Mohawk castle and their property, I conceive they are founded on misinformation given to that gentleman; these Indians have peaceably remained there under the sanction of the public faith repeatedly given them by the Commissioners of Indian affairs, on condition of peaceable demeanor; this contract they have not violated to our knowledge. It is therefore incumbent on us, as servants of the public, to keep the public faith inviolate; and we therefore entreat you to postpone the sending the Indians from hence until the pleasure of his excellency Gen. Washington can be obtained, and a letter is already dispatched to him on the occasion, and in which we have mentioned this application to you."

The country of the Onondagas, the Cayugas, and the Senecas, the three western tribes, was completely overrun and laid waste. To a person reading the foregoing journal, it may seem that too much severity was exercised in the burning of the Indian towns, and that corn, &c. was wantonly destroyed; but it must be borne in mind that this was not a bare retaliatory measure, though as such it might have been justified by the previous conduct of the Indians; their towns were their retreats, and from thence they made incursions into the settlements; driven back to Niagara, and rendered dependent upon the English for supplies of provisions, they would necessarily be much crippled in their future operations. Though, as we shall see, this campaign did not put a stop to the ravages of the Indians, yet they never recovered from the severe chastisement which they received.

A part only of the Indians ever returned to their old settlements, from which they were driven; some of them obtained permission to locate in the extreme western part of the State; during the following winter, 1779–80, they remained in and about Fort Niagara. Provisions were scarce; those they received were salt, a kind to which the Indians were unaccustomed. They took the scurvy and died in great numbers. The winter was unusually cold, which increased the difficulties of their situation.

CHAPTER VII.

"And now no scenes had brighter smiled,
No skies with purer splendor mild,
No greener wreath had crowned the spring,
No sweeter breezes spread the wing,
Nor streams through gayer margins rolled,
Nor harvests waved with richer gold,
Nor flocks on brighter hillocks played,
Nor groves entwined a safer shade:
But o'er her plains, infernal war
Has whirled the terrors of his car,
The vengeance poured of wasting flame,
And blackened man with endless shame."

At the commencement of the Revolution, the whole country now embraced within the limits of the county of Schoharie, contained scarcely one thousand inhabitants; the greater part of these inhabited the valley of the Schoharie Creek. Their settlements commenced about 20 miles above the junction of that stream with the Mohawk River, and extended along its valley 15 miles.* The breadth of this valley va-

* A part only of the settlements of Schoharie was embraced within the county of Tryon; but their revolutionary history is connected with that of Tryon County; and I have concluded to give it in this chapter. The facts were principally furnished by a friend, since the other chapters were written. I have in many cases adopted his language and sentiments. Some allusions have been made in the foregoing chapters to these settlements; but I trust I shall be excused for giving a more minute account of them.

ries from two to three miles, and both in the richness of its soil, and in the beauty of its scenery, is scarcely equalled in the State. The history of its settlement, and the incidents that occurred there during the war of the Revolution, is lost, so far as written documents are concerned; and all that can be known respecting it must be collected from tradition, and the oral accounts of the survivors. Before commencing a narration of the events of the Revolution in Schoharie, it may be well to relate what tradition has preserved of its early history.

In the year 1709, a number of families from the Palatinates in Germany, induced by the liberal offers made by Queen Anne, embarked for New York, and having proceeded up the Hudson as far as Albany, landed and selected a few of their number to choose a place for a settlement. Of these, some went to Schenectady, and thence up the Mohawk, where a settlement of Germans had been formed a few years previous; the others, hearing of a beautiful country to the southwest, penetrated the wilderness in that direction; and after travelling through a hilly, and in some parts mountainous country, arrived the second day on the height of land east of the Scoharie Creek.

Here a scene of extraordinary beauty, and to them entirely new, burst upon their sight; at their feet, and far below them, was a plain of limited extent, embosomed by hills, in some places rising abruptly to the height of 1000 feet, and in others of more gentle ascent, and broken by deep ravines. The declivity of the hills was covered with a stinted growth of oak, too scanty to hide even from a distant view the rocks amid which they grew, and forming a striking contrast with the stately forest and luxuriant vegetation of the plain below. The valley had been partially cleared, and the alternate spots of woodland and meadow, interspersed with clumps of trees, added variety and richness to the landscape. Along its western boundary ran the Schoharie Creek, now washing the base of the hill, now meandering through the flats; its course marked through the woodlands by the deep green of the trees along its bank, and through the meadows by the elms that lined its borders; sometimes its course was hidden from the view by the thick foliage, and again, as its channel spread out wider, or its course inclined to the east, its clear waters were seen glittering in the sunbeams. No traces of any occupants of this valley were seen, except here and there the ruins of a deserted wigwam.

The travellers returned to Albany, and gave so flattering an account of the country which they had visited, that the whole company started immediately for Schoharie, without waiting for the return of their friends from the Mohawk. The place they chose for a settlement had formerly been occupied by a part of the Mohawk tribe of Indians; but they had most of them now left it.

The settlers were illy provided with implements of husbandry, and with many of the necessaries of life; which wants were very severely felt during many years. Whether they paid the Mohawks an equivalent for the land, tradition does not inform us. It was not, however, until several years after, that they obtained a grant from government.

A commission was sent to grant them a title in the name of the crown, and to extend to them the protection of the laws. Believing this to be a pretense for exacting taxes from them, and remembering their former oppression, they drove off the commissioner, and refused to accept his proposals. A part left the settlement and went up the Mohawk, and the remainder were finally prevailed upon by threats and persuasion to accept the terms offered by the government agent.

From this period down to 1775, nothing of importance happened in the settlement. When the first steps were taken to resist the enforcement of the acts of Parliament, a majority of the inhabitants determined to support the colonial cause. A committee of safety was appointed, which exercised the powers mentioned in the previous account of these bodies.

In the fall of 1777 the inhabitants began to suffer from the inroads of straggling parties of Indians, and the committee turned their attention to devising some mode of defense. Aid was sought from government, and three forts were erected, called the Upper, Middle, and Lower Forts. The Middle Fort was near where the village of Middleburgh now stands; the Upper Fort was five miles above, and the Lower Fort six miles below; they consisted of intrenchments of earth and wood thrown up in the usual form, around some building, which served as a shelter for the women and children. In the Middle Fort, this building was a stone dwelling-house; in the Lower a stone church. The forts were garrisoned with a few continental soldiers, and each furnished with a small field-piece. Many of the inhabitants repaired to the forts at night, and returned in the morning to their employment on their farms.

During two or three subsequent years, no powerful party of the enemy laid their whole settlement in ruins; but individual after individual, and family after family, were missing along its outskirts. The smoking ruins of their dwellings, the charred bones of their inmates, and the dead bodies of domestic animals killed by the enemy, were all that were left to record their fate, until the return of some captive, or the narration of a prisoner taken from the enemy, revealed the secret of their destruction.

The Tories, who often commanded the Indians, were the most barbarous. There is a story told of an act in a settlement adjoining Schoharie, which, for the honor of humanity, would not be believed were it not supported by undoubted testimony. A party of Indians had entered a house, and killed and scalped a mother and a large family of children. They had just completed their work of death when some royalists belonging to their party came up, and discovered an infant still alive in the cradle. An Indian warrior, noted for his barbarity, approached the cradle with his uplifted hatchet. The babe looked up in his face and smiled; the feelings of nature triumphed over the ferocity of the savage; the hatchet fell from his hand, and he was in the act of stooping down to take the infant in his arms, when one of the royalists, cursing the Indian for his humanity, took it up on the point of his bayonet, and holding it up struggling in the agonies of death, exclaimed—"*this too is a rebel.*"

But the inhabitants were not the only sufferers. When contending with equal numbers, they generally defeated the enemy, and often the Indians found their antagonists their superiors in stratagem as well as in bravery. Seven Indians meeting with a man by the name of Sawyer, took him prisoner, and having gone eight or ten miles, bound him, and laid down to sleep. In the night, he succeeded in loosing his hands, and then silently taking out of the belt of the nearest savage his hatchet, killed with it six of them. The seventh made his escape wounded. Sawyet returned home in safety.

The following account is given by the Rev. Mr. Fenn, the former clergyman of Harpersfield, who received the information from Col. Harper.

In the year 1778, M'Donald, a Tory of some enterprise and activity, had collected about 300 Indians and Tories, and was committing great depredations on the frontiers. He fell down upon the Dutch settlements of Schoharie, with all his barbarity and exterminating rage: Col. Vrooman commanded in the fort at Schoharrie at this time: they saw the enemy wantonly destroying everything on which they could lay their hand. The garrison were so weak that they could spare no men from the fort to protect the inhabitants, or secure the crops. "What shall be done?" says Col. Harper. "Oh, nothing at all," says Col. Vrooman; "we be so weak we cannot do anything."

Col. Harper ordered his horse, and laid his course for Albany; rode right down through the enemy, who were scattered over all the country: at Fox's

Creek, put up at a Tory tavern for the night; he retired to bed after having locked his door; soon there was a loud rapping at the door. "What is wanted?" "We want to see Col. Harper." The colonel arose and unlocked the door; seated himself on the bed; and laid his sword and pistols before him: in stepped four men. "Step one inch over that mark," said the colonel, "and you are dead men." After talking a little time with him, they left the room; he again secured the door, and sat on his bed until daylight appeared; he then ordered his horse, mounted, and rode for Albany, and the enemy were round the house. An Indian followed the colonel almost into Albany; and when the colonel would wheel his horse and present his pistol, the Indian would turn and run with all his might. When the colonel arrived at Albany, he called on Col. Gansevoort, stated the distressed situation of Schoharie, and prayed for help; a squadron of horse was immediately provided, and they rode all night, and appeared in Schoharie in the morning; and the first knowledge that the people had that any relief was expected, they heard a tremendous shrieking and yelling, and looked out and saw Col. Harper with his troop of horse welting up the enemy. The men in the fort rushed out, and joined in the attack, and the country was soon cleared of the enemy, and the inhabitants had peace and rest, and could collect their harvest in safety.

The massacres at Wyoming and Cherry Valley had employed most of the Indians during 1778, and in 1779 the western tribes were driven back by Gen. Sullivan. During the latter summer, a party of the

Onondagas, after the destruction of their town by Col. Van Schaick, made an incursion into Schoharie.

There was, at this time, a little settlement, consisting of only nineteen families, on the Cobbleskill Creek, ten miles west of Schoharie. Though they had erected no fortifications, they had prepared for defense, by organizing a company of militia, and procuring arms and ammunition. About the middle of May, it was reported at a meeting of the militia, that some straggling Indians had been seen in the neighborhood, and a scout of three men, one of whom was suspected of being secretly a royalist, was sent out into the forest. On the return of the scout, they met two Indians near the settlement, who accosting them in friendly terms, and pretending to be hunting, were suffered to pass. The Indians took a circuitous route, and in a short time met them again. The suspected individual had now disappeared, having taken a different path to the settlement. The Indians still pretended friendship; one of them familiarly took the musket from one of the men, and knocking out the flint, handed it back. The other attempted the same thing, but his adversary perceiving his intention, shot him. His companion fled, and the men returned to the settlement.

This circumstance, together with a rumor that a large body of Indians were on their march for Schoharie, excited fears that this little settlement would be the first object of their revenge. They immediately despatched a messenger to Schoharie with the intelligence, and directed him to ask for assistance. A part of a company of continental soldiers, under the command of Capt. Patrick, was sent the same day to Cobbleskill. The next morning a party of Indians were seen to cross the creek and return again into the woods. A small detachment of men were sent in pursuit. These were soon driven back by superior force. Capt. Patrick then marched the whole of his little band, and 15 volunteers of the militia, to their support. The Indians were driven back, but soon made a stand, and after firing again retreated. They continued to retreat, disputing the ground at every step, evidently increasing in number, until the conflict became exceedingly fierce. Capt. Patrick was at first wounded, and afterwards killed, when his men sought safety in flight. The Indians immediately pursued them, and at the same instant the main body, which had been concealed in the thickets, rushed forth, and with deafening yells poured a shower of rifle-balls upon the fugitives; their number, as afterwards ascertained, was about 300.

The death of Capt. Patrick alone saved his men from entire destruction; in a few moments more they would have been surrounded, and their retreat cut off.

The inhabitants of the settlement, as soon as they saw the fugitives emerging from the woods, pursued by the Indians, fled in an opposite direction, and all arrived safe at Schoharie; their escape was favored by the desperate resistance of seven of the soldiers, who, taking possession of a house, fired from the windows, and checked the pursuit of the enemy. The Indians at length succeeded in setting the house on fire, and six of its brave defenders perished in the flames; the other was afterward found a few rods distant, much burned, and horribly mutilated; a roll of continental money was put in his hand, as if in derision of the cause which he supported. The enemy set fire to the buildings in the vicinity, and after burying the dead, and mangling the dead bodies of the soldiers, retired without pursuing the fugitives further.

Of the 45 who went out, 21 escaped, 22 were killed, and 2 taken prisoners. The Indians suffered severely, according to the account of the prisoners who afterward returned. They were accompanied by a few Tories, and commanded by a Tory, who took this method to obtain revenge for an unsuccessful attempt to arrest him the previous year; he afterward returned to his former home upon Charlotte River, and was killed by the celebrated Murphy, who was one of a party sent to bring him into the fort.*

---

* Murphy, who was of great service to the inhabitants of Schoharie, was a native of Virginia, and had belonged to Morgan's rifle corps, in which he had distinguished himself as a marksman. After the capture of Burgoyne, the company to which he belonged was ordered to Schoharie, where it remained until their term of service expired.

When the company was disbanded, Murphy and some others remained, and served in the militia. His skill in the desultory war which the Indians carry on, gave him so high a reputation, that though not nominally the commander, he usually directed all the movements of the scouts that were sent out, and on many important occasions the commanding officers found it dangerous to neglect his advice. His double rifle, his skill as a marksman, and his fleetness either in retreat or pursuit, made him an object both of dread and of vengeance to the Indians. They formed many plans to destroy him, but he always eluded them, and sometimes made them suffer for their temerity.

He fought the Indians in their own way, and with their own weapons. When circumstances permitted he tomahawked and scalped his fallen enemy. He boasted after the war that he had slain forty of the en-

In the fall of 1780, the enemy, about 800 strong, under Sir John Johnson, made preparations for destroying Schoharie and the Mohawk valley. The forces, consisting of British regulars, loyalists, and Tories, assembled on the Tioga, and marched thence up along the eastern branch of the Susquehanna, and crossed thence to Schoharie. Col. Harper, with a small body of men, annoyed them on their march, watched all their movements, and gave timely notice

---

emy with his own hand, more than half of whom he scalped. He took delight in perilous adventures, and seemed "to love danger for danger's sake." Tradition has preserved the account of many of his exploits; but there are so many versions of the same story, and so much evident fiction mixed with the truth, that we shall give but a single instance as a proof of the dread with which he was regarded by the Indians.

They were unable to conjecture how he could discharge his rifle twice without having time to reload; and his singular good fortune in escaping unhurt, led them to suppose that he was attended by some invisible being who warded off their bullets, and sped his with unerring certainty to the mark. When they had learned the mystery of his double-barreled gun, they were careful not to expose themselves too much until he had fired twice, knowing that he must have time to reload his piece before he could do them further injury.

One day, having separated from his party, he was pursued by a number of Indians, all of whom he outran excepting one; Murphy turned round, fired upon this Indian, and killed him. Supposing that the others had given up the pursuit, he stopped to strip the dead, when the rest of his pursuers came in sight. He snatched the rifle of his fallen foe, and with it killed one of his pursuers; the rest, now sure of their prey, with a yell of joy heedlessly rushed on, hoping to make him their prisoner; he was ready to drop down with fatigue, and was likely to be overtaken, when turning round, he discharged the remaining barrel of his rifle, and killed the foremost Indian; the rest, astonished at his firing three times in succession, fled, crying out that he could shoot all day without loading.

of their approach. On the 16th of October they encamped about four miles from the Upper Fort. It was their intention to pass the Upper Fort in the night, and to attack the Middle Fort at daybreak. As it was expected that the Upper Fort would be the first object of attack, they hoped to surprise the Middle Fort by this unexpected movement. Sir John had ordered his troops to be put in motion at four in the morning, but from some mistake it was five before they began their march. The main body passed the Upper Fort undiscovered; but the rear-guard was discovered by the sentinels, and the alarm gun immediately fired; the alarm was quickly answered from the other forts, and 20 riflemen were sent out from the Middle Fort to watch the motions of the enemy; they soon fell in with an advanced party, and retreated back to the fort. The firing of the alarm gun disappointing the enemy, became the signal for them to commence the destruction of the settlement; houses, barns, and stacks of hay were burned, and cattle, sheep, and horses killed or driven away. Sir John gave orders that the church should be spared; but he found that with such an army he had only the power of doing injury, and contrary orders were never obeyed —it too was burned.

About 8 o'clock the enemy commenced a regular attack on the fort; the regular troops fired a few cannon-shot, and threw a number of shells; but for want of skill in the gunners, the shot either fell short or flew over, and the shells exploded high in the air. The Indians retreated behind a row of willow-trees, and kept up a constant fire with small-arms, but at too great a distance to take effect.

In the fort all was gloom and despondency; the garrison amounted to no more than 150 regular troops, and about 100 militia. It is said that there was but a single pound of powder in the magazine; their ammunition wagons had been sent to Albany for a supply, but had been detained beyond their usual time. Two men had been sent through the woods the day before to bring powder on their backs, but they had not had time to complete their journey. The regular soldiers had but a few cartridges apiece; the militia were better supplied. To attempt to defend the fort appeared to be madness; to surrender, was to deliver up themselves, their wives, and their children, to immediate death, or at least to a long captivity. Major Woolsey, who commanded the continental troops, was inclined to surrender on the first appearance of the enemy, but was prevented by the officers of the militia, who resolved to defend the fort. Woolsey's presence of mind forsook him in the hour of danger; he concealed himself at first with the women and children in the house, and when driven out by the ridicule of his new associates, he crawled round the intrenchments on his hands and knees, amid the jeers and bravos of the militia, who felt their courage revive as their laughter was excited by the cowardice of the major. In times of extreme danger, everything which has a tendency to destroy reflection by exciting risibility has a good effect.

The enemy, perceiving that their shot and shells did little or no execution, formed under shelter of a small building near the fort, and prepared to carry the works by assault. While the preparations were making, a flag was seen to approach the fort; all seemed inclined to admit it, when Murphy, who suspected that it was only an artifice to learn the actual strength of the garrison, and aware that for him, at least, there was no safety in capitulation, fired upon the flag. The flag retired, and some soldiers were ordered to arrest Murphy; but so great was his popularity among the militia, that no one dared to obey. The flag approached a second time, and was a second time driven back by Murphy and his adherents. A white flag was then ordered to be raised in the fort, but Murphy threatened with instant death any one who should obey. The enemy sent a flag a third time, which was again compelled to retire. The British officers now held a council of war, and after a short consultation withdrew, and proceeded down the Schoharie Creek, burning and destroying everything in their way.

The loss of the garrison in this affair was only one killed and two wounded, one mortally. It is not known what loss the enemy sustained, or why they retreated so hastily. It was said by some, that a pretended royalist had given them exaggerated accounts of the strength of the garrison; by others, that a rumor reached them that the militia were advancing from Albany. The latter was probably the true cause. Perhaps the determined spirit of resistance manifested in firing upon the flag, led them to suppose the defense would be obstinate. The Tory leaders, satiated with blood, may have been unwilling to act over the tragedies of Wyoming and Cherry Valley.

When they arrived at the Lower Fort, they showed

little disposition to attack it, although its garrison did not amount to 100 men. They separated into two divisions, the regular troops marching along the bank of the creek, and the Indians filing off about half a mile to the east of the fort. The regulars fired a few cannon-shot without effect, one only lodging in the corner of the church; and then, after sinking one of their field-pieces in a morass, marched round to the north of the fort, where they were joined by the Indians. Here they fired a few shot with small-arms, and a few of the Indians approached near enough to throw their bullets into the tower of the church, where some marksmen had been stationed. A discharge of grape from the fort drove them back, and they continued their march through the woods to Fort Hunter, on the Mohawk, near the mouth of Schoharie Creek, where they arrived after dark. The ravages of this army, as they passed up the valley of the Mohawk, and the battles fought with the militia, will be given in a subsequent chapter.

The beautiful valley of Schoharie Creek presented a scene of devastation, on the night of the 17th of October, not easily described. Houses, barns, and numerous stacks of hay and grain were consumed; domestic animals lay dead everywhere over the fields; a few buildings belonging to the royalists had been spared, but the militia, sallying out, set fire to them in revenge. After the burning of Schoharie, this settlement ceased to be so much an object of Tory vengeance; and during the years 1781 and 1782, though there were frequent alarms, little damage was done by the enemy. The Indians appeared once in considerable numbers at Cobbleskill, burned a few buildings, killed one man, and carried off five prisoners; but the body of the inhabitants hàd taken refuge in a fort which they had built on their return from Schoharie in 1781, and were safe.

CHAPTER VIII.

"Here too, those warrior sires with honor rest,
Who braved in freedom's cause the valiant breast,
Sprang from their half-drawn furrow, as the cry
Of threatened liberty came thrilling by;
Looked to their God, and reared in bulwark round
Breasts free from guile, and hands with toil embrowned,
And bade a monarch's thousand banners yield—
Firm at the plough, and giorious in the field;
Lo! here they rest, who every danger braved,
Unmarked, untrophied, 'mid the soil they saved."

In 1768, William, John, Alexander, and Joseph Harper, with eighteen other individuals, obtained a patent for twenty-two thousand acres of land lying in the now county of Delaware. The Harpers removed from Cherry Valley soon after, and made a settlement there which was called Harpersfield. This settlement had begun to flourish at the commencement of the war. Col. John Harper, who has been often mentioned in the foregoing chapters, had the command of one of the forts in Schoharie.

The following account of a successful enterprise of Col. Harper, was also furnished by the Rev. Mr. Fenn, who received the information from him. "He informed me that in the year 1777, he had command of the fort in Schoharie, and of all the frontier stations in this region. He left the fort in Schoharie, and came out through the woods to Harpersfield in the time of making sugar, and from thence laid his course for Cherry Valley to investigate the state of things there; and as he was pursuing a blind kind of Indian trail, and was ascending what are now called Decatur Hills, he cast his eye forward and saw a company of men coming directly toward him, who had the appearance of Indians. He knew that if he attempted to flee from them they would shoot him down; he resolved to advance right up to them, and make the best shift for himself he could. As soon as he came near enough to discern the white of their eyes, he knew the head man and several others; the head man's name was Peter, an Indian with whom Col. Harper had often traded at Oquago, before the Revolution began. The colonel had his great-coat on, so that his regimentals were concealed, and he was not recognized; the first word of address on Col. Harper's part was, "How do you do, brothers?" the reply was, "Well—how do you do, brother? which way are you bound, brother?" "On a secret expedition—and which way are you bound, brothers?" "Down the Susquehanna to cut off the Johnstone settlement." (Parson Johnstone, and a number of Scotch families, had settled down the Susquehanna, at what is now called Sidney Plains, and these were the people whom they were about to destroy.) Says the colonel, "Where do you lodge to-night?" "At the mouth of Scheneva's creek," was the reply. Then shaking hands with them, he bid them good speed, and proceeded on his journey.

"He had gone but a little way from them before he took a circuit through the woods, a distance of eight or ten miles, on to the head of Charlotte River, where were a number of men making sugar; ordered them to take their arms, two days' provisions, a canteen of rum, and a rope, and meet him down the Charlotte, at a small clearing called Evans's place, at a certain hour that afternoon; then rode with all speed through the woods to Harpersfield; collected all the men who were there making sugar, and being armed and victualled, with each man his rope, laid his course for Charlotte; when he arrived at Evans's place, he found the Charlotte men there in good spirits; and when he mustered his men, there were fifteen, including himself, exactly the same number as there were of the enemy; then the colonel made his men acquainted with his enterprise.

"They marched down the river a little distance, and then bent their course across the hill to the mouth of Schenevas Creek; when they arrived at the brow of the hill where they could overlook the valley where the Schenevas flows, they cast their eyes down upon the flat, and discovered the fire around which the enemy lay encamped. 'There they are,' said Col. Harper. They descended with great stillness, forded the creek, which was breast-high to a man; after advancing a few hundred yards, they took some refreshment, and then prepared for the contest—daylight was just beginning to appear in the east. When they came to the enemy, they lay in a circle, with their feet toward the fire, in a deep sleep; their arms, and all their implements of death, were all stacked up according to the Indian custom when they lay themselves down for the night: these the colonel secured by carrying them off a distance, and laying them down: then each man, taking his rope in his hand, placed himself by his fellow; the colonel rapped his man softly, and said, 'Come, it is time for men of business to be on their way;' and then each one sprung upon his man, and after a most severe struggle they secured the whole number of the enemy.

"After they were all safely bound, and the morning had so far advanced that they could discover objects distinctly, says the Indian, Peter—'Ha! Col. Harper! now I know thee—why did I not know thee yesterday?' 'Some policy in war, Peter.' 'Ah, me find em so now.' The colonel marched the men to Albany, delivered them up to the commanding officer there, and by this bold and well-executed feat of valor he saved the whole Scotch settlement from a wanton destruction."

Early in the spring of 1780, a party of Tories and Indians, under the command of Brant, destroyed Harpersfield. The inhabitants had generally left the place; but a few of the men were at the time engaged in making maple sugar. Nineteen were taken prisoners, and several killed. A consultation was held in the Indian language in presence of the prisoners, relative to a contemplated attack upon the Upper Fort in Schoharie; the Indians, satisfied with the booty and prisoners already obtained, were unwilling to risk anything in an uncertain expedition; some of the Tories represented the plan as promising success, and advised the Indians to kill the prisoners, that they might not be encumbered with them. Brant came up to Capt. Alexander Harper, one of the prisoners, and drawing his sword, asked him if there were any troops in the fort; saying his life should be taken if he did not inform him correctly. Harper knew enough of the Indian language to have learned the subject of the foregoing conversation, and immediately answered, that it was well garrisoned, believing that they would all be killed should they answer differently. Another prisoner, not knowing the determination of the Indians, and fearing their vengeance should the falsehood be detected, stated truly that there were few if any troops in the fort. Harper insisted that his statement was true; he was believed, and they returned to Niagara. The last night of their journey they encamped a short distance from the fort. In the morning the prisoners were to run the gauntlet. Harper, knowing the hostility of the Indians toward him, and fearing they might take his life, requested Brant to interfere and protect him, which he promised to do. The Indians arranged themselves in two parallel lines, facing inwards, with clubs and whips in their hands.

Harper was selected first; he was a tall, athletic man, and on the first signal sprang from the mark with extraordinary swiftness. An Indian near the end of the line, fearing he might escape with little injury, stepped before him. Harper struck him a blow with his fist, and then springing over him ran toward the fort; the Indians, enraged, broke their ranks and followed him. The garrison, who had been apprised of the movements of the Indians, were upon the walls; when they saw Harper approaching, they threw open the gate, and he rushed in, when they immediately closed it. It was with difficulty that they could keep the Indians back. The other prisoners took different courses, and got into the fort without passing through this, if not fiery, yet bloody ordeal.*

---

* William Harper was an active member of the Provincial Congress, and after the war was several times a member of the State Legislature. When Otsego County was formed, he was appointed one of the assistant judges; William Cooper, Esq., being first judge. He lived to a great age, and died a few years since at Milford, in Otsego County, retaining to the last that strong desire for information which had characterized his public life. Col. John Harper died in Harpersfield, and Alexander and Joseph, soon after the war, obtained a grant of some land in the western part of the State of Ohio, whither they removed. The quiet of the country, and the approach of civilization, was not congenial to them; they preferred the life of a borderer, and sought it amid the boundless forests which then covered that beautiful State.

CHAPTER IX.

> " And Vengeance striding from his grisly den,
> With fell impatience grinds his iron teeth ;
> And Massacre, unchidden, cloys his famine,
> And quaffs the blood of nations."

WE will now return to the valley of the Mohawk, which we left with the retreat of St. Leger, and the close of the campaign of 1777.

During the fall and the following year, Indian scouts infested the country around Fort Schuyler and the western settlements, cutting off supplies and massacreing the inhabitants and soldiers, when small parties of the latter happened to pass beyond the limits of the fort.

The following narrative is given by Dr. Dwight: "In the autumn, when the siege of Fort Stanwix was raised, the following occurrence took place here. Capt. Greg, one of the American officers left in the garrison, went out one afternoon with a corporal belonging to the same corps to shoot pigeons. When the day was far advanced, Greg, knowing that the savages were at times prowling round the fort, determined to return. At that moment a small flock of pigeons alighted upon a tree in that vicinity. The corporal proposed to try a shot at them ; and having approached sufficiently near, was in the act of elevating his piece towards the pigeons, when the report of two muskets, discharged by unknown hands, at a small distance, was heard ; the same instant, Greg saw his companion fall, and felt himself badly wounded in the side. He tried to stand, but speedily fell, and in a moment perceived a huge Indian taking long strides toward him with a tomahawk in his hand. The savage struck him several blows on the head, drew his knife, cut a circle through the skin from his forehead to the crown, and then drew off the scalp with his teeth.

"At the approach of the savage, Greg had counterfeited the appearance of being dead with as much address as he could use, and succeeded so far as to persuade his butcher that he was really dead ; otherwise measures still more effectual would have been employed to dispatch him. It is hardly necessary to observe, that the pain produced by these wounds was intense and dreadful ; those on the head were, however, far the most excruciating, although that in his side was believed by him to be mortal. The savages having finished their bloody business, withdrew.

"As soon as they were fairly gone, Greg, who had seen his companion fall, determined if possible to make his way to the spot where he lay ; from a persuasion that if he could place his head upon the corporal's body, it would in some degree relieve his excessive anguish. Accordingly he made an effort to rise, and having with great difficulty succeeded, immediately fell. He was not only weak and distressed, but had been deprived of the power of self-command by the blows of the tomahawk. Strongly prompted, however, by this little hope of mitigating his sufferings, he made a second attempt and again fell. After several unsuccessful efforts, he finally regained possession of his feet, and, staggering slowly through the forest, he at length reached the spot where the corporal lay. The Indian who had marked him for his prey, took a surer aim than his fellow, and killed him outright. Greg found him lifeless and scalped. With some difficulty he laid his own head upon the body of his companion, and, as he had hoped, found considerable relief from this position.

"While he was enjoying this little comfort, he met with trouble from a new quarter. A small dog which belonged to him, and had accompanied him in his hunting, but to which he had been hitherto inattentive, now came up to him in apparent agony, and leaping around him in a variety of involuntary motions, yelped, whined, and cried in an unusual manner, to the no small molestation of his master. Greg was not in a situation to bear the disturbance even of affection. He tried in every way which he could think of to force the dog from him, but he tried in vain. At length, wearied by his cries and agitations, and not knowing how to put an end to them, he addressed the animal as if he had been a rational being. 'If you wish so much to help me, go and call some one to my relief.' At these words the creature instantly left him, and ran through the forest at full speed, to the great comfort of his master, who now hoped to die quietly.

"The dog made his way directly to three men belonging to the garrison, who were fishing at the distance of a mile from the scene of this tragedy; as soon as he came up to them, he began to cry in the same afflicting manner, and advancing near them, turned and went slowly back toward the point where his master lay, keeping his eye continually on the men; all this he repeated several times. At length one of the men observed to his companions, that there was something very extraordinary in the actions of the dog, and that in his opinion they ought to find out the cause; his companions were of the same mind, and they immediately set out with an intention to follow the animal whither he should lead them. After they had pursued him some distance, and found nothing, they became discouraged. The sun had set, and the forest was dangerous; they therefore determined to return. The moment the dog saw them wheel about, he began to cry with increased violence, and coming up to the men, took hold of the skirts of their coats with his teeth, and attempted to pull them toward the point to which he had before directed their course. When they stopped again, he leaned his back against the back part of their legs, as if endeavoring to push them onward to his master. Astonished at this conduct of the dog, they agreed, after a little deliberation, to follow him until he should stop. The animal directed them directly to his master. They found him still living, and, after burying the corporal as well as they could, they carried Greg to the fort; here his wounds were dressed with the utmost care, and such assistance was rendered to him as proved the means of restoring him to perfect health. This story," says the Doctor, "I received from Captain

Edward Buckley, who received the account from Greg a few days before."

In the spring of 1778 Lafayette was stationed at Albany; in March he went up to Johnstown, from which place he wrote to Col. Gansevoort a letter, dated March 6th, 1778. This letter was enclosed in a letter from Col. Livingston of the same date, of which the following is an extract:

"Enclosed you have a letter from Major Gen. Marquis de Lafayette, relative to Col. Carleton, nephew to Gen. Carleton, who has for some time been in this part of the country as a spy. The general apprehends he has taken his route by the way of Oswego, and begs you'll send out such parties as you may judge necessary for apprehending him."

The following is the letter of Lafayette:

"Sir,

"As the taking of Col. Carleton is of the greatest importance, I wish you would try every means in your power to have him apprehended. I have desired Col. Livingston, who knows him, to let you have any intelligence he can give, and to join to them those I have got by a Tory about the dress and figure of Carleton. You may send as many parties as you please, and every where you'll think proper, and do every convenient thing for discovering him. I dare say he knows that we are after him, and has nothing in view but to escape, which I beg you to prevent by all means. You may promise, in my name, fifty guineas, hard money, besides all money, &c. they can find about Carleton, to any party of soldiers or

Indians who will bring him alive. As every one knows now what we send for, there is no inconvenience to scatter them in the country, which reward is promised in order to stimulate the Indians.

I have the honor to be, sir,

Your most obedient servant,

The Marquis DE LAFAYETTE."

Col. Carleton, it is believed, was not apprehended. The Indians and Tories found employment in the destruction of Wyoming and Cherry Valley; and the valley of the Mohawk, with the exception of an incursion into the German Flats, was unmolested during the summer of 1778. The following letter was written by Major Robert Cochran, then commanding at Fort Schuyler, to Col. Gansevoort, dated

"*Fort Schuyler, Sept.* 18*th*, 1778.

"DEAR COLONEL,

"Since my last, the sachems and warriors of the Oneida and Tuscarora nations, with Col. Lewee, arrived at this fort, with a formal speech from both nations. They informed me of their great uneasiness in regard to the matter of scalping, which had so lately happened about this fort, and were sorry any suspicions should be entertained that they had the least knowledge of any thing being intended against any body here; that they had from the beginning of the present dispute declined acting against us; that they had been used well at first by Col. Dayton, then by Col. Elmore; afterward Col. Gansevoort came to this fort, a native of Albany, from whom we expected much, as the Commissioners of Indian affairs noticed him in particular; but we are sorry he has not noticed us much for some time past; we are sorry you neglect us now; when your affairs were in a worse situation, you courted us and our interest; but now you are prosperous you don't know us; you know we are one; that we have made an agreement with Gen. Schuyler and the other commissioners, that we would be friendly, and not strike the axe at each other.

"The next morning I answered them as follows: 'That I was glad to see them here, and that I had taken particular notice of all they had said; and further, that we were inclined to give them assurance of our friendly dispositions to them, and were sorry that any uneasiness should arise in their minds; and in regard to what some bad soldiers might say, that they would not regard it, as all societies have their bad people among them.'

To which they replied: 'They would not regard what the soldiers should say, but would apply to the head when occasion might require.' I fed them plentifully, and gave them drink also, which I thought was best at present for the public service; and they went off greatly satisfied."

Sometime in the summer of 1778 the enemy made an incursion into the western part of the county, and destroyed the settlements of German Flats. This fine, fertile section of country was laid waste. About one hundred houses were burned, a few persons were killed and taken, but most of the inhabitants escaped.

Early in the spring of 1779, as before stated, General Clinton, with two regiments of the New York line, moved up the Mohawk, and encamped at Canajoharie. During this summer also, little mischief was done in the valley of the Mohawk. In the spring of 1780, the Indians again made their appearance, infuriated, rather than humbled, by the destruction of their villages and grain the previous summer.

General Clinton gave the following orders to Colonel Gansevoort, dated

"*Albany*, *June* 6, 1780.

"SIR,

"You will proceed with your regiment as soon as possible to Fort Plank, where you will find a quantity of provisions, destined for the use of the garrison at Fort Schuyler, which you will take into your charge and escort to that post.

"As the enemy are said to be out in force on the Mohawk River, it is absolutely necessary that you should pay the strictest attention to prevent a surprise; and, in case of attack, to defend the stores to the last extremity; the present situation of the garrison points out the absolute necessity of this caution.

"You will receive a supply of provisions before you march, for the use of your troops, to the end that you may not make use of that destined for the garrison. If you should fall short, you must impress from the inhabitants, avoiding every degree of irregularity."

Brant, sagacious, and generally successful where he directed, had caused a rumor to be circulated that he intended to capture the batteaux, in order to divert attention from other points of attack. This plan succeeded in August following; when, on account of a similar report, the militia of Canajoharie were ordered out to guard a number of batteaux to Fort Schuyler. Brant made a circuit through the woods, and coming in the rear of them, laid waste the whole country around Canajoharie.

The following account of this movement is given by Col. Samuel Clyde, in a letter to Gov. George Clinton, dated

"*Canajoharie, August 6th,* 1780.

"Sir,

"I here send you an account of the fate of our district. On the second day of this inst., Joseph Brant, at the head of about four or five hundred Indians and Tories, broke in upon the settlements, and laid the best part of the district in ashes, and killed sixteen of the inhabitants that we have found; took between fifty and sixty prisoners, mostly women and children, twelve of whom they have sent back. They have killed and drove away with them upwards of three hundred head of cattle and horses; have burnt fifty-three dwelling-houses, beside some outhouses, and as many barns, one very elegant church, and one grist-mill, and two small forts that the women fled out of. They have burnt all the inhabitants' weapons and implements for husbandry, so that they are left in a miserable condition. They have nothing left to support themselves but what grain they have growing, and that they cannot get saved for want of tools to work with, and very few to be got here.

"This affair happened at a very unfortunate hour, when all the militia of the county were called up to Fort Schuyler to guard nine batteaux about half laden. It was said the enemy intended to take them on their passing to Fort Schuyler. There was scarce a man left that was able to go. It seems that every thing conspired for our destruction in this quarter; one whole district almost destroyed, and the best regiment of militia in the county rendered unable to help themselves or the public. This I refer you to Gen. Rensselaer for the truth of.

"This spring, when we found that we were not likely to get any assistance, and knew that we were not able to withstand the enemy, we were obliged to work and build ourselves forts for our defense, which we had nearly completed, and could have had our lives and effects secure, had we got liberty to have made use of them. But that must not be, we must turn out of them; not that we have anything against assisting the general to open the communication to Fort Schuyler, but still doubted what has happened while we were gone. But it was still insisted on that there was no danger when we were all out; that in my opinion there never has been such a blunder committed in the conuty since the war commenced, nor the militia so much put out; and to send generals here without men, is like sending a man to the woods to chop without an axe. I am sensible, had the general had sufficient men, that he would have been able to have given satisfaction both to the public and inhabitants here."

We have already given an account of the ravages of Sir John Johnson, in the fall of 1780, along the valley of the Schoharie Creek. The day after the burning of Schoharie, that is, the 18th of October, he burned Caughnawaga. Col. Fisher, residing near this place, after defending himself in his house, with two brothers, both of whom were killed, fled from it, and was pursued and overtaken by the Indians. They tomahawked and scalped him, and left him, as they supposed, dead. The next day he was found by a friend, who carried him to his house. He recovered and lived long after the war, a useful member of society, and a monument of Indian barbarity.

From Caughnawaga, Johnson passed up on the north side of the Mohawk, ravaging and burning every thing in his course. Gen. Van Rensselaer, who had been apprised of his movements, collected the militia from Claverack and Schenectady, and pursued him. From Caughnawaga, Gen. Van Rensselaer wrote to Col. Brown, commanding at Stone Arabia, with a small force of 130 men stationed in a fort there, to turn out and check the advance of the enemy, and he would support him from the rear. Col. Brown obeyed the orders, but owing to some delay of Gen. Van Rensselaer's, was not supported by him. He fell, fighting manfully at the head of his little band, with 30 or 40 of his followers. The rest, unable to oppose any longer a force so much superior, retreated.

Sir John Johnson settled at Fox's Mills, about eight miles above Fort Plank, (or as it is now called Fort Plain,) and two miles below the upper Mohawk castle. On the north side and on a flat, partly surrounded by a bend of the river, he posted his regiment of regulars and Tories. . A small breastwork was thrown across the neck of land. The Indians occupied a tract of elevated land to the north and in the immediate vicinity, which was covered with a thick growth of shrub-oak. In this position Sir John awaited the approach of Gen. Van Rensselaer, who was joined by the Canajoharie militia and the Tories from Fort Plain under Col. Du Bois. After a slight skirmish the Indians were driven from their position, and fled up the river to the fording place, near the castle, where they crossed, and directed their course toward the Susquehanna. Sir John's troops made a more effective resistance, though they were almost exhausted by the forced marches which they had made, and the labors they had performed. The attack had been commenced late in the day. Though it was conducted with considerable spirit, night came on before the works of Sir John were carried. In this situation Gen. Van Rensselaer ordered his troops to fall back a mile and encamp. Many of the militia were enraged on account of this order, and refused to obey it. They remained during most of the night, and took several prisoners, who informed them that the enemy were on the point of offering to capitulate, when Gen. Van Rensselaer ordered his troops to fall back. A detachment of the Canajoharie militia, under Col.Clyde, took one of their field-pieces during the night.

On the following morning, when Gen. Van Rensselaer advanced with his troops, the enemy had entirely disappeared. They had left their ground, and retreated up the river a short distance, and then crossed to the south. The river was deep and rapid where it formed the bend, which would have ensured Gen. Van Rensselaer a complete victory had he prosecuted his attack with more vigor. A detachment was sent in pursuit, who discovered in the trail of the enemy evidence of the extreme state to which they were reduced by hunger and fatigue. The whole country on the north side of the river, from Caughnawaga to Stone Arabia and Palatine, had been devastated, which, with the ravages of Brant on the south side of the river, in the previous August, almost completed the destruction of the Mohawk settlements.

If here and there a little settlement escaped their ravages, each were like an oasis in the desert, affording temporary shelter and protection, and, like them, liable to be destroyed or buried up by the next whirlwind which should sweep over the land.

But these incursions of the enemy were not made without loss on their part. The militia hastily collected, hung upon their rear, and often attacked them, and checked and diverted their course; and there were instances of individual resistance—of men standing between the enemy and their wives and children, upon whose scalps the Indians might well have painted *the little red foot*,* indicating that they fell fighting bravely in their defense.

---

* See Appendix—Notes I, K.

CHAPTER X.

"Still in your prostrate land there shall be some
Proud hearts, the shrines of Freedom's vestal flame;
Long trains of ill may pass unheeded, dumb,
But vengeance is behind, and justice is to come."

THE following letter was written by Major Nicholas Fish to Gen. Clinton, under date of

Schenectady, March 6th, 1781.

"DEAR GENERAL,

"The enclosed letters from Col. Cortland announce the disagreeable tale of the capture of fifteen men of our regiment and murder of one, by which the inhabitants of this town, and doubtless of the upper settlements, have their fears very considerably alarmed.

"In consequence of your intention, communicated to me when last in Albany, I wrote to the justices at Canajoharie for a warrant to impress twenty sleighs, for the purpose of transporting another supply of provision to Fort Schuyler, and ordered the officer commanding at Fort Rensselaer to furnish men to execute the warrant on Tuesday morning, and forward the sleighs to this place to-morrow evening. Perhaps this disaster may put it out of his power to procure the number ordered; but should the sleighs arrive, I wish to have particular instructions whether to prosecute the first plan of sending on the provision or not; and if you should judge it expedient to send on the provision, notwithstanding the misfortune, I would be happy to know what number the escort must consist of, and from what posts it must be furnished. The company with me amounts to about forty men fit for duty; the companies above average about the same number; to lessen either, you will readily believe, sir, would increase the uneasiness of the inhabitants.

"P. S. If the present moment for sending an additional supply to the fort is to be embraced, would it not be advisable to call in some aid from the militia?"

To this letter Gen. Clinton returned, on the same day, the following answer, dated

"*Albany.*

"Yours of this day's date has been received. The intelligence from Fort Schuyler is too disagreeable to dwell upon; I hope it may put us so much on our guard as to prevent similar accidents. I sincerely wish sleighs could be procured nearer hand than those at Canajoharie. The provision, I should think, ought at least to be sent as far as that settlement by sleighs from the vicinity of Schenectady. However, if a sufficient number are not furnished from that quarter, Mr. Glenn must procure them nearer home. I do not imagine the present escort will run so great a risk as the last; yet I would not wish to subject such an important transport to the least uncertainty. You will therefore detach the company under your immediate command to Johnstown; and as they have been up lately, and consequently fatigued, you will direct them to remain there, and send on the company now stationed there, with twenty men from each of the other companies, and officers proportionate, which will complete the escort to eighty men; the inhabitants in their absence must turn out and defend their posts."

This expedition was undertaken by Major Fish, and the provision safely conveyed to Fort Schuyler; but the labor of transporting it was extremely severe. The snow was so deep that the road was almost impassable, and in many places above Canajoharie no path had been made. Some days they advanced only two or three miles. This labor of transporting and guarding provision and ammunition for Forts Plain, Dayton,* and Schuyler, was very oppressive upon the inhabitants of the frontier.

---

* Fort Dayton was built 1776, at German Flats, and named in honor of Col. Dayton. The old fort at German Flats was called Fort Herkimer; and in 1758 was commanded by Col. Charles Clinton, father of Gen. James and Governor George Clinton, and grandfather of De Witt Clinton, who was a son of General James Clinton. This officer marched from this fort in the summer of 1758, under Gen. Bradstreet, to Oswego, and went thence to the siege of Fort Frontenac. This expedition was completely successful; the French were not apprised of their approach until they saw them before the walls of their fortress. Among the persons who were afterward distinguished, who accompanied Gen. Bradstreet, were Horatio Gates, then a captain, and Nathaniel Woodhull, then a major, afterward first president of the New York Provincial Congress, and who in the Revolution was a general, and sealed his attachment to the cause of his country with his blood. Col. Charles Clinton wrote a very interesting account of this expedition against Fort Fontenac, which has been preserved, and is in possession of his great grandson, Charles Clinton, Esq., of New York. Though not belonging to the period of which I am writing, yet I will insert the account which he gives of the capture of this fort.

"The fort of Frontenac was a regular square, built on the entrance in the Lake Ontario, on the northwest side of the river. It was built of

During the early part of the summer of 1781, a constant warfare was carried on in the vicinity of the forts; small parties of Indians hovered about Fort Plain, and cut off every soldier or inhabitant who was so careless or unfortunate as to stray beyond its walls.

Col. Willet, who now commanded at this fort, in July sent Lieut. Gros, with thirty-six men, as a secret scout, into Durlagh, now the town of Sharon, in Schoharie County. They discovered, near the borders of that settlement, an Indian trail, and followed it in the direction the Indians had gone. The scout

---

stone and lime, about fifteen feet high; had all round a platform of timber, boarded with thick plank, on which their cannon were mounted; the embrasures were too narrow to admit of the cannon to be brought to bear on one point. The situation was bad, for it stood in a low place, and rising ground northwest of it; and little hollows, by which we made our approaches with so little loss. The first day we made no intrenchments, but from behind one of these little heights fired with our cannon upon them. It was well supplied with all sorts of warlike stores; had above sixty pieces of cannon, and a vast number of beautiful small-arms, and powder and ball of all sorts. We brought off from it a large quantity of powder, but the garrison, not expecting the English would ever venture to pay them a visit there, had sent their men to other places of more danger. I cannot tell how many was in it; we saw but about a hundred; but when they found that the place would be taken, the Indians (and no doubt many of the French) went away, as did the men on board the brig and schooner. I believe the garrison might consist of 200. The destruction of this place, and of the shipping, artillery, and stores, is one of the greatest blows the French have met with in America, considering the consequence of it; as it was the store out of which all the forts to the southward were supplied, and the shipping destroyed those they employed in that service.

"It was concerted and agreed upon in an instant, (though looked upon by some as a chimerical, wild, improbable undertaking,) carried on so secretly that the French never heard of our coming till they saw us where we came to at an island, the evening before we landed. The

fell in file alongside of the path made by the Indians, and by this means ascertained that the force of the enemy was very considerable. Three men were sent on to make further discoveries. After pursuing the trail a short distance, they arrived upon the border of a thick cedar swamp, five or six miles to the north-east of Cherry Valley; here they found the camp of the enemy, in which a few sentinels only were stationed. The main body of the enemy were out on some expedition. One of the men stole up and took a blanket from beneath a tent, without being dis-

---

siege was carried on so vigorously that we invested the place the 26th of August, and took it the 27th, about the same time. Here I must observe, that the governor of Fort Frontenac was let go home in exchange for Col. Schuyler; and for the other prisoners, they are to send us as many of ours from Canada, in exchange.—28th. Having the evening before put our plunder on board our shipping and batteaux, we set sail, and left that neat, handsome garrison and good buildings (where the French lived well) in a heap of rubbish. By this we paid them for the demolition of Oswego, which they served the same way, with this difference, that we neither insulted nor injured any one of the prisoners, but rather treated them with more humanity than that nation deserved whose ambition has embroiled all Europe in war for many years.

"I will conclude my narrative of the taking of Frontenac, by relating a piece of papist superstition, told us by a young man, one of Captain Oglevie's men, who was taken by the Indians, and sold to the governor of Fort Frontenac, and was in his service when he took the place: He says, that when we invested the place, the priests, or some of their people, set the Lady Mary's image on a table, standing, and a number of the people were praying earnestly to her to deliver and save them and the garrison from us heretics; but in the height of their devotion a bomb fell near the place, burst, and broke into the windows, and, without any regard to the image, drove it in pieces off the table. This struck them with such terror, they all looked up, and cried, Mon Dieu! mon Dieu! all was lost, the Virgin Mary was gone, the heretics would take the place."

covered. Having made the necessary observations, they followed the remainder of the scout back to Fort Plain. It was almost night when the scout arrived, but Col. Willet added seventy men, and ordered an immediate march. They were joined by Major Robert M'Kean, with about thirty men, making their force one hundred and fifty. M'Kean informed Col. Willet that the enemy were about three hundred strong, principally Indians, under the command of a Tory, by the name of John Doxtader; and that the day previous they had destroyed Currytown, a small settlement near the Mohawk, a short distance above Schenectady. The night was very dark, and there was no road, nothing but a path through the woods. Their progress was very slow. About daylight they came in sight of the camp. A scout sent forward reported that the enemy had just returned. Col. Willet drew up his men in two parallel lines, and then ordered them to fall back and conceal themselves behind the trees. His plan was favored by the thick cedar swamp in the neighborhood of the enemy's camp. Major M'Kean with fifty men occupied the right, and Col. Willet commanded the left body, composed of his one hundred men. Two men were then sent forward to pass over a piece of open ground in sight of the enemy. When discovered, they were directed to lead in between the two lines. The expectations of Col. Willet were realized; the Indians, as soon as they saw these men, raised their war-cry and commenced an immediate pursuit. As they followed in, the troops of Major M'Kean opened a galling and destructive fire upon them, which was warmly seconded by Col. Willet's men on the left. The Indians were beaten at their own game; they sought shelter behind the trees, but were driven back and routed at the point of the bayonet. Col. Willet led the van, and waving his hat cheered on his men. The camp of the enemy and all their plunder was taken. They retreated down toward the Susquehanna, and were pursued with considerable loss. Shortly after the first fire, Major M'Kean received two severe wounds, but he continued his command until the rout of the enemy was complete. His faithful soldiers carried him back to Fort Plain, where he survived but a day or two. The victory was dearly won by the loss of this brave and hardy chieftain.

In August following, Major Ross and Walter Butler came from Canada by the way of Sacondaga to Johnstown, with 607 men—477 British and Tories, and 130 Indians. They encamped on the elevated ground a little to the north of Johnson Hall. This edifice, erected by Sir William Johnson, and in which he resided at the time of his death, is situated about one mile distant from the court-house, in the centre of the village, and upon ground descending gradually from the northwest to the south and southeast. The village plot descends to the north, thus forming a small valley between the Hall and village. To a person in the village, Johnson Hall appears to be situated on a lawn, beyond which no prospect opens to the sight. When arrived at the Hall, he perceives in an easterly direction, about nine miles distant, the range of Mayfield hills or mountains, while to the south are seen Anthony's Nose, on the Mohawk; beyond that

Charleton, and, still further on, the hills between Canajoharie and Cherry Valley; and, at a distance of between thirty and forty miles, the blue, cloud-like mountains leading to the Catskill and Delaware.

Col. Willet moved from Fort Plain with about 300 levies. On the 22d of August he determined to attack the enemy in their camp. He detached 100 men under Colonel Harper to make a circuit through the woods and fall upon the enemy's rear, while he should attack them in front. A short distance above the Hall, Col. Willet was met by Ross with all his force, and his men on the first fire gave way and retreated. Willet endeavored to rally them at the Hall, but failed. At the village he succeeded in stopping them; here he was joined by 200 militia just arrived. The detachment under Harper had gained the rear, and had now opened a fire upon the enemy. The attack was now renewed by Colonel Willet, and the enemy were finally driven from their ground with loss. Thirteen Americans, and seventeen British and Indians were killed.

Major Ross retreated up the north side of the Mohawk, marching all night, after the battle. In the morning he was pursued by Col. Willet, but was not overtaken. The region of country over which Ross retreated after he had passed the settlements, lies twenty or thirty miles north of Fort Schuyler, and at that time was uncultivated and desolate; his army suffered much from hunger.

It was on this retreat that Walter Butler was killed; he was pursued by a small party of Oneida Indians; when he arrived at West Canada Creek, about fifteen miles above Herkimer, he swam his horse across the stream, and then turning round, defied his pursuers, who were on the opposite side. An Oneida immediately discharged his rifle, and wounded him, and he fell. Throwing down his rifle and his blanket, the Indian plunged into the creek and swam across; as soon as he had gained the opposite bank, he raised his tomahawk, and with a yell, sprang, like a tiger, upon his fallen foe; Butler supplicated, though in vain, for mercy; the Oneida, with his uplifted axe, shouted in his broken English: "Sherry Valley! remember Sherry Valley!" and then buried it in his brains. He tore the scalp from the head of his victim, still quivering in the agonies of death, and ere the remainder of the Oneidas had joined him, the spirit of Walter Butler had gone to give up his account. The place where he crossed is called *Butler's Ford* to this day.

Col. John Butler had some good traits of character, and in his calmer moments would regret the ravages committed by the Indians and Tories; but Walter Butler was distinguished from youth for his severe, acrimonious disposition. After the massacre at Cherry Valley he went to Quebec; but Gen. Haldiman, governor of Canada, gave out that he did not wish to see him.*

---

* Col. Stone, in his Life of Brant, has in one or two instances attempted a justification or rather palliation of the conduct of Walter Butler, and says that the history of the events was written too soon to be entirely impartial. One of the letters of Butler, which he gives as proof, and which will be found in Vol. I, pages 377, 378, closes with this threat: "But be assured that if you persevere in detaining my father's family

It may be remarked here, that many of the British officers did not approve of the conduct of the Indians and Tories. In that war, though we had many a bitter, we had also many a generous and warm-hearted foe. They said it was a disgrace to the English army, thus to carry on this predatory warfare, and to make prisoners of women and children.

In the winter of 1781–2, Col. Willet* undertook a

---

with you, that *we shall no longer take the same pains to restrain the Indians from prisoners, women and children*, that we have heretofore done. I am your humble servant,

WALTER N. BUTLER,
GENERAL SCHUYLER." *Capt. Com. of the Rangers.*

The language of that letter needs no comment. It was written the day after the massacre at Cherry Valley, and it was answered by Gen. James Clinton. Gen. Clinton in his reply says:

"Do not flatter yourself, sir, that your father's family have been detained on account of any consequence they were supposed to be of, or that it is determined they should be exchanged in consideration of the *threat* contained in your letter. I should hope for the sake of human nature, and the honor of civilized nations, that the British officers had exerted themselves in restraining the barbarity of the savages."

The wife of Col. John Butler was, with some of her children, detained as a hostage by the committee of safety, and they were afterward exchanged for the wife and children of Col. Samuel Campbell, who were taken prisoners at Cherry Valley.

* Col. Marinus Willet died at New York, August 22, 1830—the anniversary of his battle with Major Ross and Walter Butler—aged 90 years. The following notice appeared in one of the city papers:

"The coffin of Col. Willet, who died recently in the city of New York, was made of pieces of wood collected by himself, many years ago, from different revolutionary battle-grounds. The corpse, in compliance with a written request of the deceased, was habited in a complete suit of ancient citizen's apparel, including an old-fashioned three-cornered hat, which had been preserved for that purpose. It is estimated that several thousand persons passed through the house for the purpose of viewing the remains."

hazardous expedition—an expedition suited to his bold, persevering genius. He marched a body of his men, in the dead of winter, from Fort Plain to Oswego, passing up the Mohawk on the ice, and using snow-shoes the remainder of the way; his object was the capture of Fort Oswego; but on his arrival near the fort, he learned that the preliminary treaty of peace had been signed; he therefore immediately abandoned the enterprise.

The incursion of Ross and Butler was the last made into the county of Tryon. Indeed, there was no longer anything to destroy. The inhabitants lost all but the soil which they cultivated; their beautiful county, except in the vicinity of the forts, was turned into a wilderness. During the war, famine sometimes appeared inevitable, and it was with difficulty that they preserved from the ravages of the enemy sufficient grain to support their families during the winter. The resistance of the inhabitants of the frontier settlements, however unimportant it may seem, because no great battles were fought, or important victories won, was of very considerable moment in the cause for which they struggled; they kept back the enemy from the towns on the Hudson, and thus frustrated the plan of the British for establishing a line of posts along that river. And while we admire the heroism and patriotism of those worthies of the Revolution whose names have come down to us surrounded with a halo of glory, we should not withhold our praise from those obscure individuals in the frontier settlements, who, amid the most appalling dangers, surrounded on all sides by enemies and traitors, still refused to submit to oppression and arbitrary exactions, though allured by assurances of safety and promises of reward. Many left their homes; many fell in battle in the regular army, and in skirmishes and battles with the enemy at home; and many fell silently, by the rifle, the tomahawk, and the scalping-knife of the Indian.

"Their ashes flew, no marble tells us whither."

CHAPTER XI.

"'Tis faith thus wrought, whose fearful mysteries
Yield e'en weak women strength for deeds like these."

It has been stated in a preceding chapter, that Mrs. Campbell and her children were carried captives into the Indian country. Soon after her arrival at Canadaseago, the capital of the Seneca nation, she was given to a family to fill the place left vacant by the death of one of its members. This family was composed of females, with the exception of one aged warrior, who no longer went forth either to the chase or to war; this circumstance enabled her to render herself useful to them. The Indians knew little of the most common arts of life; few of the Indian women could make even an ordinary calico garment. She made garments not only for the family to which she belonged, but also for the neighboring families, who in return sent corn and venison for their support. By reason of these services, she was under no restraint, but was free to come or go as she pleased.

The Indians paid no regard to the Sabbath, but pursued their usual avocations on that day; on her informing them that she kept that day sacred, they did not ask her to do any work, and gave strict orders to the children to remain silent while in her presence.

An Indian one day came into the house where she was, and asked her why she wore caps, saying, "Indians do not do so." She replied it was the custom of her countrywomen. "Well, come to my house, and I will give you a cap." Her adopted mother motioned to her to follow him. As soon as they had entered the house, he pulled from behind a beam a cap of a smoky color, and handed it to her, saying in English, "I got that cap in Cherry Valley; I took it from the head of a woman." On examination she recognized it as having belonged to the unfortunate Jane Wells; and was no doubt the one she had on when she was so barbarously murdered, as it had a cut in the crown made by the tomahawk, and was spotted with blood. She could not but drop a tear to her memory, for she had known her from infancy—a pattern of virtue and loveliness. In the Indian who stood before her she perceived the murderer of her friend. She turned from him with horror. Returning to her cabin, she tore off the lace border, and washing it carefully, though she could not efface the stains of blood, laid it away with the intention of giving it to some of the friends of Miss Wells, if any had been fortunate enough to escape. She afterward gave it to Miss Ramsay, a cousin, whom she found at Fort Niagara, and who, together with her mother, melted into tears as they beheld this little relic, spotted with the blood of their kinswoman.

Early in the winter the nation assembled at Canadaseago to hold a general council, and to celebrate their late successes. This village was laid out with some regularity, and in almost a circular form, enclosing a large green. The houses were generally built of bark, after the rude style of the Indians. A few were of hewn logs. The ceremony was commenced by a sacrifice. A white dog was killed and borne along in procession to a large fire kindled in the centre of the village. In the mean time others went round to every house with a basket, in which each individual was required to deposit something. This basket, with all its contents, was first cast into the fire. Afterward the dog was laid on and thoroughly roasted, and was then eaten. This was followed by eating, drinking and dancing, which continued for several days.*

When Col. Butler went to Canada he left his wife and children in the county. The committee afterward refused permission to them to join him. Captain Walter Butler, her son, wrote a letter by the prisoners who returned to Cherry Valley, to Col. Campbell, proposing an exchange of Mrs. Campbell and her children for his mother and brothers. This letter was laid by him before Gov. Clinton and Gen. Schuyler, and the proposed exchange was agreed to by them.

Early in the spring Col. Campbell dispatched an Indian messenger to Col. Butler at Fort Niagara, informing him that the proposition was acceded to. Col. Butler soon after came to Canadaseago to confer with the Indians in reference to their giving up their prisoners. When prisoners have been given to a family, that family return them with great reluctance. They usually fill the places of deceased relatives. To

---

* See Appendix—Note K.

return them for money, or any other compensation, would be equivalent to selling their relatives. A council was called, which continued sitting for several days. Col. Butler urged with great earnestness the Indians to give up the prisoners in exchange for his wife and children. The assent of the council was finally obtained. The residence of Mrs. C. was intended to have been only temporary at Canadaseago. This spring she was to have been placed in a family in the Genesee village, who were kinsfolk of the family with whom she lived at this time, and also of Guyanguahta, or, as he was usually called, Grahta, the Seneca king. It was necessary to obtain their assent, and the old king himself set out on this errand. Having succeeded, he returned to Canadaseago, and immediately informed Mrs. C. that she was now free. The good old king had always been kind to her. Though considerably advanced in life, so that he did not join in the war, yet he performed this journey on foot. Before her departure for Niagara, he came up from his residence near the outlet of the Seneca Lake, to bid her adieu, and to wish her success on her journey. "You are now about to return to your home and friends, I rejoice. You live a great way, many days' journey from here. I am an old man, and do not know that I shall live to the end of this war; if I do, when the war is over I will come and see you." This was spoken through an interpreter. A circumstance occurred about the same time, which deserves notice. It has been observed that the Oneidas passed through the country of the other nations unmolested. One of them came into the village of Canadaseago. Among the prisoners in the village was a Mr. Piper, who had been taken in the valley of the Mohawk. He sought an interview with the Indian. The Indian, informed of this, called upon him, and addressed him in English in a very grave tone: "You wished to see me—I have come—what do you want?" "I wished to request you, when you return, to go to my family and inform them that I am alive." "Is that all?" said the generous Oneida; "I supposed you wanted me to conduct you back to your home." "I dare not leave," was the reply; "I would be pursued and overtaken, and probably killed." "I can lead you safe, by paths which they do not know. If you will go with me, I am sure I can conduct you home in safety." Mr. Piper was advanced in life, and preferred waiting until some exchange should be made, to hazarding his life by an attempt to escape. This conversation had been over-heard. Col. Butler, fearing lest he might escape, ordered him forward to Niagara. Col. Butler remained in the Indian country with his rangers. He was joined by Brant and the Indians, in all about 800, who made a stand, as before mentioned, at Newtown. Mrs. Campbell, shortly after the return of the old king, was also sent to Niagara, where she arrived in June, 1779. Soon after the British at that fort received information of the march of Gen. Sullivan. The fort at this time was in a poor condition to resist an attack. A regiment was ordered up from Canada to aid in repairing and garrisoning it. The men were almost constantly on fatigue duty during the summer. The most vigorous preparations were made to give Gen. Sullivan a warm reception, should the capture of this fort be the object of the campaign.

Among the persons driven into the fort by the American army, was Catrine Montour, who had signalized herself by her inhumanity at Wyoming. She had two sons, who were the leaders of bands, and who consequently imparted additional consequence to her. This creature was treated with considerable attention by some of the officers. It has already been remarked, however, in justice to that body of men, that the indiscriminate war which was carried on along the border was not generally sanctioned or approved of by them.

A son of Catrine Montour took prisoner, in Cherry Valley, Mr. Cannon, the father of Mrs. Campbell. Mr. Cannon was severely wounded by a musket ball, and was also advanced in life; but he had been a committee-man, and had taken an active part in the war. He was therefore taken along a prisoner, for the purpose of exchange. On the return of the party into the Indian country, Catrine addressed her son in English, and, in the presence of Mr. Cannon, reproached him for having acted humanely. "Why did you bring that old man a prisoner? Why did you not kill him when you first took him?" Another person was Molly, the sister of Joseph Brant, and mistress of Sir William Johnson. Lieut. Col. Stacia, who had been taken prisoner at Cherry Valley, was also at the fort. Molly Brant had, from some cause, a deadly hostility to him. She resorted to the Indian method of dreaming. She informed Col. Butler that she dreamed she had the Yankee's head, and that she and the Indians were kicking it about the fort. Col. Butler ordered a small keg of rum to be painted and given to her. This for a short time appeased her, but she dreamed the second time that she had the Yankee's head, with his hat on, and she and the Indians were kicking it about the fort for a football. Col. Butler ordered another keg of rum to be given to her, and then told her, decidedly, that Col. Stacia should not be given up to the Indians. Apart from this circumstance, I know nothing disreputable of Molly Brant; on the contrary, she appears to have had just views of her duties. She was careful of the education of her children, some of whom were respectably married.

The Indians having been driven into Fort Niagara, Col. Butler was enabled to get from them all Mrs. Campbell's children. She was sent down to Montreal in June, 1780, a year after her arrival at the fort. Here she found Mrs. Butler and children, and one of her own sons, a child about seven years of age.* He had been with the Caughnawagas, a branch of the Mohawk tribe, settled in Canada. Mrs. Butler had taken off his Indian dress, and had clad him in the green uniform of Col. Butler's Rangers. It was, however, only the appearance of the child which she had altered; for he could speak nothing but the

---

* James S. Campbell, Esq. was the second son of Col. Samuel Campbell, and is still living at Cherry Valley, on the old homestead which he inherited from his father. He has long since forgotten the Indian tongue. Indeed, as he has often stated to me, he forgot it as readily as he learned it.

Mohawk tongue, having entirely forgotten the English. Mrs. C. had not seen him since the day of their captivity at Cherry Valley. Though his habits had changed with his language, she rejoiced, for he had not forgotten her.

At Montreal, several other prisoners were collected, previous to their being exchanged. They were detained here several months waiting for their passports. They repeatedly made inquiries of, and remonstrated to Gen. Haldiman, the Governor. He said it was not in his power to grant them, but he would write to the commander-in-chief at Quebec; which he accordingly did. The passports were soon after obtained, and the prisoners were sent to Crown Point, where a batteaux lay which had brought from the States several loyalist families. Before their arrival, a British vessel had come into the port from Canada, and the sailors commenced telling the people on the wharf, and in the other vessels, that expeditions were fitting out in Canada against Fort George and Fort Ann. The Americans in the batteau overheard this conversation. When the prisoners left St. John's, the commander at that place wrote to Crown Point, ordering the commander there to permit the batteau to return. This letter was to have been carried by them; but by accident it was sent forward and reached Crown Point before they did, and the batteau immediately departed. They were then sent back to Port Affair and detained there. They saw the expedition going down the lake, and though at that time they did not know that the sailors on board the batteau had overheard the conversation relative to it, yet they consoled themselves with the idea that *they* must have received some intimation of it, and would apprise the inhabitants. But the spies returned, saying all was silent and no attack was apprehended. Shortly after the batteau returned with another cargo of loyalist families. The batteaumen had given no intimation of the contemplated invasion. It was supposed they preferred the hard dollars which they received in pay for their labor, to the welfare of their country. They excused themselves by saying they considered it a sailor's story, and entitled to no credit.

One party of Indians and Tories in this expedition was commanded by Captain Johnson, a brother of Guy Johnson, who, on account of his ferocious conduct, was called "Savage Johnson." When this expedition returned, poles were erected in the sterns of the boats, from which were suspended the scalps of persons whom they had killed. According to the account given by them, the number killed was about fifty.

The prisoners were now sent down to Crown Point—the batteau was dismissed, and they passed the lake. In their passage they were the cause of alarm to the inhabitants who had so recently been visited. The men were clad in blanket coats, and some of the women wore red cloaks. A scout had discovered them on the lake, and taking them for a party of Indians and Tories, gave the alarm, and before their arrival more than a thousand militia had collected, under Col. Ethan Allen. While stopping at a small fortress, eight miles from Castleton, it was announced that a flag was approaching. It was supposed to be sent to demand the surrender of the fortress. Col. Herrick, of the militia, struck his sword upon the ground with such force that he broke it in pieces, saying it should not be surrendered. Col. Allen told the prisoners that they should not again fall into the hands of the enemy, and immediately mounting them upon horseback, sent them off toward Albany, with an escort of a hundred men. This flag was sent for the following reason. It had been rumored that the inhabitants in that section had said that if they were not protected from the incursions of the Indians and Tories, they would seek protection elsewhere. It is perhaps needless to add, that this flag was sent to offer them the protection of Great Britain, which was indignantly rejected.

Shortly after her arrival at Albany, Mrs. Campbell was joined by Mr. Campbell, who had been in Fort Schuyler during most of the time since 1778. They removed up the river to where now is situated the village of West Troy. On the east side of the river there were but two houses, where is now situated the beautiful city of Troy.

It was not until the spring of 1784, that they returned to Cherry Valley. They were now almost penniless, their lands had gone to waste, and were covered with underbush, and overrun with wild beasts. With a large family, and without a shelter, save a little log cabin, hastily put up, they felt for a time that their lot had been a hard one. But the consciousness that they had done their duty to their country, and that that country was now free, bore them up under their misfortunes. Toward the close of summer, Mr. C. had succeeded in erecting a comfortable log-house, and his farm began to assume again the aspect of cultivation. He received information that General Washington and several other distinguished persons were passing up the Mohawk, and would visit Cherry Valley. When they arrived, he had no place, save his log-house, in which to receive them. But most of them had been accustomed to the camp, and dreaded no inconvenience from this source. General Washington was accompanied by Gov. George Clinton, Gen. Hand, and many officers of the New York line. Gov. Clinton immediately inquired for Robert Shankland, who had married a distant connection of his, and with whom he was acquainted. Before introducing him, it may be well to give some account of this brave and hardy borderer. From the first he had espoused the colonial cause; and being an Irishman by birth, maintained it with the characteristic warmth of his countrymen. He lived in a remote part of the town, but while the garrison was kept, he came almost daily to inquire as to the state of affairs at home and abroad. He was accustomed to pass by the farm of a Mr. Coonrad, a townsman, whom he found always engaged in his usual farming business. Believing that a man could not be a good Whig, who appeared so indifferent to what was doing in the country, he one day accosted him. Armed, as was his custom, with a musket and a large basket-hilted sword, he drew up before him, when the following dialogue was held: "Mr. Coonrad, are you a Whig?" he asked, sternly. "Yes, Mr. Shankland,

I am as good a Whig as you are." "And why don't you arm yourself in defense of your country, as I do, then?" Throwing up his musket and striking his hand upon his sword, he marched toward the fort, leaving Mr. Coonrad somewhat surprised at this, though not unusual, yet searching question. Mr. Coonrad was afterward an active partisan soldier.

When Cherry Valley was destroyed, the house of Mr. Shankland, by renson of its remoteness, was not burned. He fled, however, with his family to the Mohawk River. The following summer he returned with his son Thomas, a lad about fourteen years of age. They were awakened one morning a little before daylight by a violent pounding at the door, with a demand of admittance, made in broken English. Mr. Shankland arose, and taking down his guns, directed his son to load them as fast as they should be discharged by him. Upon listening, he ascertained that the demand was made by Indians, who were endeavoring to hew down the door with their tomahawks. With a spear in his hand he now carefully unbarred his door and charged upon them. Surprised by this sudden and unexpected attack, they fell back. One of the Indians whom he pursued in his retreat fell over a log which lay near the door and into which he struck his spear. He drew it back suddenly, when the blade parted from the handle and remained in the wood. He seized the blade in his hand and wrested it out, and then retreated into the house. Not a gun was fired nor a tomahawk thrown at him in this sortie. The Indians now commenced firing through the door and in the windows, which was returned by Mr. S., though with no effect on the part of the Indians, and with little on his. One or two of the Indians were slightly wounded. His son, who was frightened, made his escape through the window, and ran toward the woods. He was discovered, pursued and taken. When Mr. S. learned from their shouts that this was the case, he determined to sally out again and sell his life as dearly as possible. But upon reflection, fearing it might endanger the life of his son, whom they might otherwise save alive, he concluded to remain and defend his house to the last. The Indians, who were few in number, finding themselves unable to effect an entrance into the house, hit upon another method of attack. They gathered combustible materials, and placing them at a side of the house where there were no windows, and where they could not be annoyed by Mr. S., set fire to them. In a few minutes the whole side of the house was enveloped in flames. There was but one way of escape. He had sown a field of hemp, which came up to his house on one side, and luckily the side in which was the cellar door. The prospect of a successful defense being now over, he went into the cellar, and having gained the woods through the hemp, made his way to the Mohawk in safety. The Indians waited until the house was burned down, supposing him to have been burned in it, and then, raising their shout of victory, departed, taking their prisoner along with them into the western part of the State.

When Mr. Shankland had been introduced to the company, he was requested to relate some of his adventures, and the foregoing was a part of his narration.

He stood up in the centre of the little log-cabin, and so far as space would allow, "fought his battle o'er." His audience listened with great attention, though their faculties were occasionally excited by his drolleries. Such a group would form no mean subject for the pencil.

An object of some interest also to the party, was a gun which formerly belonged to Joseph Mayall, and the notice of which arose from the following circumstance. Mayall lived in the town of Laurens, in the now county of Otsego. Though an Englishman by birth, he had sided with the colonies. He had returned home during the summer, and was hunting, when he was accosted by three men, who requested him to pilot them a short distance down the Susquehanna to the fording place. He did so; but the men, abusing his confidence, took his gun from him, and having taken off the lock returned it to him. They then informed him that he must accompany them to Canada. He remonstrated, saying that peace had been declared, and they had no right to detain him a prisoner. Finding argument unavailing he concluded to submit until an opportunity to escape should offer. When crossing a branch of the Susquehanna, the better to secure their prisoner, one of the men passed to the opposite side of the stream—one stationed himself in the middle, and one was to accompany Mayall. Seizing upon this advantage, Mayall struck the man who was with him on the bank a violent blow with his gun, which felled him to the earth; and then seizing quickly his gun, fired at and wounded the one in the stream. The third fired at, but missed Mayall, and then fled.

Mayall returned and came to Cherry Valley, bringing the guns of the two men, together with his own, which he deposited with Mr. Campbell. Mayall was a stout, athletic man, and the barrel of his gun was bent almost to a semicircle by the violence of the blow.

The ensuing morning, Gov. Clinton, seeing several boys, inquired of Mrs. C. how many children she had: having told him, he added, "they will make fine soldiers in time." She replied, "she hoped her country would never need their services." "I hope so too, madam," said Gen. Washington, "for I have seen enough of war." They visited Otsego Lake and outlet, where Gen. Sullivan threw a dam across, and afterward passed down to join Gen. Sullivan. The following letter was written by Gen. Washington to the Marquis of Chastelleux, a foreigner who was in pursuit of literary and military fame.

"I have lately made a tour through the lakes George and Champlain as far as Crown Point, then returning to Schenectady I proceeded up the Mohawk River to Fort Schuyler, crossed over to Wood Creek, which empties into the Oneida Lake, and affords the water communication with Ontario. I then traversed the country to the head of the eastern branch of the Susquehanna, and viewed the Lake Otsego and the portage between that lake and the Mohawk River at Canajoharie. Prompted by these actual observations, I could not help taking a more contemplative and extensive view of the vast inland navigation of these United States, and could not but be struck with the immense diffusion and importance of it, and with the goodness of that Providence which has dealt his favors to us with so profuse a hand. Would to God we may have wisdom enough to improve them. I shall not rest contented until I have explored the western country, and traversed those lines (or great part of them) which have given bounds to a new empire."

At the close of the war most of the surviving inhabitants of Cherry Valley, and of the valley of the Mohawk, returned to their former homes.* Many of them had been scattered in different provinces and along the sea-board. The places of some were not occupied, and many a tear was shed as their friends lamented their death,

> ——"Recalling with a sigh
> Dim recollected pleasures of the days of youth,
> And early love."

Many of the soldiers who were at the close of the war without homes, and who had been stationed along the frontier, returned and settled upon the places of their former trials and sufferings. The fertility of the western part of the State had been discovered by Sullivan's expedition. These and other subsequent circumstances produced a tide of emigration to the west, which has not yet ceased to flow, which still pours on its flood into the far unbroken wilderness. Who that looked upon central and western New York then, would have dreamed of its sudden growth and pros-

* On the 4th day of July, 1840, the inhabitants of Cherry Valley celebrated the anniversary of the one hundredth year of their settlement. The centennial discourse of the author will be found in the Appendix; and with it the writer feels that he has done with the history of his native town. The men of other generations must continue it.

perity—that in fifty years it would teem with more than a million of inhabitants, rich in education, rich in morals, rich in enterprise, both civil and religious, in all that adorns a State! When however I look over this land, the domain of the once proud and noble Iroquois, and remember how in the days of their glory they defended this infant colony from the ravages of the French, and contrast their former state, numerous, powerful, and respected, with their present condition, I feel almost disposed to blot out the record which I have made of their subsequent cruelties. They are passing away from among us, without leaving upon the land which they inhabited any mementoes of their greatness. No Brant has written the history of the Six Nations, and left for our perusal "the story of their wrongs."

> "Their yell of vengeance was their trump of fame,
> Their monument, a grave without a name."

I here close this little sketch of our border warfare. Every person will readily perceive how difficult it is to collect materials for even such a sketch, where the few tattered and moth-eaten documents are to be sought for among many persons, and when the authenticity of many events, long gone by, rests upon the frail basis of human memory. It is very possible, therefore, yea, very probable, there are omissions, perhaps errors, in this volume of Annals. I shall be satisfied, however, if I shall have succeeded in rescuing from oblivion any materials, however few or small, which shall be useful and important for the future historian of this State; for that architect whose lot it shall be to rear a monument more durable than those of stone—"that loftier monument on which, not the rays of the setting sun, but the rays of a nation's glory, as long as letters shall endure, will continue to 'play and linger on its summit.'"

Since 1776, revolution has followed revolution; but however splendid in their commencement, or successful in their termination, in the eye of the American, they eclipse not that which terminated in his country's independence. Far from becoming stale, it increases in interest as we recede from it. As our numbers and resources increase, we wonder that so much was done; and when the few remnants of those times shall be gathered to their companions in peace, we shall regret but too late that we had not honored them more.

APPENDIX.

APPENDIX.

Note A.

"The most remarkable difference existed between the confederates and the other Indian nations with respect to eloquence. You may search in vain in the records and writings of the past, or in events of the present times, for a single model of eloquence among the Algonkins, the Abenaquis, the Delawares, the Shawanese, or any other nation of Indians, except the Iroquois. The few scintillations of intellectual light; the faint glimmerings of genius, which are sometimes to be found in their speeches, are evidently derivative, and borrowed from the confederates."

Speech of the Mohawk Chiefs to the Magistrates of Albany, on the 25th of March, 1689–90, after the destruction of Schenectady.

"*Brethren!*—The murder of our brethren at Schenectady by the French, grieves us as much as if it had been done to ourselves, for we are in the same chain; and no doubt our brethren of New England will be likewise sadly affected with this cruel action of the French. The French on this occasion have not acted like brave men, but like thieves and robbers. Be not therefore discouraged. We give this belt to wipe away your tears.

"*Brethren!*—We lament the death of so many of our brethren, whose blood has been shed at Schenectady. We don't think that what the French have done can be called a victory; it is only a farther proof of their cruel deceit. The governor of Canada sends to Onondaga, and talks to us of peace with our whole house, but war was in his heart, as you may now see by woful experience. He did the same formerly at Cadarackui, and in the Senecas country. This is the third time he has acted so deceitfully. He has broken open our house at both ends, formerly in the Senecas country, and now here. We hope, however, to be revenged of them. One hundred of our bravest young men are in pursuit of them; they are brisk fellows, and they will follow the French to their doors. We will beset them so closely, that not a man in Canada shall dare to step out of doors to cut a stick of wood; but now we gather up our dead to bury them by this second belt.

"*Brethren!*—We came from our castles with tears in our eyes, to bemoan the blood shed at Schenectady by the perfidious French. While we bury our dead murdered at Schenectady, we know not what may have befallen our own people that are in pursuit of the enemy; they may be dead. What has befallen you may happen to us; and therefore, we come to bury our brethren at Schenectady with this third belt.

"Great and sudden is the mischief, as if it had fallen from Heaven upon us. Our forefathers taught us to go with all speed to bemoan and lament with our brethren, when any disaster or misfortune happens to any in our chain. Take this belt of vigilance, that you may be more watchful for the future. We give our brethren eye-water to make them sharp-sighted. (Giving a fourth belt.)

"We now come to the house where we usually renew the chain; but alas! we find the house polluted with blood. All the Five Nations have heard of this, and we are come to wipe away the blood, and clean the house. We come to invite Corlear, and every one of you, and Quider, (calling to every one of the principal men present by their names,) to be revenged of the enemy, by this fifth belt.

"*Brethren!*—Be not discouraged; we are strong enough. This is the beginning of your war, and the whole house have their eyes fixed upon you at this time, to observe your behavior. They wait your motion, and are ready to join in any resolute measures.

"Our chain is a strong chain; it is a silver chain; it can neither rust nor be broken. We, as to our parts, are resolute to continue the war.

"We will never desist, so long as a man of us remains. Take heart; do not pack up and go away;*

* This was spoken to the English, who were about removing from Albany.

this will give heart to a dastardly enemy. We are of the race of the bear; and a bear, you know, never yields, while one drop of blood is left. We must all be bears. (Giving a sixth belt.)

"*Brethren!*—Be patient; this disaster is an affliction which has fallen from heaven upon us. The sun, which hath been cloudy, and sent this disaster, will shine again with its pleasant beams. Take courage, courage. (Repeating the word several times as they gave a seventh belt.)

(*To the English.*)

"*Brethren!*—Three years ago we were engaged in a bloody war with the French, and you encouraged us to proceed in it. Our success answered our expectation; but we were not well begun, when Corlear stopped us from going on. Had you permitted us to go on, the French would not now have been able to do us the mischief they have done; we would have prevented their sowing, planting, or reaping.

"We would have humbled them effectually, but now we die. The obstructions you then made now ruin us. Let us after this be steady, and take no such false measures for the future, but prosecute the war vigorously. (Giving a beaver skin.)

"The brethren must keep good watch, and if the enemy come again, send more speedily to us. Don't desert Schenectady. The enemy will glory in seeing it desolate. It will give them courage that had none before. Fortify the place; it is not well fortified now; the stockadoes are too short; the Indians can jump over them. (Gave a beaver skin.)

"*Brethren!*—The mischief done at Schenectady cannot be helped now; but for the future, when the enemy appears any where, let nothing hinder your sending to us by expresses, and fire great guns, that all may be alarmed. We advise you to bring all the River Indians under your subjection, to live near Albany, to be ready on all occasions.

"Send to New England; tell them what has happened to you. They will undoubtedly awake, and lend us their helping hand. It is their interest, as much as ours, to push the war to a speedy conclusion. Be not discouraged; the French are not so numerous as some people talk. If we but heartily unite to push on the war, and mind our business, the French will soon be subdued."

The magistrates having returned an answer on the twenty-seventh, to the satisfaction of the Indians, they repeated it all over, word by word, to let the magistrates see how carefully they minded, and then added—

"*Brethren!*—We are glad to find you are not discouraged. The best and wisest men sometimes make mistakes. Let us now pursue the war vigorously. We have a hundred men out; they are good scouts. We expect to meet all the sachems of the other nations, as they come to condole with you. You need not fear our being ready at the first notice. Our axe is always in our hands; but take care that you be timely ready. Your ships, that must do the principal work, are long a fitting out. We do not design to go out with a small company, or in skulking parties; but as soon as the nations can meet, we shall be ready with our whole force. If you would bring this war to a happy issue you must begin soon—before the French can recover the losses they have received from us, and get new vigor and life; therefore send in all haste to New England. Neither you nor we can continue long in the condition we are now in; we must order matters so that the French be kept in continual fear and alarm at home; for this is the only way to be secure, and in peace here.

"The Scatikok Indians, in our opinion, are well placed where they are, (to the northward of Albany;) they are a good out-guard; they are our children, and we must take care that they do their duty: but you must take care of the Indians below the town; place them near the town, so as they may be of more service to you."

NOTE B.

SKETCH OF THE LIFE OF SIR WILLIAM JOHNSON.

A CONSIDERABLE part of the following sketch of the life of Sir William Johnson is taken from the travels of Dr. Dwight. In the main, it is believed to be correct, though perhaps he has not done him justice in the remarks which he makes relative to his command at Lake George. He is supported, however, by an article supposed to have been written by Gov. Livingston, and published in the seventh volume of the Collections of the Massachusetts Historical Society.

"The sight of Sir William Johnson's mansion, in this vicinity, awakened in my mind a variety of interesting reflections. This gentleman was born in Ireland, about the year 1714. Sir Peter Warren having married an American lady, purchased a large estate on and near the Mohawk. In the year 1734 he sent for Mr. Johnson, who was his nephew, to come and superintend the property. To fulfill the duties of the commission Mr. Johnson seated himself in this spot—here he became, of course, extensively acquainted with the Six Nations. He studied their character, and acquired their language; carried on an extensive trade with them, and by a course of sagacious measures made himself so agreeable and useful to them, that for many years he possessed an influence over them, such as was never gained by any other white man.

"His constitution was unusually firm, and his mind hardy, coarse and vigorous. Unsusceptible of those delicate feelings by which minds of a softer mould are in a great measure governed, destitute of those refined attachments which are derived from a correspondence with elegant society, and unconfined by those moral restraints which bridle men of tender consciences, he here saw the path open to wealth and distinction, and determined to make the utmost of his opportunity. In troublesome times, an active, ambitious man hardly ever fails to acquire some degree of consequence. Such were the times in which Mr. Johnson resided at this place, and so persevering and successful was he in turning them to his advantage, that he rose from the station of a common soldier to the command of an army, and from the class of yeomen to the title of baronet.

"In the year 1757 he led the provincial army to Lake George, where was achieved the first victory gained on the British side in the war commencing at that period. For this victory, toward which he did little more than barely hold the place of commander-in-chief, he received from the House of Commons £5,000 sterling, and from the King the title of baronet and the office of superintendent of Indian affairs.

"In the year 1759, being at the head of the provincial troops employed under Brigadier Gen. Prideaux to besiege Fort Niagara, he became, upon the death of that officer, commander-in-chief of the whole army, and directed the siege with activity and skill. On the 24th of July a body of French and Indian assailants approached to raise the siege ; Sir William marched out to meet them and gained a complete victory. The next morning the fort itself surrendered, and the garrison were made prisoners of war.

"In 1760 he led 1000 Iroquois to join the army of Gen. Amherst at Oswego. With this body he proceeded under the command of that illustrious man to Montreal. Here he concluded his military career with honor, being present and active in a distinguished station at the surrender of Canada.

"The services which he rendered to the British colonists were important, and will be long as well as deservedly remembered. The property which he amassed here was very great. At the time when he came into America a considerable part of the cultivated, and much of the uncultivated land in the province of New York, was divided into large manorial possessions, obtained successively from the government by men of superior sagacity and influence. Sir William followed the custom of the country, and by a succession of ingenious and industrious exertions secured to himself vast tracts of valuable land.*

* The following story of Sir William's ingenuity has been frequently related. Old King Hendrick, of the Mohawks, was at his house at the time Sir William received two or three rich suits of military clothes. The old king, a short time afterward, came to Sir Willliam and said: "I dream." "Well, what did you dream?" "I dream you give me one suit of clothes." "Well, I suppose you must have it," and accordingly he gave him one. Some time after Sir William met Hen-

"As these were always exposed to French and Indian incursions, they were obtained for trifling sums,

---

drick, and said, "I dreamed last night." "Did you; what you dream?" "I dreamed you gave me a tract of land," describing it. After a pause, "I suppose you must have it, but," and he raised his finger significantly, "you must not dream again." This tract of land extended from the East to West Canada Creek, in the now county of Herkimer, and was about twelve miles square. The title was afterward confirmed by the King of England, and it was justly called the "Royal Grant."

Old King Hendrick, or as he was sometimes called, the great Hendrick, lived in the now town of Minden in Herkimer County, and near the upper Mohawk castle. "The site of his house," says Dr. Dwight, "is a handsome elevation, commanding a considerable prospect of the neighboring country. It will be sufficient to observe here, that for capacity, bravery, vigor of mind, and immovable integrity united, he excelled all the Aboriginal inhabitants of the United States of whom any knowledge has come down to the present time. A gentleman of a very respectable character, who was present at a council held with the Six Nations, by the Governor of New York, and several agents of distinction from New England, informed me that his figure and countenance were singularly inpressive and commanding; that his eloquence was of the same superior character, and that he appeared as if born to con rol other men, and possessed an air of majesty unrivalled within his knowledge." In the French wars he led forth his Mohawk warriors and fought side by side with Sir William Johnson. Through all the intrigues of the French he remained faithful to his alliance. He was also highly esteemed by the white inhabitants. During some of the negotiations with the Indians of Pennsylvania and the inhabitants of that state, Hendrick was present at Philadelphia. His likeness was taken, and a wax figure afterward made, which was a very good imitation. After the death of Hendrick, an old friend, a white man, visited Philadelphia, and among other things was shown this wax figure. It occupied a niche, and was not observed by him until he had approached within a few feet. The friendship of former days came fresh over his memory, and forgetting for the moment Hendrick's death, he rushed forward and clasped in his arms the frail, icy image of the chieftain.

being considered by most men as of very little value. In consequence of the peace of Paris, and the subsequent increase of the settlements in the province, they rose, as he had foreseen, from being of little value to such a price as to constitute an immense fortune.

"By Lady Johnson he had three children; two daughters, one married to Col. Claus, the other to Col. Guy Johnson, and a son afterward, Sir John Johnson. Of the first of these gentlemen I have no further information. The two last took the British side of the question in the Revolutionary war.

"Sir William built a house at the village of Johnstown, where he chiefly lived during the latter part of his life. The house which he built on this road (along the Mohawk River) was occupied by Sir John. Colonel Guy Johnson built a house on the opposite side of the road a little further down the river. Here these men lived, essentially in the rank, and with not a small part of the splendor of noblemen. But when they joined the British standard their property vanished in a moment, and with it their consequence, their enjoyments, and probably their hopes."

Many accounts are still given of the rustic sports encouraged by Sir William, and of the influence which he exerted over the Indians and white inhabitants. He died July 11th, 1774, aged 59 years. There is something still mysterious connected with his death. He had been out to England, and returned the previous spring. During a visit which he made shortly after to Mr. Campbell, an intimate friend of his at Schenectady, the conversation turned upon the subject of the disputes between the colonies and the mother country. He then said *he should never live to see them in a state of open war.* At a court held in Johnstown for Tryon County, he received a foreign package. He was in the court-house when it was handed him. He immediately left the house and walked over to the Hall. This package was afterward understood to have contained instructions to him to use his influence in engaging the Indians in favor of England, in case a war should break out. If such were the instructions to Sir William, his situation was indeed trying. On the one side was the English government, which had so highly honored and enriched him, and on the other his own adopted country, whose armies he had led to victory, with many warm personal friends who entertained a great respect for him, and who had fought by his side during the previous wars. A spirit like his could not but have foreseen the dreadful consequences of employing such a a force as the Indians in such a war. His death followed immediately before the rising of the court. Rumor said he died by poison, administered by himself; but perhaps extreme excitement of mind thus suddenly put an end to a life already protracted to a middling old age. He was buried under the old stone church at Johnstown. His bones were taken up in 1806, and redeposited. In the coffin was found the ball with which he was wounded at Lake George, which had never been extracted, and which ever after occasioned lameness. His most valuable papers, including his will, (said to be a very singular document,) were buried in an iron chest in his garden, where they were much injured by the dampness of the earth. They were taken away by his son, Sir John, during the war.

Note C.

SKETCH OF THE LIFE AND CHARACTER OF JOSEPH BRANT.

Joseph Brant, whose name has so often been mentioned in the foregoing pages, was a Mohawk sachem, of great celebrity and influence in his tribe. The time of his birth I do not know. In July, 1761, he was sent, by Sir William Johnson, to the "Moor's Charity School," at Lebanon, Connecticut, established by the Rev. Dr. Wheelock, which was afterward removed to Hanover, and became the foundation of Dartmouth College. The following mention of him is made in the memoirs of that gentleman:

"Sir William Johnson, Superintendent of Indian Affairs in North America, was very friendly to the design of Mr. Wheelock, and, at his request, sent to the school, at various times, several boys of the Mohawks to be instructed. One of them was the since celebrated Joseph Brant; who, after receiving his education, was particularly noticed by Sir William Johnson, and employed by him in public business. He has been very useful in advancing the civilization of his countrymen, and for a long time past has been a military officer of extensive influence among the Indians in Upper Canada."

In confirmation of one of the statements in the above notice, it may be here added, that in 1787 he translated the book of Mark into the Mohawk tongue; and, as is mentioned in the letter hereafter inserted, contemplated writing a history of the Six Nations.

The movements of Brant during the war have been detailed, at considerable length, in the foregoing historical sketch of Tryon County. Combining the natural sagacity of the Indian with the skill and science of the civilized man, he was a formidable foe. He was a dreadful terror to the frontiers. His passions were strong. In his intercourse he was affable and polite, and communicated freely relative to his conduct. He often said that during the war he had killed but one man in cold blood, and that act he ever after regretted. He said he had taken a man prisoner, and was examining him; the prisoner hesitated, and, as he thought, equivocated. Enraged at what he considered obstinacy, he struck him down. It turned out that the man's apparent obstinacy arose from a natural hesitancy of speech.

The following is the account, given by an European traveller, Mr. Weld, which is alluded to in the letter of Thomas Campbell. "With a considerable body of his troops, he joined the forces under the command of Sir John Johnson. A skirmish took place with a body of American troops; the action was warm, and Brant was shot by a musket ball in his heel, but the Americans in the end were defeated, and an officer, with sixty men, were taken prisoners. The officer, after having delivered up his sword, had entered into conversation with Sir John Johnson, who commanded the British troops, and they were talking together in the most friendly manner, when Brant, having stolen slily behind them, laid the American officer low with a blow of his tomahawk. The indignation of Sir John Johnson, as may be readily supposed, was roused by such an act of treachery, and he resented it in the warmest terms. Brant listened to him unconcernedly, and when he had finished, told him, that he was sorry for his displeasure, but that indeed his heel was extremely painful at the moment, and he could not help revenging himself on the only chief of the party that he saw taken. Since he had killed the officer, he added, his heel was much less painful to him than it had been before." There were doubtless some grounds for such statements as that above; though probably very much exaggerated. I have heard a story somewhat similar told of him, but it was said that the officer was killed to prevent his being retaken by the Americans, who were in pursuit of the Indians. In the retreat he would not keep up with them.

Brant stated, and it is believed to be true, that on the morning of the day on which Cherry Valley was destroyed, he left the main body of the enemy, and, by a different route, endeavored to arrive first at the house of Mr. Wells, for the purpose of protecting the family; but that he found on his route, and a little way from the house, a large ploughed field to cross, which hindered him, so that he did not arrive until it was too late.

In person, Brant was about the middling size, of a square, stout build, fitted rather for enduring hardships than for quick movements. His complexion was lighter than that of most of the Indians, which resulted, perhaps, from his less exposed manner of living. This circumstance, probably, gave rise to a statement, which has been often repeated, that he was of mixed origin. He was married in the winter of 1779 to a daughter of Col. Croghan by an Indian woman. The circumstances of his marriage are somewhat singular. He was present at the wedding of Miss Moore from Cherry Valley, who had been carried away a prisoner, and who married an officer of the garrison at Fort Niagara.

Brant had lived with his wife for some time previous, according to the Indian custom, without marriage; but now insisted that the marriage ceremony should be performed. This was accordingly done by Col. Butler, who was still considered a magistrate. After the war he removed, with his nation, to Canada. There he was employed in transacting important business for his tribe. He went out to England, after the war, and was honorably received there. He died about ten or fifteen years since, at Brantford, Haldiman County, Upper Canada, where his family now reside. One of his sons, a very intelligent man, has been returned to the Colonial Assembly. This son, a few years since, when in London, in company with Capt. Robert Carr, a grandson of Sir William Johnson, laid before Thomas Campbell written documents, which changed Mr. Campbell's opinion of his father, and led to an *exposé* of his views, in a letter to him.

For the correct understanding of the following letter, by those who have not read that beautiful poem, "Gertrude of Wyoming," (if there are any such,) and who may not have a copy at hand, I will insert the objectionable stanzas—one of them has already been given in part. The speech is that of an Oneida chief, who is made to say, immediately preceding the battle or massacre at Wyoming:

"But this is not a time—he started up,
And smote his breast with wo-denouncing hand—
This is no time to fill the joyous cup;
The mammoth comes—the foe—the monster, Brant,
With all his howling, desolating band;
These eyes have seen their blade, and burning pine;
Awake at once, and silence half your land.
Red is the cup they drink; but not with wine:
Awake, and watch to-night, or see no morning shine.

"Scorning to wield the hatchet for his tribe,
'Gainst Brant himself I went to battle forth:
Accursed Brant! he left of all my tribe
Nor man, nor child, nor thing of living birth:
No! not the dog that watched my household hearth,
Escaped that night of blood upon our plains:
All perished! I alone am left on earth!
To whom nor relative, nor blood remains—
No, not a kindred drop that runs in human veins."

Letter to the Mohawk Chief, Ahyonwaeghs, commonly called John Brant, Esq. of the Grand River, Upper Canada, from Thomas Campbell.

"*London, January* 20, 1822.

"SIR,

"Ten days ago I was not aware that such a person existed as the son of the Indian leader, Brant, who is mentioned in my poem, "Gertrude of Wyoming." Last week, however, Mr. S. Bannister, of Lincoln's Inn, called to inform me of your being in London, and of your having documents in your possession which he believed would change my opinion of your father's memory, and induce me to do it justice. Mr. Bannister distinctly assured me that no declaration of my sentiments on the subject was desired, but such as should spontaneously flow from my own judgment of the papers that were to be submitted to me.

"I could not be deaf to such an appeal. It was my duty to inspect the justification of a man whose memory I had reprobated, and I felt a satisfaction at the prospect of his character being redressed, which was not likely to have been felt by one who had willingly wronged it. As far as any intention to wound the feelings of the living was concerned, I really knew not, when I wrote my poem, that the son and daughter of an Indian chief were ever likely to peruse it, or be affected by its contents; and I have observed most persons to whom I have mentioned the circumstance of your appeal to me, smile with the same surprise which I experienced on first receiving it. With regard to your father's character, I took it as I found it in popular history. Among the documents in his favor, I own that you have shown me one which I regret that I never saw before, though I might have seen it; viz. the Duke of Rochefoucault's honorable mention of the chief in his travels.* Without mean-

* The following testimony is borne to his fair name by Rochefoucault, whose ability and means of forming a correct judgment will not

ing, however, in the least to invalidate that nobleman's respectable authority, I must say, that even if I had met with it, it would have still offered only a general and presumptive vindication of your father, and not such a specific one as I now recognize. On the other hand, judge how naturally I adopted accusations against him which had stood in the Annual Register of 1779, as far as I knew, uncontradicted, for thirty years. A number of authors had repeated them with a confidence which beguiled at last my suspicion, and I believe that of the public at large. Among these authors were Gordon, Ramsay, Marshall, Belsham, and Weld. The most of them, you may tell me, perhaps, wrote with zeal against the American war. Well, but Mr. John Adolphus was never suspected of any such zeal, and yet he had said in his history of England, &c. (Vol. III, p. 110,) 'a force of sixteen hundred savages and Americans in disguise, headed by an Indian, Col. Butler, and a half-Indian of extraordinary ferocity, named Brant, lulling the fears of

---

be denied. "Colonel Brant is an Indian by birth. In the American war he fought under the English banner, and he has since been in England, where he was most graciously received by the king, and met with a kind reception from all classes of people. His manners are semi-European. He is attended by two negroes; has established himself in the English way; has a garden and a farm; dresses after the European fashion, and, nevertheless, possesses much influence over the Indians. He assists at present (1795) at the Miami treaty, which the United States are concluding with the western Indians. He is also much respected by the Americans; and, in general, bears so excellent a name, that I regret I could not see and become acquainted with him."—*Rochefoucault's Travels in North America.*

the inhabitants (of Wyoming) by treachery, suddenly possessed themselves of two forts and massacred the garrison.' He says farther, 'that all were involved in unsparing slaughter, and that even the devices of torment were exhausted.' He possessed, if I possessed them, the means of consulting better authorities; yet he has never, to my knowledge, made any atonement to your father's memory. When your Canadian friends, therefore, call me to trial for having defamed the warrior Brant, I beg that Mr. John Adolphus may be also included in the summons. And, after his own defense and acquittal, I think he is bound, having been one of my historical misleaders, to stand up as my gratuitous counsel, and say—'Gentlemen, you must acquit my client, for he has only fallen into an error which even my judgment could not escape.'

"In short, I imbibed my conception of your father from accounts of him that were published when I was scarcely out of my cradle. And if there were any public, direct, and specific challenge to those accounts in England, ten years ago, I am yet to learn where they existed.

"I rose from perusing the papers you submitted to me, certainly with an altered impression of his character. I find that the unfavorable accounts of him were erroneous, even on points not immediately connected with his reputation. It turns out, for instance, that he was a Mohawk Indian, of unmixed parentage. This circumstance, however, ought not to be overlooked in estimating the merits of his attainments. He spoke and wrote our language with force and facility, and had enlarged views of the union and policy of the Indian tribes. A gentleman who had been in America, and from whom I sought information respecting him in consequence of your interesting message, told me, that though he could not pretend to appreciate his character entirely, he had been struck by the *naiveté* and eloquence of his conversation. They had talked of music, and Brant said, 'I like the harpsichord well, and the organ still better; but I like the drum and trumpet best of all, for they make my heart beat quick.' This gentleman also described to me the enthusiasm with which he spoke of written records. Brant projected at that time to have written a history of the Six Nations. The genius of history should be rather partial to such a man.

"I find that when he came to England, after the peace of 1783, the most distinguished individuals of all parties and professions treated him with the utmost kindness. Among these were the late Bishop of London, the late Duke of Northumberland, and Charles Fox. Lord Rawdon, now Marquis of Hastings, gave him his picture. This circumstance argues recommendations from America founded in personal friendship. In Canada the memorials of his moral character represent it as naturally ingenuous and generous. The evidence afforded induces me to believe that he often strove to mitigate the cruelty of Indian warfare.

"Lastly, you affirm that he was not within many miles of the spot when the battle which decided the fate of Wyoming took place, and from your offer of reference to living witnesses, I cannot but admit the assertion. Had I learned all this of your father when I was writing my poem, he should not have figured in it as the hero of mischief. I cannot, indeed, answer by anticipation what the writers who have either to retract or defend what they may have said about him, may have to allege; I can only say that my own opinion about him is changed. I am now inclined exceedingly to doubt Mr. Weld's anecdote, and for this reason: Brant was not only trusted, consulted, and distinguished by several eminent British officers in America, but personally beloved by them.

"Now I could conceive men in power, for defensible reasons of state politics, to have officially trusted, and even publicly distinguished at courts or levees, an active and sagacious Indian chief, of whose private character they might nevertheless still entertain a very indifferent opinion. But I cannot imagine high-minded and high-bred British officers, forming individual and fond friendship for a man of ferocious character. It comes within my express knowledge that the late Gen. Sir Charles Stuart, fourth son of the Earl of Bute, the father of our present ambassador at Paris, the officer who took Minorca and Calvi, and who commanded our army in Portugal, knew your father in America, often slept under the same tent with him, and had the warmest regard for him. It seems but charity to suppose the man who attracted the esteem of Lord Rawdon and Gen. Stuart, to have possessed amiable qualities, so that I believe you when you affirm that he was merciful as brave. And now I leave the world to judge whether the change of opinion, with which I am touched, arises from false delicacy and flexibility of mind, or from a sense of honor and justice.

"Here, properly speaking, ends my reckoning with you about your father's memory; but, as the Canadian newspapers have made some remarks on the subject of Wyoming, with which I cannot fully coincide, and as this letter will probably be read in Canada, I cannot conclude it without a few more words, in case my silence would seem to admit of propositions which are rather beyond the stretch of my creed. I will not, however, give any plain truths which I have to offer to the Canadian writers, the slightest seasonings of bitterness, for they have alluded to me, on the whole, in a friendly and liberal tone. But when they regret my departure from historical truth, I join in their regret only in as far as I have unconsciously misunderstood the character of Brant, and the share of the Indians in the transaction, which I have now reason to suspect, was much less than that of the white men. In other circumstances, I took the liberty of a versifier, to run away from fact into fancy, like a school-boy, who never dreams that he is a truant when he rambles on a holyday from school. It seems, however, that I falsely represented Wyoming to have been a terrestrial paradise. It was not so, say the Canadian papers, because it contained a great number of Tories; and undoubtedly that cause goes far to account for the fact. Earthly paradises, however, are but earthly things, and Tempe and Arcadia may have had their drawbacks on happiness as well as Wyoming. I must, nevertheless, still believe that it was a flourishing colony, and that its destruction furnished a just warning to human beings against war and revenge. But the whole catastrophe is affirmed in a

Canadian newspaper to have been nothing more than a fair battle. If this be the fact, let accredited signatures come forward to attest it, and vindicate the innocence and honorableness of the whole transaction, as your father's character has been vidicated. An error about him by no means proves the whole account of the business to be a fiction. Who would not wish its atrocities to be disproved? But who can think it disproved by a single defender, who writes anonymously, and without definable weight or authority?

"In another part of the Canadian newspapers, my theme has been regretted as dishonorable to England. Then it was, at all events, no fable. But how far was the truth dishonorable to England? American settlers, and not Englishmen, were chiefly the white men, calling themselves Christians, who were engaged in this affair. I shall be reminded, perhaps, that they also called themselves Loyalists. But for Heaven's sake, let not English loyalty be dragged down to palliate atrocities, or English delicacy be invoked to conceal them. I may be told that England permitted the war, and was therefore responsible for its occurrences. Not surely, universally, nor directly. I should be unwilling to make even Lord North's administration answerable for all the actions of Butler's Rangers; and I should be still more sorry to make all England amenable either for Lord North's administration or for Butler's Rangers. Was the American war an unanimous and heartfelt war of the people? Were the best patriots and the brightest luminaries of our senate for, or against it? Chatham declared, that if America fell she would fall like the strong man—that she would embrace the pillars of our constitution, and perish beneath its ruins. Burke, Fox, and Barre kindled even the breasts of St. Stephen's Chapel against it; and William Pitt pronounced it a war against the sacred cause of Liberty. If so, the loss of our colonies was a blessing, compared with the triumph of those principles that would have brought Washington home in chains. If Chatham and Pitt were our friends in denouncing the injustice of this war, then Washington was only nominally our foe in resisting it; and he was as much the enemy of the worst enemies of our constitution, as if he had fought against the return of the Stuarts on the banks of the Spey or the Thames. I say, therefore, with full and free charity to those who think differently, that the American war was disgraceful only to those who were its abettors, and that the honor of Englishmen is redeemed in proportion as they deprecate its principles and deplore its details. Had my theme even involved English character more than it does, I could still defend it. If my Canadian critic alleges that a poet may not blame the actions of his country, I meet his allegation and deny it. No doubt a poet ought not forever to harp and carp upon the faults of his country, but he may be her moral censor, and he must not be her parasite. If an English poet under Edward III. had only dared to leave one generous line of commiseration to the memory of Sir William Wallace, how much he would have raised our estimation of the moral character of the age! There is a present and a future in national character, as well as a past; and the character of the present age is best provided for by impartial and generous sentiments respecting the past. The twentieth century will not think the worse of the nineteenth for regretting the American war. I know the slender importance of my own works. I am contending, however, against a false principle of delicacy, that would degrade poetry itself if it were adopted; but it will never be adopted.

"I therefore regret nothing in the historical allusions of my poem, except the mistake about your father. Nor, though I have spoken freely of American affairs, do I mean to deny that your native tribes may have had a just cause of quarrel with the American colonists. And I regard it as a mark of their gratitude that they adhered to the royal cause, because the governors acting in the king's name had been their most constant friends, and the colonial subjects possibly, at times, their treacherous invaders. I could say much of European injustice toward your tribes, but in spite of all that I could say, I must still deplore the event of Christians having adopted their mode of warfare, and, as circumstances then stood, of their having invoked their alliance. If the Indians thirsted for vengeance on the colonists, that should have been the very circumstance to deter us from blending their arms with ours. I trust you will understand this declaration to be made in the spirit of frankness, and not of mean and inhospitable arrogance. If I were to speak to you in that spirit, how easily and how truly could you tell me that the American Indians have departed faster from their old practices of warfare, than Christians have departed from their habits of religious persecution! If I were to preach to you about European humanity, you might ask me how long the ashes of the Inquisition have been cold, and whether the slave-trade be yet abolished? You might demand how-many—no, how few generations have elapsed since our old women were burned for imaginary commerce with the devil, and whether the houses be not yet standing from which our great grandmothers may have looked on the hurdles passing to the place of execution, whilst they blessed themselves that they were not witches? A horrible occurrence of this nature took place in Scotland during my own grandfather's lifetime. As to warlike customs, I should be exceedingly sorry if you were to press me even on those of my brave old ancestors, the Scottish Highlanders. I can nevertheless recollect the energy, faith, hospitality of those ancestors, and at the same time I am not forgetful of the simple virtues of yours.*

---

* "Considering the filial motives of the young chief's appeal to me, I am not afraid that any part of this letter, immediately relating to him, will be thought ostentatious or prolix. And, if charitably judged, I hope that what I have said of myself and my poem will not be felt as offensive egotism. The public has never been troubled with any defense of mine against any attacks on my poetry that were merely literary, although I may have been as far as authors generally are from bowing to the injustice of hostile criticism. To show that I have not been over-anxious about publicity, I must mention a misrepresentation respecting my poem on Wyoming, which I have suffered to remain uncorrected for ten years. Mr. Washington Irving, in a biographical sketch prefixed to it in an American edition, described me as having injured the composition of the poem, by showing it to friends, who struck out its best passages. Now I read it to very few friends, and to none at whose suggestion I ever struck out a single line. Nor did

"I have been thus special in addressing you, from a wish to vindicate my own consistency, as well as to do justice to you in your present circumstances, which are peculiarly and publicly interesting. The chief of an aboriginal tribe now settled under the protection of our sovereign in Canada, you are anxious to lead on your people in a train of civilization that is already begun. It is impossible that the British community should not be touched with regard for an Indian stranger of respectable private character, possessing such useful and honorable views. Trusting that you will amply succeed in them, and long live to promote improvement and happiness amidst the residue of your ancient race,

I remain your sincere well-wisher,

THOMAS CAMPBELL."

I ever lean on the taste of others with that miserable distrust of my own judgment which the anecdote conveys. I knew that Mr. Irving was the last man in the world to make such a misrepresentation intentionally, and that I could easily contradict it; but from aversion to bring a petty anecdote about myself before the world, I forbore to say anything about it. The case was different when a Canadian writer hinted at the patriotism of my subject. There he touched on my principles, and I have defended them, contending that on the supposition of the story of Wyoming being true, it is a higher compliment to British feelings to reveal, than palliate or hide it."

Note D.

SKENANDO.

The following account of the death of this chief was published in the Utica Patriot, March 19, 1816:

"Died at his residence, near Oneida Castle, on Monday, 11th inst., Skenando, the celebrated Oneida chief, aged 110 years; well known in the wars which occurred while we were British colonies, and in the contest which issued in our independence, as the undeviating friend of the people of the United States. He was very savage and addicted to drunkenness* in his youth, but by his own reflections and the benevolent instruction of the late Rev. Mr. Kirkland, missionary to his tribe, he lived a reformed man for more than sixty years, and died in Christian hope. From attachment to Mr. Kirkland he had always expressed a strong desire to be buried near his minister

* In the year 1755, Skenando was present at a treaty made in Albany. At night he was excessively drunk, and in the morning found himself in the street, stripped of all his ornaments and every article of clothing. His pride revolted at his self-degradation, and he resolved that he would never again deliver himself over to the power of *strong water*.

and father, that he might (to use his own expression) '*go up with him at the great resurrection.*' At the approach of death, after listening to the prayers which were read at his bedside by his great granddaughter, he again repeated the request. Accordingly, the family of Mr. Kirkland having received information by a runner that Skenando was dead, in compliance with a previous promise sent assistance to the Indians, that the corpse might be carried to the village of Clinton for burial. Divine service was attended at the meeting-house in Clinton on Wednesday at two o'clock, P. M. An address was made to the Indians by the Rev. Dr. Backus, President of Hamilton College, which was interpreted by Judge Deane, of Westmoreland. Prayer was then offered and appropriate psalms sung. After service, the concourse which had assembled from respect to the deceased chief, or from the singularity of the occasion, moved to the grave in the following order:

STUDENTS OF HAMILTON COLLEGE,

CORPSE,

INDIANS,

MRS. KIRKLAND AND FAMILY,

JUDGE DEANE, REV. DR. NORTON, REV. MR. AYRE,

OFFICERS OF HAMILTON COLLEGE,

CITIZENS.

" After interment, the only surviving son of the deceased, self-moved, returned thanks, through Judge Deane as interpreter, to the people for the respect shown to his father on the occasion, and to Mrs. Kirkland and family for their kind and friendly attention.

"Skenando's person was tall, well made, and robust. His countenance was intelligent, and displayed all the peculiar dignity of an Indian chief. In his youth he was a brave and intrepid warrior, and in his riper years one of the noblest counsellors among the North American tribes; he possessed a vigorous mind, and was alike sagacious, active and persevering. As an enemy he was terrible. As a friend and ally he was mild and gentle in his disposition, and faithful to his engagements. His vigilance once preserved from massacre the inhabitants of the little settlement at German Flats. In the Revolutionary war his influence induced the Oneidas to take up arms in favor of the Americans. Among the Indians he was distinguished by the appellation of the 'white man's friend.'

"Although he could speak but little English, and in his extreme old age was blind, yet his company was sought. In conversation he was highly decorous, evincing that he had profited by seeing civilized and polished society, and by mingling with good company in his better days.

"To a friend who called on him a short time since, he thus expressed himself by an interpreter: 'I am an aged hemlock. The winds of an hundred winters have whistled through my branches; I am dead at the top. The generation to which I belonged have run away and left me; why I live the great Good Spirit only knows. Pray to my Jesus that I may have patience to wait for my appointed time to die.'

"Honored chief! His prayer was answered; he was cheerful and resigned to the last. For several years he kept his dress for the grave prepared. Once and again, and again he came to Clinton to die; longing that his soul might be with Christ, and his body in the narrow house near his beloved Christian teacher.

"While the ambitious but vulgar great look principally to sculptured monuments and to riches in the temple of earthly fame, Skenando, in the spirit of the only real nobility, stood with his loins girded, waiting the coming of the Lord. His Lord has come, and the day approaches when the green hillock that covers his dust will be more respected than the Pyramids, the Mausolea, and the Pantheons of the proud and imperious. His simple turf and stone will be viewed with veneration when their tawdry ornaments shall awaken only pity and disgust.

'Indulge my native land, indulge the tear
That steals impassioned o'er a nation's doom;
To me each twig from Adam's stock is dear,
And sorrows fall upon an Indian's tomb."

Clinton, March 14th, 1816."

Note E.

MOSES YOUNGLOVE.

Dr. Younglove, after his return from captivity, wrote a poem describing some of the scenes which he had witnessed, and detailing his wanderings and sufferings. I shall make some extracts from this poem, not that they contain many poetic beauties, but because they delineate some striking customs of the Indians. The poem comes from the pen of the hero himself, who might with truth exclaim, "pars magna fui." The first extract is a description of the battle of Oriskany.

The time and place of our unhappy fight,
To you at large were needless to recite;
When in the wood our fierce, inhuman foes,
With piercing yell from circling ambush rose:
A sudden volley rends the vaulted sky;
Their painted bodies hideous to the eye;
They rush like hellish furies on our bands,
Their slaughter weapons brandished in their hands.
Then we with equal fury join the fight,
Ere *Phœbus* gained his full meridian height;

Nor ceased the horrors of the bloody fray,
Till he had journeyed half his evening way.
Now hand to hand, the contest is for life,
With bayonet, tomahawk, sword, and scalping-knife;
No more remote the work of death we ply,
And thick as hail the showering bullets fly:
Full many a hardy warrior sinks supine,
Yells, shrieks, groans, shouts, and thundering volleys join;
The dismal din the ringing forest fills,
The sounding echo roars along the hills.
Our friends and foes lie struggling in their blood,
An undistinguished carnage strews the wood;
And every streamlet drinks the crimson flood.
True valor, stubbornness, and fury here,
There fell revenge, despair, and spite appear;
Long raged surrounding death, and no deliverance near;
While mangled friends, not fated yet to die,
Implore our aid in vain with feeble cry.
Of two departments were the assailing foes:
Wild savage natives lead the first of those;
Their almost naked frames, of various dyes,
And rings of black and red surround their eyes.
On one side they present a shaven head,
The naked half of the vermilion red;
In spots the party-colored face they drew,
Beyond description horrible to view;
Their ebon locks in braid, with paint overspread;
The silvered ears depending from the head;
Their gaudery my descriptive power exceeds,
In plumes of feathers, glittering plates and beads.
With them, of parricides a bloody band,
Assist the ravage of their parent land;
With equal dress, and arms, and savage arts,
But more than savage rancor in their hearts.

These for the first attack their force unite,
And most sustain the fury of the fight,
Their rule of warfare, devastation dire,
By undistinguished plunder, death, and fire;
They torture man and beast with barbarous rage,
Nor tender infant spare, nor reverend sage.
O'er them a horrid monster bore command,
Whose inauspicious birth disgraced our land;
By malice urged to every barbarous art;
Of cruel temper, but of coward heart.
The second was a renegado crew,
Who arm and dress as Christian nations do,
Led by a chief who bore the first command;
A bold invader of his native land.
Such was the bloody fight, and such the foe;
Our smaller force returned them blow for blow,
By turns successfully their forced defied,
And conquest wavering seemed from side to side.

The following is a description of a scene the night after the battle:

Not half the savages returned from fight;
They to their native wilds had sped their flight:
Those that remained a long encampment made,
And rising fires illumined all the shade;
In vengeance for their numerous brothers slain,
For torture sundry prisoners they retain;
And three fell monsters, horrible to view,
A fellow-prisoner from the sentries drew;
The guards before received their chief's command,
To not withhold us from the slaughtering band;
But now the sufferer's fate they sympathize,
And for him supplicate with earnest cries.

I saw thc General slowly passing by;
The sergeant on his knees, with tearful eye,
Implored the guards might wrest him from their hands,
Since now the troops could awe their lessened bands.
With lifted cane the General thus replies,
(While indignation sparkles from his eyes,)
"Go, sirrah! mind your orders given before,
And for infernal rebels plead no more!"
For help the wretched victim vainly cries,
With supplicating voice and ardent eyes;
With horror chilled, I turn away my face,
While instantly they bear him from the place.
Dread scene! with anguish stung I inly groan,
To think the next hard lot may be my own;
And now I poring sit, now sudden start,
Through anxious agitation of my heart;
In every bush the coming foe appear,
Their sound in every breeze I seem to hear.

Nocturnal shades at length involve the sky,
The planets faintly glimmer from on high;
When through the grove the flaming fires arise,
And loud resound the tortured prisoners' cries;
Still as their pangs are more or less extreme,
The bitter groan is heard, or sudden scream;
But when their natures failed, and death drew near,
Their screeches faintly sounded in the ear.

Tremendous night of woe beyond compare!
I beg for death, in anguish of despair;
No gleam of hope, no rest my soul could find;
Approaching torture gnawing on my mind;
Until *Aurora* purpled o'er the skies,
Then gentle slumber sealed awhile my eyes;

But troubled dreams arising in my head,
My fancy to the scene of battle led.
The fatal wood my weeping eyes survey,
Where pale in death my slaughtered neighbors lay;
A long adieu, I cried, my brethren slain;
No more to joy my longing soul again!
Who shall protect your wives with guardian care,
And babes abandoned to the rage of war?
Decrepit parents, with the feeble groan,
Shall wail your fate, their country's, and their own;
While, lost to all, you here unburied lay,
To feast the ravens and the beasts of prey;
Yet, by your slaughter, safe arrived on shore,
The storms of war shall break your peace no more;
Each honest soul your memory shall revere,
And pay the tribute of a tender tear.
Oh! had I too partook your calm repose,
In safe retreat, beyond the power of foes,
I had avoided, by a milder fate,
Dread horrors past, and tortures that await.

His own day of trial and suffering at length came on, and he thus describes it:

Now did the dreadful morn at length arise,
And *Sol* through mists reluctant climbed the skies,
When savages, for horrid sport prepared,
Demand another prisoner from the guard.
We saw their feared approach with mortal fright,
Their scalping-knives they sharpened in our sight;
Beside the guard they sat them on the ground,
And viewed, with piercing eyes, the prisoners round.
As when a panther grim, with furious eye,
Surveys the tender lad he dooms to die;

The lad beholds him, shivering with affright,
Sees all resistance vain, despairs of flight;
So they on me their glaring eyelids roll,
And such the feelings of my suddering soul.
At length one, rising, seized me by the hand;
By him drawn forth, on trembling knees I stand;
I bid my fellows all a long adieu;
With answering grief my wretched case they view.

They led me, bound, along the winding flood,
Far in the gloomy bosomof the wood;
There (horrid sight!) a prisoner roasted lay,
The carving-knife had cut his flesh away.
Against a tree erect I there was bound,
While they regaled themselves upon the ground;
Their shell of spirits went from hand to hand,
Their friends collecting still, a numerous band.

So passed the day. What terrors in me reign!
I supplicate for instant death in vain.
I think upon this breach of nature's laws,
My family, my friends, my country's cause;
Around me still collect my bloody foes,
Still in my mind approaching torture rose;
The skeleton in open prospect lay,
Chaos of woful thought employed my wretched day.

Now on a neighboring green, high jutting o'er,
Where underneath the rapid waters roar,
There, round a fire, their heaps of fuel rise,
Nocturnal shadows thickening in the skies.
Beside the fire I tremble at the stake;
The numerous herd a spacious circle make;
And as the flames, advancing, rise in air,
Within the ring my torturers repair;

With whoop and dance they tune the deathful song,
Along the margin crowd the sportive throng;
When lo! the failing bank, beneath the load,
Broke short and plunged us headlong in the flood.
In transport down the stream my course I made;
With dismal cries resounds the gloomy shade;
The floating stake adhering by a thong,
With nose above the stream I steal along.
Through all the vale a fruitless search they made,
And fearful howlings rung along the shade.
When to the camp again their way they steer,
Their distant clamor murmuring in my ear,
Far down the stream, where lies a naked strand,
With shivering limbs, I softly crept to land.
The stake upon the shore I trailed along;
Then joyfully unbound each fettering thong,
And for the neighboring road in haste depart,
The hope of freedom dawning in my heart.
Through gloomy thickets, far, I grope my way,
And briery heaths, where pines extended lay;
Now thoughts of home my ravished soul delight,
Now distant, savage yells my mind affright;
Still I my way with all my power pursued,
Still did the road my anxious search elude.
Long time I groped the rough, uncertain way;
Through erring course, I wandered far astray;
Nor moon, nor star, would lend a friendly ray;
Then laid me down, dejected and forlorn,
To rest my weary limbs, and wait the morn;
Ere long my leafy couch I there had pressed,
Exhausted nature sunk to quiet rest.

He was retaken and carried to the far west by a different tribe. The following is a description of the arrival of the tribe at their village, and of his running the gauntlet:

Their glad return through all the place was told;
Next morning they convene both young and old.
The band, equipped in all their war parade,
Into the town a formal entry made;
They led me up, triumphing with delight,
With all their spoils and trophies of the fight,
Except the scalps; for these they had their pay,
From British agents ere they came away,
They end their march, where, high upon the green,
A numerous crowd of every age was seen;
The hoary parent bowing down with years,
The mother with her tender train appears;
The youthful archer bends his little bow,
And sportive striplings gambol in the row;
Warriors and hunters tricked in best array,
And youthful maids their tawny charms display,
With scarlet cloth, rings, beads, and ribbons gay.
I trembled when I to the crowd was brought,
The stake and flames arising in my thought;
But soon my guard, approaching to my ear,
Bid me confide in him, and nothing fear.
There, in a spacious hut, on either hand,
Two lengthy rows with sticks and weapons stand;
Then stripped I was to pass between the rows,
And each inflict at pleasure wounds and blows;
My keeper gently struck, then urged my flight;
Between the ranks I fled with all my might.
As when some farmer, blest with plenteous yield,
His crop of buckwheat thrashes in the field,
The men and boys with flail in hand around,
Clap after clap loud constant clatterings sound,

The straw all crushed in broken pieces lie,
The grains around the thrashers' faces fly;
So, as with naked frame I pass along,
Resound the strokes of all the furious throng;
So by their blows my mangled skin is broke,
And so the sputtering blood pursues the stroke.
  Two female furies at the further end,
Their brother slain in fight, my death intend;
Enraged, they maul with clubs my bleeding head,
And doubtless would erelong have laid me dead;
But quickly did their father interpose,
And then my keeper fended off their blows.
I blessed the thought that once his death withstood,
And checked my hand, when raised to shed his blood.
The aged sire adopts me for his son;
Rejoiced, I put the savage habit on;
With honorary paint, in blanket dressed,
I stand installed an Indian with the rest.
The sire in gayest fashion shaved my head,
Then to his home, rejoicing, I was led.
  They used me tenderly, my wounds they healed,
But deeper wounds within remain concealed;
My wife, my country, friends, and blooming child;
Exchanged for captive bands in regions wild;
These thoughts incessant did my bosom rend,
And often did the painful tear descend.

Note F.

BIOGRAPHICAL SKETCH OF GOVERNOR GEORGE CLINTON.

George Clinton, formerly Governor of the State of New York, and Vice President of the United States, was born on the 26th July, 1739, in the county of Ulster, in the colony of New York. He was the youngest son of Colonel Charles Clinton, an emigrant from Ireland, and a gentleman of distinguished worth and high consideration.

He was educated, principally, under the eye of his father, and received the instruction of a learned minister of the Presbyterian church, who had graduated in the university of Aberdeen; and, after reading law in the office of William Smith, afterward chief justice of Canada, he settled himself in that profession in the county of his nativity, where he rose to eminence.

In 1768, he took his seat as one of the members of the Colonial Assembly for the county of Ulster, and he continued an active member of that body until it was merged in the Revolution. His energy of character, discriminating intellect, and undaunted courage, placed him among the chiefs of the Whig party; and he was always considered possessed of a superior mind and master spirit, on which his country might rely, as an asylum in the most gloomy periods of her fortunes.

On the 22d of April, 1775, he was chosen by the Provincial Convention of New York one of the delegates to the Continental Congress, and took his seat in that illustrious body on the 15th of May. On the 4th of July, 1776, he was present at the glorious declaration of independence, and assented with his usual energy and decision to that measure; but having been appointed a brigadier general in the militia, and also in the army, the exigencies of his country, at that trying hour, rendered it necessary for him to take the field in person, and he therefore retired from Congress immediately after his vote was given, and before the instrument was transcribed for the signature of the members; for which reason his name does not appear among the signers.

A constitution having been adopted for the State of New York, on the 20th April, 1777, he was chosen, at the first election under it, both governor and lieutenant governor, and he was continued in the former office for eighteen years, by triennial elections; when, owing to ill health, and a respect for the republican principle of rotation in office, he declined a re-election.

During the Revolutionary war, he cordially co-operated with the immortal Washington, and, without his aid, the army would have been disbanded, and the northern separated from the southern States, by the intervention of British troops. He was always at his post in the times that tried men's souls; at one period repelling the advances of the enemy from Canada, and at another meeting them in battle when approaching from the south. His gallant defense of Fort Montgomery, with a handful of men, against a powerful force commanded by Sir Henry Clinton, was equally honorable to his intrepidity and his skill.

The following are the particulars of his gallant conduct at the storming of Forts Montgomery and Clinton, in October, 1777:

"When the British reinforcements, under General Robertson, amounting to nearly two thousand men, arrived from Europe, Sir Henry Clinton used the greatest exertion, and availed himself of every favorable circumstance, to put these troops into immediate operation. Many were sent to suitable vessels, and united in the expedition, which consisted of about four thousand men, against the forts in the Highlands. Having made the necessary arrangements, he moved up the North River, and landed on the 4th of October at Tarrytown, purposely to impress General Putnam, under whose command a thousand continental troops had been left, with a belief that his post at Peekskill was the object of attack. At eight o'clock at night the general communicated the intelligence to Governor Clinton, of the arrival of the British, and at the same time expressed his opinion respecting their destination. The designs of Sir Henry were immediately perceived by the governor, who prorogued the Assembly on the following day, and arrived that night at Fort Montgomery. The British troops, in the mean time, were secretly conveyed across the river, and assaults upon our forts were meditated to be made on the 6th, which were accordingly put in execution, by attacking the American advanced party at Doodletown, about two miles and a half from Fort Montgomery. The Americans received the fire of the British, and retreated to Fort Clinton. The enemy then advanced to the west side of the mountain, in order to attack our troops in the rear. Governor Clinton immediately ordered out a detachment of one hundred men toward Doodletown, and another of sixty, with a brass field-piece, to an elegible spot on another road. They were both soon attacked by the whole force of the enemy, and compelled to fall back. It has been remarked that the talents, as well as the temper of a commander, are put to as severe a test in conducting a retreat, as in achieving a victory. The truth of this Governor Clinton experienced, when, with great bravery, and the most perfect order, he retired till he reached the fort. He lost no time in placing his men in the best manner that circumstances would permit. His post, however, as well as Fort Clinton, in a few minutes were invaded on every side. In the midst of this disheartening and appalling disaster he was summoned, when the sun was only an hour high, to surrender; but his gallant spirit sternly refused to obey the call. In a short time after the British made a general and most desperate attack on both posts, which was received by the Americans with undismayed courage and resistance. Officers and men, militia and continentals, all behaved alike brave. An incessant fire was kept up till dusk, when our troops were overpowered by numbers, who forced the lines and redoubts at both posts. Many of the Americans fought their way out; others accidentally mixed with the enemy, and thus made their escape effectually; for, besides being favored by the night, they knew the various avenues in the mountains. The Governor, as well as his brother, General James Clinton, who was wounded, were not taken."

The administration of Governor Clinton was characterized by wisdom and patriotism. He was a republican in principle and practice. After a retirement of five years, he was called by the citizens of the city and county of New York to represent them in the Assembly of the State; and to his influence and popularity may be ascribed, in a great degree, the change in his native State, which finally produced the important political revolution of 1801.

At that period, much against his inclination, but from motives of patriotism, he consented to an election as governor and in 1805 he was chosen Vice President of the United States, in which office he continued until his death, presiding with great dignity in the Senate, and evincing, by his votes and his opinions, his decided hostility to constructive authority, and to innovations on the established principles of republican government.

He died at Washington, when attending to his duties as Vice President, and was interred in that city, where a monument was erected by the filial piety of his children, with this inscription, written by his nephew:

"To the memory of George Clinton. He was born

in the State of New York on the 26th of July, 1739, and died in the city of Washington, on the 20th of April, 1812, in the seventy-third year of his age. He was a soldier and statesman of the Revolution. Eminent in council, and distinguished in war, he filled with unexampled usefulness, purity, and ability, among many other offices, those of Governor of his native State, and of Vice-President of the United States. While he lived, his virtue, wisdom, and valor were the pride, the ornament, and security of his country; and when he died, he left an illustrious example of a well-spent life, worthy of all imitation.

"There are few men who will occupy as renowned a place in the history of his country as George Clinton; and the progress of time will increase the public veneration, and thicken the laurels that cover his monument."*

* American Biographical Dictionary.

Note G.

BIOGRAPHICAL SKETCH OF GENERAL PHILIP SCHUYLER.

The following Biographical Sketch of Gen. Philip Schuyler is taken from the Address of Chancellor Kent before the New York Historical Society. It is a beautiful outline of the life of that distinguished man; and I trust that no apology is necessary for inserting it at length.

The Dutch family of Schuyler stands conspicuous in our colonial annals. Col. Peter Schuyler was mayor of Albany, and commander of the northern militia in 1690. He was distinguished for his probity and activity in all the various duties of civil and military life. No man understood better the relation of the colony with the Five Nations of Indians, or had more decided influence with that confederacy. He had frequently chastised the Canadian French for their destructive incursions upon the frontier settlements; and his zeal and energy were rewarded by a seat in the provincial council; and the House of Assembly gave their testimony to the British court of his faithful services and good reputation. It was this same vigilant officer who gave intelligence to the inhabitants of Deerfield, on Connecticut River, of the designs of the French and Indians upon them, some short time before the destruction of that village in 1704. In 1720, as president of the council, he became acting governor of the colony for a short time, previous to the accession of Gov. Burnet. His son, Col. Philip Schuyler, was an active and efficient member of Assembly, for the city and county of Albany, in 1743. But the Philip Schuyler to whom I particularly allude, and who in a subsequent age shed such signal lustre upon the family name, was born at Albany in the year 1733, and at an early age he began to display his active mind and military spirit. He was a captain in the New York levies at Fort Edward, in 1755, and accompanied the British army in the expedition down Lake George, in the summer of 1758. He was with Lord Howe when he fell by the fire of the enemy, on landing at the north end of the lake, and he was appointed (as he himself informed me) to convey the body of that young and lamented nobleman to Albany, where he was buried, with appropriate solemnities, in the Episcopal Church.

We next find him under the title of Col. Schuyler, in company with his compatriot, George Clinton, in the year 1768, on the floor of the House of Assembly, taking an active share in all their vehement discussions. Neither of them was to be overawed or seduced from a bold and determined defense of the constitutional rights of the colonies, and of an adherence to the letter and spirit of the councils of the union. The struggle in the House of Assembly between the ministerial and the whig parties, was brought to a crisis in the months of February and March, 1775; and in that memorable contest, Philip Schuyler and George Clinton, together with Nathaniel Woodhull, of Long Island, acted distinguished parts. On the motions to give the thanks of the House to the delegates from the colony in the Continental Congress of September, 1774, and to thank the merchants and inhabitants of the colony for their adherence to the non-importation, and the association recommended by Congress, those patriots found themselves in the minority. But their courage and resolution gained strength from defeat.

On the 3d of March, Col. Schuyler moved declaratory resolutions that the act 4 Geo. III. imposing duties for raising a revenue in America; and for the extending the jurisdiction of Admiralty courts; and for depriving his majesty's subjects in America of trial by jury; and for holding up an injurious discrimination between the subjects of Great Britain and those of the colonies, were great grievances. The government party seem to have fled the question, and to have left in the House only the scanty number of nine members, and the resolutions were carried by a vote of seven to two. But their opponents immediately rallied, and eleven distinct divisions, on different motions, were afterwards taken in the course of that single day, and entered on the journal; and they related to all the momentous points then in controversy between Great Britain and the United Colonies. It was a sharp and hard-fought contest for fundamental principles; and a more solemn and eventful debate rarely ever happened on the floor of a deliberative assembly.

The House consisted on that day of twenty-four members, and the ministerial majority was exactly in the ratio of two to one; and the intrepidity, talents, and services of the three members I have named, and especially of Schuyler and Clinton, were above all praise, and laid the foundation for those lavish marks of honor and confidence which their countrymen were afterward so eager to bestow.

The resistance of the majority of the House was fairly broken down, and essentially controlled by the efforts of the minority and the energy of public opinion. A series of resolutions, declaratory of American grievances, were passed, and petitions to the King and Parliament adopted, not indeed in all respects such as the leaders of the minority wished, (for all their amendments were voted down,) but they were nevertheless grounded upon the principles of the American Revolution. They declared that the claims of taxation and absolute sovereignty, on the part of the British Parliament, and the extension of admiralty jurisdiction, were grievances, and unconstitutional measures; and that the act of Parliament, shutting up the port of Boston, and altering the charter of that colony, also was a grievance.

These were the last proceedings of the General Assembly of the colony of New York, which now closed its existence forever. More perilous scenes, and new and brighter paths of glory, were opening upon the vision of those illustrious patriots.

The delegates from this colony to the first Continental Congress in 1774, were not chosen by the General Assembly, but by the suffrages of the people, manifested in some sufficiently authentic shape in the several counties.

The delegates to the second constitutional Congress, which met in May, 1775, were chosen by a Provincial Congress, which the people of the colony had already created, and which was held in this city, in April of that year, and had virtually assumed the powers of government. The names of the delegates from this colony, to this second congress, were John Jay, John Alsop, James Duane, Philip Schuyler, George Clinton, Lewis Morris, and Robert R. Livingston; and the weight of their talents and character may be inferred from the fact, that Mr. Jay, Mr. Livingston, Mr. Duane, and Mr. Schuyler were early placed upon committees, charged with the most arduous and responsible duties. We find Washington and Schuyler associated together in the committee, appointed on the 14th of June, 1775, to prepare rules and regulations for the government of the army. This association of those great men, commenced at such a critical moment, was the beginning of a mutual confidence, respect, and admiration, which continued with uninterrupted and unabated vividness during the remainder of their lives. An allusion is made to this friendship in the memoir of a former president of this society, and the allusion is remarkable for its strength and pathos. After mentioning General Schuyler, he adds, "I have placed thee, my friend, by the side of him who knew thee; thy intelligence to discern, thy zeal to promote thy country's good, and knowing thee, prized thee. Let this be thy eulogy. I add, and with truth, peculiarly thine—content it should be mine to have expressed it."

The congress of this colony, during the year 1775 and 1776, had to meet difficulties and dangers almost sufficient to subdue the firmest resolution. The population of the colony was short of 200,000 souls. It had a vast body of disaffected inhabitants within its own bosom. It had numerous tribes of hostile savages on its extended frontier. The bonds of society seemed to have been broken up, and society itself resolved into its primitive elements. There was no civil government, but such as had been introduced by the Provincial Congress and county committees, as temporary expedients. It had an enemy's province in the rear, strengthened by large and well-appointed forces. It had an open and exposed sea-port without any adequate means to defend it. In the summer of 1776, the state was actually invaded, not only upon our Canadian, but upon our Atlantic frontier, by a formidable fleet and army, calculated by the power that sent them to be sufficient to annihilate at once all our infant republics.

In the midst of this appalling storm, the virtue of our people, animated by a host of intrepid patriots, the mention of whose names is enough to kindle enthusiasm in the breast of the present generation, remained glowing, unmoved, and invincible. It would be difficult to find any other people who have been put to a severer test, or on trial gave higher proofs of courage and capacity.

On the 19th of June, 1775, Philip Schuyler was appointed by Congress the third major general in the armies of the United Colonies; and such was his singular promptitude, that, in eleven days from this appointment, we find him in acual service, corresponding with Congress from a distance, on business that required and received immediate attention. In July, 1775, he was placed at the head of a board of commissioners for the northern department, and empowered to employ all the troops in that department at his discretion, subject to the future orders of the commander-in-chief. He was authorized, if he should find it practicable and expedient, to take possession of St. Johns and Montreal, and pursue any other measure in Canada having a tendency, in his judgment, to promote the peace and security of the United Colonies.

In September, 1775, Gen. Schuyler was acting under positive instructions to enter Canada, and he proceeded, with Generals Montgomery and Wooster under his command, to the Isle au Noix. He had at that time become extremely ill, and he was obliged to leave the command of the expedition to devolve upon Gen. Montgomery. The latter, under his orders, captured the garrisons of Chambly and St. Johns, and pressed forward to Montreal and Quebec. Montreal was entered on the 12th of November, 1775, by the troops under the immediate orders of Montgomery, and in the same month a committee from Congress was appointed to confer with General Schuyler, relative to raising troops in Canada for the possession and security of that province. His activity, skill, and zeal shone conspicuously throughout that arduous northern campaign; and his unremitting correspondence with Congress received the most prompt and marked consideration.

While the expedition under Montgomery was employed in Canada, Gen. Schuyler was called to exercise his influence and power in another quarter of his military district. On the 30th of December, 1775, he was ordered to disarm the disaffected inhabitants of Tryon County, then under the influence of Sir John Johnson; and on the 18th of January following, he made a treaty with the disaffected portion of the people in that western part of the state. The Continental Congress were so highly satisfied with his conduct in that delicate and meritorious service, as to declare, by a special resolution, that he had executed his trust with fidelity, prudence and dispatch; and they ordered a publication of the narrative of his march in depth of winter into the regions bordering on the middle and upper Mohawk. The duties imposed upon that officer were so various, multiplied, and incessant, as to require rapid movements,sufficient to distract and confound an ordinary mind. Thus, on the 30th of December, 1775, he was ordered to disarm the Tories in Tryon County. On the 8th of January, 1776, he was ordered to have the river St. Lawrence, above and below Quebec, well explored. On the 25th of January, he was ordered to have the fortress of Ticonderoga repaired and made defensible, and on the 17th of February he was directed to take the command of the forces, and conduct the military operations at the city of New York. All these cumulative and conflicting orders from Congress, were made upon him in the course of six weeks, and they were occasioned by the embarrassments and distresses of the times.

In March, 1776, Congress changed their plan of operation, and directed Gen. Schuyler to establish his head-quarters at Albany, and superintend the army destined for Canada. He was instructed to take such orders as he should deem expedient, respecting the very perplexing and all-important subject of the supplies for the troops in Canada, and those orders as to the supplies were repeated in April, and again in May, 1776. The duty of procuring supplies, though less splendid in its effects, is often more effectual to the safety and success of an army than prowess in the field. Gen. Schuyler, by his thorough business habits, his precise attention to details, and by his skill and science in every duty connected with the equipment of an army, was admirably fitted to be at the head of the commissariat; and he gave life and vigor to every branch of the service. His versatile talents, equally adapted to investigation and action, rendered his merits as an officer of transcendent value.

On the 14th of June, 1776, he was ordered by Congress to hold a treaty with the Six Nations, and engage them in the interest of the colonies, and to treat with them on the principles, and in the decisive manner, which he had suggested. His preparations for taking immediate possession of Fort Stanwix, and erecting a fortification there, received the approbation of Congress, and their records afford the most satisfactory evidence that his comprehensive and accurate mind had anticipated and suggested the most essential measures, which he afterward diligently executed throughout the whole northern department. But within three days after the order for the treaty, Congress directed his operations to a different quarter of his command. He was ordered, on the 17th of June, to clear Wood Creek, and construct a lock upon the creek at Skeensborough, (now Whitehall,) and to take the level of the waters falling into the Hudson at Fort Edward, and into Wood Creek. There can be no doubt that those orders were all founded upon his previous suggestions, and they afford demonstrative proof of the views entertained by him, at that early day, of the practicability and importance of canal navigation. He was likewise directed to cause armed vessels to be built, so as to secure the mastery of the waters of the northern lakes. He was to judge of the expediency of a temporary fortification or intrenched camp on the heights opposite Ticonderoga. Captain Graydon visited Gen. Schuyler early in the summer of 1776, at his head-quarters on Lake George; and he speaks of him, in the very interesting memoirs of his own life, as an officer thoroughly devoted to business, and being, at the same time, a gentleman of polished, courteous manners. On the 1st of August following, he was on the upper Mohawk, providing for its defense and security, and again in October we find him on the upper Hudson, and calling upon the Eastern States for their militia.

There can be no doubt that the northern frontier, in the campaign of 1776, was indebted for its extraordinary quiet and security to the ceaseless activity of Gen. Schuyler. At the close of that year he was further instructed to build a floating battery on the lake, at the foot of Mount Independence, and also to strengthen the works at Fort Stanwix.

In the midst of such conflicting and harassing services, he had excited much popular jealousy and ill will, arising from the energy of his character, and the dignity of his deportment. He was likewise disgusted at what he deemed injustice, in the irregularity of appointing other and junior officers in separate and independent commands within what was considered to be his military district. He accordingly, in October, 1776, tendered to Congress the resignation of his commission. But when Congress came to investigate his services, they found them, says the historian of Washington, far to exceed in value any estimate which had been made of them. They declared that they could not dispense with his services, during the then situation of affairs; and they directed the president of Congress to request him to continue in his command, and they declared their high sense of his services, and their unabated confidence in his attachment to the cause of freedom.

A governor and legislature were chosen in the summer of 1777, and in that trying season there was not a county in this State, as it then existed, which escaped a visit from the arms of the enemy. To add to the embarrassment of our councils in the extremity of their distress, the inhabitants of the northeast part of the State, (now Vermont,) which had been represented in the convention, and just then ingrafted into the constitution, under the names of the counties of Cumberland and Gloucester, renounced their allegiance, and set up for an independent state. On the 30th of

June, in that year, they were knocking at the door of Congress for a recognition of their independence, and an admission into the Union.

The memorable campaign of 1777 was opened by an expedition of the enemy from New York to Danbury in Connecticut, and the destruction of large quantities of provisions, and military means collected and deposited in that town. In the northern quarter, Gen. Burgoyne advanced from Canada through the lakes, with a well-appointed army of 10,000 men; and for a time he dissipated all opposition, and swept every obstacle before him. Gen. Schuyler was still in the command of the whole northern department, and he made every exertion to check the progress of the enemy. He visited in person the different forts, and used the utmost activity in obtaining supplies, to enable them to sustain a siege. While at Albany, (which was his head-quarters, as previously fixed by Congress,) busy in accelerating the equipment and march of troops, Ticonderoga being assailed, was suddenly evacuated by Gen. St. Clair. Gen. Schuyler met on the upper Hudson the news of the retreat, and he displayed, says the candid and accurate historian of Washington, the utmost diligence and judgment in that gloomy state of things. He effectually impeded the navigation of Wood Creek. He rendered the roads impassable. He removed every kind of provisions and stores beyond the reach of the enemy. He summoned the militia of New York and New England to his assistance, and he answered the proclamation of Burgoyne by a counter proclamation, equally addressed to the hopes and fears of the country. Congress, by their resolution of the 17th of July, 1777, approved all the acts of Gen. Schuyler, in reference to the army at Ticonderoga. But the evacuation of that fortress excited great discontent in the United States, and Gen. Schuyler did not escape his share of the popular clamor, and he was made a victim to appease it. It was deemed expedient to recall the general officers in the northern army, and in the month of August he was superseded in the command of that department by the arrival of Gen. Gates. The laurels which he was in preparation to win by his judicious and distinguished efforts, and which he would very shortly have attained, were by that removal intercepted from his brow.

General Schuyler felt acutely the discredit of being recalled in the most critical and interesting period of the campaign of 1777; and when the labor and activity of making preparations to repair the disaster of it had been expended by him; and when an opportunity was opening, as he observed, for that resistance and retaliation which might bring glory upon our arms. If error be attributable to the evacuation of Ticonderoga, says the historian of Washington, no portion of it was committed by Gen. Schuyler. But his removal, though unjust and severe as respected himself, was rendered expedient, according to Chief Justice Marshall, as a sacrifice to the prejudices of New England.

He was present at the capture of Burgoyne, but without any personal command; and the urbanity of his manners, and the chivalric magnanimity of his character, smarting as he was under the extent and severity of his pecuniary losses, was attested by Gen. Burgoyne himself, in his speech in 1778, in the British House of Commons. He there declared, that, by his orders, "a very good dwelling-house, exceeding large storehouses, great saw-mills, and other outbuildings, to the value altogether, perhaps, of 10,000*l*. belonging to Gen. Schuyler, at Saratoga, were destroyed by fire, a few days before the surrender." He said further, that one of the first persons he saw after the convention was signed, was Gen. Schuyler, and when expressing to him his regret at the event which had happened to his property, Gen. Schuyler desired him "to think no more of it, and that the occasion justified it, according to the principles and rules of war. He did more," said Burgoyne; "he sent an aid-de-camp to conduct me to Albany, in order, as he expressed it, to procure better quarters than a stranger might be able to find. That gentleman conducted me to a very elegant house, and, to my great surprise, presented me to Mrs. Schuyler and her family. In that house I remained during my whole stay in Albany, with a table with more than twenty covers for me and my friends, and every other possible demonstration of hospitality."

I have several times had the same relation, in substance, from Gen. Schuyler himself, and he said that he remained behind at Saratoga, under the pretext of taking care of the remains of his property, but in reality to avoid giving fresh occasions for calumny and jealousies, by appearing in person with Burgoyne, at his own house. It was not until the autumn of 1778, that the conduct of Gen. Schuyler, in the campaign of 1777, was submitted to the investigation of a court-martial. He was acquitted of every charge with the highest honors, and the sentence was confirmed by Congress. He shortly afterward, upon his earnest and repeated solicitations, had leave to retire from the army, and he devoted the remainder of his life to the service of his country in its political councils.

If the military life of Gen. Schuyler was inferior in brilliancy to that of some others of his countrymen, none of them ever surpassed him in fidelity, activity, and devotedness to the service. The characteristic of his measures was utility. They bore the stamp and unerring precision of practical science. There was nothing complicated in his character. It was chaste and severe simplicity; and, take him for all in all, he was one of the wisest and most efficient men, both in military and civil life, that the state or the nation has produced.

He had been elected to Congress in 1777, and he was re-elected in each of the three following years. On his return to Congress, after the termination of his military life, his talents, experience, and energy were put in immediate requisition; and in November, 1779, he was appointed to confer with General Washington, on the state of the southern department. In 1781, he was in the senate of this State; and wherever he was placed, and whatever might be the business before him, he gave the utmost activity to measures, and left upon them the impression of his prudence and sagacity. In 1789, he was elected to a seat in the first senate of the United States, and when his term of service expired in Congress, he was replaced in the senate of this State. In 1792, he was very active in digesting and bringing to maturity that early and great measure of State policy, the establishment of companies for inland lock navigation. The whole suggestion was the product of his fertile and calculating mind, ever busy in schemes for the public welfare. He was placed at the head of the direction of both of the navigation companies, and his mind was ardently directed for years towards the execution of those liberal plans of internal improvement. In 1796, he urged in his place in the Senate, and afterward published in a pamphlet form, his plan for the improvement of the revenue of this State, and, in 1797, his plan was almost literally adopted, and to that we owe the institution of the office of Comptroller. In 1797, he was unanimously elected by the two houses of our Legislature, a Senator in Congress; and he took leave of the Senate of this State in a liberal and affecting address, which was inserted at large upon their journals.

But the life of this great man was drawing to a close. I formed and cultivated a personal acquaintance with General Schuyler, while a member of the Legislature, in 1792, and again in 1796; and from 1799 to his death, in the autumn of 1804, I was in habits of constant and friendly intimacy with him, and was honored with the kindest and most grateful attentions. His spirits were cheerful, his conversation most eminently instructive, his manners gentle and courteous, and his whole deportment tempered with grace and dignity. His faculties seemed to retain their unimpaired vigor and untiring activity; though he had evidently lost some of his constitutional ardor of temperament and vehemence of feeling. He was sobered by age, chastened by affliction, broken by disease; and yet nothing could surpass the interest excited by the mild radiance of the evening of his days.

Note H.

WYOMING.

Among the claims set up by the State of Connecticut was the following: that by their charter they owned all lands lying between those parallels of latitude forming the northern and southern boundary of their State, and extending west to the Pacific Ocean. This claim, it will readily be perceived, would cover a large portion of the southern part of New York, and of the northern parts of Pennsylvania and Ohio. In prosecution of this claim, a colony from Windham, in Connecticut, obtained a State grant for a large tract of land lying along the Susquehanna in the State of Pennsylvania, whither they removed. The valley they occupied was called Wyoming; said to mean "Field of blood;" so called on account of a bloody battle fought in the neighborhood of the settlement by the Indians at a period anterior to the removal of the whites.

The following account of the battle and massacre is taken from an interesting history of Wyoming, written by Isaac Chapman, Esq., late of Wilkesbarre. Judge Chapman lived upon the spot, and could hardly have failed to collect accurate materials, and to give a correct narrative of the events which transpired there during the Revolutionary war. The inhabitants had collected in Forty Fort—the principal fort in the valley. The number of men in the fort was three hundred and sixty-eight.

"On the morning of the 3d of July, 1778, the officers of the garrison at Forty Fort held a council to determine on the propriety of marching from the fort, and attacking the enemy wherever found. The debates in this council of war are said to have been conducted with much warmth and animation. The ultimate determination was one on which depended the lives of the garrison and safety of the settlement. On one side it was contended that their enemies were daily increasing in numbers; that they would plunder the settlement of all kinds of property, and would accumulate the means of carrying on the war, while they themselves would become weaker; that the harvest would soon be ripe, and would be gathered or destroyed by their enemies, and all their means of sustenance during the succeeding winter would fail; that probably all their messengers were killed, and as there had been more than sufficient time, and no assistance arrived, they would probably receive none, and consequently now was the proper time to make the attack. On the other side it was argued, that probably some or all the messengers may have arrived at head-quarters, but that the absence of the commander-in-chief may have produced delay; that one or two weeks more may bring the desired assistance, and that to attack the enemy, superior as they were in number, out of the limits of their own fort, would produce almost certain destruction to the settlement and themselves, and captivity, and slavery, perhaps torture, to their wives and children. While these debates were progressing, five men belonging to Wyoming, but who at that time held commissions in the continental army, arived at the fort; they had received information that a force from Niagara had marched to destroy the settlements on the Susquehanna, and being unable to bring with them any reinforcement, they resigned their appointments, and hastened immediately to the protection of their families. They had heard nothing of the messengers, neither could they give any certain information as to the probability of relief.

"The prospect of receiving assistance became now extremely uncertain. The advocates for the attack prevailed in the council, and at dawn of day, on the morning of the 3d of July, the garrison left the fort, and began their march up the river, under the command of Col. Zebulon Butler. Having proceeded about two miles, the troops halted for the purpose of detaching a reconnoitering party, to ascertain the situation of the enemy.

"The scout found the enemy in possession of Fort Wintermoot, and occupying huts immediately around it, carousing in supposed security; but on their return to the advancing column, they met two strolling Indians, by whom they were fired upon, and upon whom they immediately returned the fire without effect. The settlers hastened their march for the attack, but the Indians had given the alarm, and the advancing troops found the enemy already formed in order of battle a small distance from their fort, with their right flank covered by a swamp, and their left resting upon the bank of a river. The settlers immediately displayed their column and formed in corresponding order, but as the enemy was much superior in numbers, their line was much more extensive. Pine woods and bushes covered the battle-ground, in consequence of which the movements of the troops could not be so quickly discovered, nor so well ascertained. Col. Zebulon Butler had command of the right, and was opposed by Col. John Butler at the head of the British troops on the left; Col. Nathan Denison commanded the left, opposed by Brant at the head of his Indians on the enemy's right. The battle commenced at about forty rods distant, and continued about fifteen minutes through the woods and brush, without much execution. At this time Brant with his Indians, having penetrated the swamp, turned the left flank of the settlers' line, and with a terrible war-whoop and savage yell made a desperate charge upon the troops composing that wing, which fell very fast, and were immediately cut to pieces with the tomahawk. Col. Denison having ascertained that the savages were gaining the rear of the left, gave orders for that wing *to fall back*. At the same time Col. John Butler, finding that the line of the settlers did not extend as far towards the river as his own, doubled that end of his line which was protected by a thick growth of brushwood, and having brought a party of his British regulars to act in column upon that wing, threw Col. Zebulon Butler's troops into some confusion. The orders of Col. Denison for his troops to *fall back*, having been understood by many to mean a *retreat*, the troops began to retire in much disorder. The savages considered this a flight, and, commencing a most hideous yell, rushed forward with their rifles and tomahawks, and cut the retiring line to pieces. In this situation it was found impossible to rally and form the troops, and the rout became general throughout the line. The settlers fled in every direction, and were instantly followed by the savages, who killed or took prisoners whoever came within their reach. Some succeeded in reaching the river, and escaped by swimming across; others fled to the mountains, and the savages, too much occupied with plunder, gave up the pursuit. When the first intelligence was received in the village of Wilkes-barre that the battle was lost, the women fled with their children to the mountains, on their way to the settlements on the Delaware, where many of them at length arrived after suffering extreme hardships. Many of the men who escaped the battle, together with their women and children, who were unable to travel on foot, took refuge in Wyoming fort, and on the following day, (July the 4th,) Butler and Brant, at the head of their combined forces, appeared before the fort, and demanded its surrender. The garrison being without any efficient means of defense, surrendered the fort on articles of capitulation, by which the settlers, upon giving up their fortifications, prisoners, and miltary stores, were to remain in the country unmolested, provided they did not again take up arms.

"In this battle about three hundred of the settlers were killed or missing, and from a great part of whom no intelligence was ever afterward received.

"The conditions of the capitulation were entirely

disregarded by the British and savage forces, and after the fort was delivered up, all kinds of barbarities were committed by them. The village of Wilkesbarre, consisting of twenty-three houses, was burned; men and their wives were separated from each other, and carried into captivity; their property was plundered, and the settlement laid waste. The remainder of the inhabitants were driven from the valley, and compelled to proceed on foot sixty miles through the great swamp, almost without food or clothing. A number perished in the journey, principally women and children; some died of their wounds; others wandered from the path in search of food, and were lost, and those who survived called the wilderness through which they passed *the shades of death*, an appellation which it has since retained."

Catrine Montour, who might well be termed a fury, acted a conspicuous part in this tragedy. She followed in the train of the victorious army, ransacking the heaps of slain, and, with her arms covered with gore, barbarously murdering the wounded, who in vain supplicated for their lives.

Halleck, in allusion to the massacre at Wyoming, has the following interesting lines:

"There is a woman, widowed, gray, and old,
Who tells you where the foot of battle stept
Upon their day of massacre. She told
Its tale, and pointed to the spot, and wept,
Whereon her father and five brothers slept
Shroudless, the bright dreamed slumbers of the brave,
When all the land a funeral mourning kept.
And there wild laurels planted on the grave,
By Nature's hand in air their pale red blossoms wave."

"MASSACRE OF WYOMING. (Pa.)

"Perhaps the last survivor of this event, which has been made the subject of the interesting poem of the gifted Campbell, is the person whose death is recorded in the annexed notice. The actual horrors of the scene of death and conflagration, or the dramatic incident embodied in the fiction founded upon it, must be vivid in the recollection of our readers.

"A MOTHER OF WYOMING

"We find in a Connecticut paper, an account of the recent decease of Mrs. Esther Skinner, of Torringford, in the one hundredth year of her age. Mrs. S. lost a husband, a brother, and two sons, in the war of the American Revolution. She, with her family, was a resident of Wyoming, at the massacre of its inhabitants by D. and T. and the Indians and Tories. Her two sons fell beneath the tomahawk, but the mother, almost by miracle, escaped with six of her children. Her son-in-law was the only man that escaped out of twenty, who threw themselves into the river, and attempted to hide themselves beneath the foliage that overhung the banks. All the others were successively massacred as they hung by the branches in the river. He alone was undiscovered. The mother travelled back to Torringford, where she has led a useful life ever since—often cheerful, though the cloud of pensiveness, brought on by her sorrows, was never entirely dissipated. But one of her children survives her."—*Journal of Commerce, Aug.* 16, 1831.

NOTE I.

Extract of a Letter from Captain Courish, of the New England militia, dated Albany, March 7th, 1782.

THE following interesting document was originally copied by the author from a newspaper published in the county of Dutchess during the Revolution. It appeared in the paper without further note or comment than is given below. It was long supposed to be authentic. It seems, however, that the article was written by Dr. Franklin. Still it embodies only statements, the counterparts of which were constantly occurring on the frontier. The grandmother of the author, who was an Indian prisoner, and was also detained nearly a year a prisoner at Fort Niagara, saw, while in that fort, large bundles of scalps brought in by the Indians.

The peltry taken in the expedition will, as you see, amount to a good deal of money. The possession of this booty at first gave us pleasure; but we were struck with horror to find among the packages eight large ones, containing scalps of our unhappy folks taken in the three last years by the Seneca Indians, from the inhabitants of the frontiers of New York,

New Jersey, Pennsylvania, and Virginia, and sent by them as a present to Col. Haldiman, Governor of Canada, in order to be by him transmitted to England. They were accompanied by the following curious letter to that gentleman:

"*Tioga, January* 3*d*, 1782.

"May it please your Excellency—

"At the request of the Seneca chiefs, I send herewith to your Excellency, under the care of James Boyd, eight packs of scalps, cured, dried, hooped, and painted with all the Indian triumphal marks, of which the following is invoice and explanation.

No. 1. Containing 43 scalps of Congress soldiers, killed in different skirmishes; these are stretched on black hoops, four inch diameter; the inside of the skin painted red, with a small black spot to note their being killed with bullets. Also 62 of farmers, killed in their houses; the hoops red; the skin painted brown, and marked with a hoe; a black circle all round to denote their being surprised in the night; and a black hatchet in the middle, signifying their being killed with that weapon.

No. 2. Containing 98 of farmers, killed in their houses; hoops red; figure of a hoe, to mark their profession; great white circle and sun, to show they were surprised in the daytime; *a little red foot*, to show they stood upon their defense, and died fighting for their lives and families.

No. 3. Containing 97 of farmers; hoops green, to show they were killed in their fields; a large white circle with a little round mark on it for the sun, to show that it was in the daytime; black bullet mark on some—hatchet on others.

No. 4. Containing 102 of farmers, mixed of the several marks above; only 18 marked with a little yellow flame, to denote their being of prisoners burnt alive, after being scalped, their nails pulled out by the roots, and other torments; one of these latter supposed to be of a rebel clergyman, his band being fixed to the hoop of his scalp. Most of the farmers appear by the hair to have been young or middle-aged men; there being but 67 very grey heads among them all; which makes the service more essential.

No. 5. Containing 88 scalps of women; hair long, braided in the Indian fashion, to show they were mothers; hoops blue; skin yellow ground, with little red tadpoles, to represent, by way of triumph, the tears of grief occasioned to their relations; a black scalping-knife or hatchet at the bottom, to mark their being killed with those instruments; 17 others, hair very gray; black hoops; plain brown color, no mark but the short club or cassetete, to show they were knocked down dead, or had their brains beat out.

No. 6. Containing 193 boys' scalps of various ages; small green hoops; whitish ground on the skin, with red tears in the middle, and black bullet marks, knife, hatchet, or club, as their deaths happened.

No. 7. 211 girls scalped, big and little; small yellow hoops; white ground; tears, hatchet, club, scalping-knife, &c.

No. 8. This package is a mixture of all the varieties abovementioned, to the number of 122; with a box of birch bark, containing 29 little infants' scalps of various sizes; small white hoops; white ground.

"With these packs the Chiefs send to your excellency the following speech, delivered by Coneiogatchie, in council, interpreted by the elder Moore, the trader, and taken down by me in writing.

"*Father!*—We send you herewith many scalps, that you may see that we are not idle friends. A blue belt.

"*Father!*—We wish you to send these scalps over the water to the great King, that he may regard them and be refreshed; and that he may see our faithfulness in destroying his enemies, and be convinced that his presents have not been made to ungrateful people. A blue and white belt with red tassels.

"*Father!*—Attend to what I am now going to say; it is a matter of much weight. The great King's enemies are many, and they grow fast in number. They were formerly like young panthers; they could neither bite nor scratch; we could play with them safely; we feared nothing they could do to us. But now their bodies are become big as the elk, and strong as the buffalo; they have also got great and sharp claws. They have driven us out of our country by taking part in your quarrel. We expect the great King will give us another country, that our children may live after us, and be his friends and children as we are. Say this for us to the great King. To enforce it we give this belt. A great white belt with blue tassels.

"*Father!*—We have only to say further, that your

traders exact more than ever for their goods; and our hunting is lessened by the war, so that we have fewer skins to give for them. This ruins us. Think of some remedy. We are poor, and you have plenty of everything. We know you will send us powder and guns, and knives, and hatchets; but we also want shirts and blankets. A little white belt."

"I do not doubt but that your excellency will think it proper to give some further encouragement to those honest people. The high prices they complain of, are the necessary effect of the war. Whatever presents may be sent for them through my hands shall be distributed with prudence and fidelity. I have the honor of being,

Your excellency's most obedient,

And most humble servant,

JAMES CRAUFURD."

NOTE J.

CHRISTIAN SHELL.

AMONG the persons who distinguished themselves by their personal courage was Christian Shell, of Shell's Bush, in the now county of Herkimer. He refused to go into any of the forts, but built a blockhouse upon his farm. These houses were usually built of hewn timber. The first story had no windows, but several loop-holes, through which those within could fire upon the enemy. The second story projected over the first two or three feet. Through this projection there were likewise apertures, through which the persons within could fire upon, or cast down missiles upon the assailants if they approached the house to force an entrance. The statements contained in the following specimen of rude poetry are true. The year following this rencontre, the Indians stole the march upon Shell, and shot him while engaged in his work on his farm. His wife and children then removed to some of the forts.

A story, a story,
Unto you I will tell,
Concerning a brave hero,
One Christian Shell,

Who was attacked by the savages
  And Tories, as is said,
But for this attack
  Most dearly they paid.

The sixth day of August,
  He went to his field,
Determined if the enemy
  Came, never to yield.

Two sons he had along with him,
  Resolved were the same;
About the middle of the afternoon,
  These invaders, they came.

He fled unto his blockhouse,
  For to save his life,
Where he had left his arms
  In the care of his wife.

The enemy took prisoners,
  Two sons that were twins,
About eight years of age;
  Soon the battle it begins.

They advanced upon him,
  And began to fire,
But Christian with his blunderbuss
  Soon made them retire.

He wounded Donald McDonald,
  And drew him in the door,
Who gave an account
  There was strength sixty-four.

They fought from two in the afternoon
  Until the closing of the light;

14*

Shell's son was slightly wounded
  Before that it was night.

The old woman she has spoiled
  Five guns, as I have since been told,
With nothing but a chopping axe,
  Which shows that she was bold.

Six there was wounded,
  And eleven there was killed,
Of this said party,
  Before they quit the field.

The Indians were forty-eight,
  And Tories full sixteen,
By old Shell and his two sons,
  Oh, the like was never seen.

Not like to get assistance,
  Nor any body's help,
They thought for to affright him
  By setting up their YELP.

But God was his assistant,
  His buckler and his shield,
He dispersed this cruel enemy,
  And made them quit the field.

Come all you Tryon County men,
  And never be dismayed,
But trust in the Lord,
  And he will be your aid.

Trust in the Lord with all your might,
  And call upon his name,
And he will help you as he did Shell
  To his immortal fame,

An account similar to the foregoing was related to me by Col. Nicholas Fish. In the spring of 1779, and a few days before the army broke up its encampment near the Hudson, the Indians and Tories burned the settlement of Warwarsing. A detachment from the army was sent to the assistance of the place. Before their arrival it was mostly destroyed. They succeeded, however, in relieving a part of the inhabitants, and especially one man, who had defended himself bravely. His house was in the woods, and in advance of all the others in the settlement. He fled into his house with his wife on the approach of the Indians. Here he defended himself with such spirit that he drove the party who had attacked him back, and forced them to seek shelter behind the trees. The Indians then collected combustibles, and setting them on fire, rushed up, and threw them on the house. The flames caught. He then took two pails, and ran to a spring several rods distant, and filling them hastily with water, returned to the house. The Indians again rushed up, determined to take him, and threw their tomahawks, and were at the door almost the same instant that it was closed. He succeeded in extinguishing the fire. At this juncture the detachment came up, and the Indians fled. The officers, as a testimony of their admiration of his courage, made a liberal present of money to him, which they raised by contribution.

NOTE K.

THE SACRIFICE OF THE SENECAS.

THE following account of the sacrifice of the Senecas, is taken from the 4th volume of Dwight's Travels, and was communicated to him by the Rev. Mr. Kirkland.

"At the time when the Senecas return from hunting in January or February, they annually keep a feast seven days; the professed object of which is, to render thanks to the Great Spirit for the benefits they have received from him during the preceding year, and to solicit the continuance of them through the year to come. On the evening before the feast commences they kill two dogs, and after painting them with various colors, and dressing them with ornaments, suspend them in the centre of the camp, or in some conspicuous place in the village.

"The whole of this solemn season is spent in feasting and dancing. Two select bands, one of men, and another of women, ornamented with a variety of trinkets, and furnished each with an ear of corn, which is held in the right hand, begin the dance at the council house. Both choirs, the men leading the way, dance in a circle around the council-fire, which is kindled for the occasion, and regulate their steps by music. Hence they proceed to every house in the village, and in the same manner dance in a circle around each fire.

"On one of the festival days they perform a peculiar religious ceremony, for the purpose of driving away evil spirits from their habitations. Three men clothe themselves in the skins of wild beasts, and cover their faces with masks of a hideous appearance, and their hands with the shell of the tortoise. In this garb they go from house to house, making a horrid noise, and in every house take the fuel from the fire and scatter the embers and ashes about the floor with their hands.

"Toward the close of the festival they erect a funeral pile, place it upon the two dogs, and set it on fire. When they are partly consumed, one of them is taken off and put into a large kettle, with vegetables of every kind which they have cultivated during the year. The other dog is consumed in the fire. The ashes of the pile are then gathered up, carried through the village and sprinkled at the door of every house. When this ceremony is ended, which is always near the close of the seventh day, all the inhabitants feast together upon the contents of the kettle; and thus the festival is terminated.

"This mode of exhibiting their gratitude is certainly far from gratifying the feelings of a Christian, yet I think several of the American States might learn from these savages the important lesson, that it becomes a people possessing the light of revelation, to render annually a public tribute of thanksgiving to the Great Benefactor of Mankind for the blessings which they have received during the year from his bountiful hand.

"This, however, is not the only religious service which has existed among the Six Nations. Mr. Kirkland informed me that while he was crossing the Oneida Lake with a fleet of canoes, a violent storm arose, from which the fleet was in the utmost danger of perishing. The chief sachem, in whose canoe Mr. Kirkland was, took from a box in the stern a small quantity of fine powder, made of a fragrant herb unknown to Mr. Kirkland, and scattered it on the water. This he found was intended as an oblation to the Deity acknowledged by the sachem."

Note L.

NUMBER OF INDIAN WARRIORS EMPLOYED IN THE REVOLUTIONARY WAR.

An estimate of the Indian nations employed by the British in the Revolutionary war, with the number of warriors annexed to each nation; by Captain Dalton, superintendent of Indian affairs for the United States, who, after being several years a prisoner with the enemy, arrived at Philadelphia, where he published the following account, 5th August, 1783.

Choctaws - - -	600	Tuscaroras - - -	200
Chickasaws - -	400	Onondagas - - -	300
Cherokees - - -	500	Cayugas - - - -	230
Creeks - - -	700	Jeneckaws (Senecas)*	400
Plankishaws - -	400	Sues and Sothuse -	1300
Oniactmaws - -	300	Putawawtawmaws -	400
Kackapoes - -	500	Tulawin - - - -	150
Munseys - - -	150	Muskulthe, or Nation of Fire - - -	250
Delawares - - -	500	Reiners, or Foxes -	300
Shawanaws - -	300		

* In 1783 Mr. Kirkland estimated the whole number of fighting men in the Seneca tribe at 600.

Mohickons - - -	60	Puyon - - -	350
Uchipweys - -	3000	Sokkie - - - -	450
Ottaways - - -	300	Abinokkie, or the St. Lawrence - -	200
Mohawks - -	300		
Oneidas* - - -	150		
		Warriors	12,690

* The Rev. Mr. Kirkland informed Dr. Stiles that there were 410 souls before the war, and that 120 joined the enemy.
10th vol. Mass. Collections, page 123.

NOTE M.

The Direct Agency of the English Government in the employment of the Indians in the Revolutionary War. By William W. Campbell. Read by Mr. Campbell, October 7th, 1845, *before the New York Historical Society.*

NEARLY forty years before the commencement of the Revolutionary war, a young man arrived in the valley of the Mohawk, who was destined to exert a greater influence than any other individual since the settlement of the province of New York, over the Indians who dwelt within its borders. He was in early manhood, but little over twenty years of age, and was entrusted with an extensive and important agency. He was of a good family—an Irishman by birth—a nephew of Sir Peter Warren, and had charge of a large landed property belonging to his uncle, which was situated in that vicinity. He rose rapidly in public estimation, for he had talent and opportunity for its exercise. He early entered the provincial army—leading sometimes the provincial troops, and sometimes the warriors of the Six Nations. In 1755 he gained a signal victory over the French on the northern frontiers of New York. The English government created him a baronet, and granted him five thousand pounds, and he was appointed a superintendent of Indian affairs for the northern provinces, with a salary of a thousand pounds a year. The fame and the fortune of Sir William Johnson were made.

He continued in the exercise of his important duties down to the period of his death. He was a man of stern and determined purpose, but urbane and conciliatory when necessary, and held a controlling influence over the Indians and most of the inhabitants of the frontier. For nearly twenty years he resided at his place, called Fort Johnson, and which is situated in the valley of the Mohawk, about three miles west of Amsterdam. He afterwards removed to Johnson Hall, near the village of Johnstown, and where he spent the remaining years of his life. In the month of July, 1774, an Indian council was called at Johnson Hall, and besides a large number of the Six Nations, there assembled at his house, Governor Franklin of New Jersey, the judges of the Supreme Court of New York, and other gentlemen of consideration and influence in the province. During the sitting of this council, on the 11th July, 1774, Sir William died suddenly. He had been, it is said, previously unwell, and the exertion which he made was greater than he could bear. It was alleged at the time, by those who espoused the American cause, that he purposely hastened his death, having determined never to lead his Indian warriors against a people with whom he had so long dwelt on the most friendly terms; and at the same time, being unwilling to disregard the instructions and wishes of a government which had so highly honored and enriched him.

An eye-witness, under date of 13th of July, 1774, thus writes: "The corpse of the late Sir William Johnson was carried from Johnson Hall to Johnstown, and deposited in the family vault in the church which he erected, attended by upwards of two thousand persons from the neighboring country, with the Indians, who all behaved with the greatest decorum, and exhibited the most lively marks of real sorrow. The pall was supported by his Excellency, the Governor of New Jersey, the Judges of the Supreme Court of New York, and other persons of note who happened to be at Johnstown at that time; and on their return from the funeral to Johnson Hall, the Indians acquainted Colonel Johnson that they would perform the ceremony of condolence the next day." They wished, they said, "to kindle up anew the fires at Johnstown and Onondaga."

Johnson Hall, the residence of Sir William at the time of his death, was situated upon an eminence, and overlooked the village and the church, from which it was distant about one mile; and the scene must have been one of an imposing character, as the long funeral procession moved slowly down the winding avenue, conveying to its last resting-place all that remained of him who had for so many years been the first man upon the borders. They who were soon after to be known as patriot and loyalist, as Whig and Tory, walked side by side, and mingled their tears together. The dusky Indian warrior bowed his head in sorrow by the side of the pale face, with whom he was not to meet again, except in the fierce and bloody contests which were soon to be waged. Some, perhaps, met for the first time afterwards in bloody strife upon the same ground over which they bore the corpse of the good old chieftain.

Thus died Sir William Johnson; and he died as he had lived, surrounded by Indian warriors. The Indian superintendency was to pass into other hands, and new and perilous scenes were preparing for the inhabitants of the frontiers of New York.

Sir William Johnson left one son, Sir John Johnson, and two daughters, one of whom was married to Colonel Daniel Claus, and the other to Colonel Guy Johnson. The latter was a distant relative of Sir William, and for thirty years had been also intimately acquainted with Indian affairs. In 1762, then being a lieutenant in the British army, he was appointed by Sir William, a deputy superintendent. For some time previous to his death, Sir William seems to have felt that his life was precarious, and deemed it a matter of great importance that a successor should be appointed. In April, 1774, a few months before his death, he wrote a pressing letter to the English government, strongly urging such an appointment at once, and recommending Colonel Guy Johnson. He spoke of the duties and fatigues growing out of his civil and military employments, and observed that they had drawn upon him a train of infirmities which had often threatened his life, and at best had rendered it precarious. "I have often," said he, "carried the most important points merely through personal influence, when all other means had failed. If, therefore, I have the least claim to indulgence in support of the application of the Indians, I cannot withhold my warmest recommendation in favor of the gentleman they wish for; and whilst I assure your lordship that I rate my present reputation and future fame too high to prostitute it for interest or partiality, would rather hazard the imputation of both than refuse my testimony towards a measure that may benefit the public when I am no more."

The recommendation of Sir William Johnson procured the appointment of Colonel Guy Johnson as his successor. The place was one of great power and responsibility. There were within the department at that time, 130,000 Indians, of whom 25,420 were fighting men. The Six Nations numbered about 10,000, and had two thousand bold and skillful warriors. The whole population of the province of New York in 1774 was 182,251, and an estimate of the militia was 32,000. In 1771, the county of Albany, then embracing all the northern and western part of the province, and extending from the banks of the Hudson on to the great cataract of Niagara, contained only 38,829 inhabitants.

In 1772, the county of Tryon, named after the then governor of the province, was formed, and it embraced the whole section of the State west of a north and south line running nearly through the centre of the present county of Schoharie. It contained, probably, a population of 10,000. Johnstown was the county town. There was no section of the country which felt so deep an interest in the movements and operations of the Indians as the inhabitants of this latter county. The population was sparse, and they were exposed upon the south, the west, and the north, and had in their midst, and immediately around them, an Indian population equal in number to their own. If we consider that there were more than twenty-five thousand Indian warriors, in some measure under the control of the superintendent, located in the valley of the Mohawk, it will at once be seen that if the Indians should be prevailed upon to take part in the contest then about commencing, the situation of the inhabitants would be one of extreme peril. It was with feelings of deep interest, therefore, that they learned that the new superintendent had called an Indian council, to be held at Guy Park, his place of residence, in the month of May, 1775.

The political elements were all in motion. Tories and Whigs were arraying themselves and preparing for the issue. As early as August, 1774, the inhabitants, at a meeting held at Palatine, had resolved, among other things, that they deeply sympathized with the inhabitants of Boston, who were suffering under the oppressive act for blocking up the port, and they added, "we will join and unite with our brethren of the rest of this colony in any thing tending to support and defend our rights and liberties."

On the 20th of May, 1775, and just previous to the Indian council at Guy Park, Col. Guy Johnson, the superintendent, addressed the following letter to the magistrates and committees of the western districts: "Gentlemen, I have lately had repeated accounts that a body of New Englanders, or other men, were to come and seize and carry away my person, and attack our family under color of malicious insinuations, that I intended to set the Indians upon the people. Men of sense and character know that my office is of the highest importance to promote peace amongst the Six Nations, and prevent their entering into any such disputes. This I effected last year, when they were much vexed about the attack made upon the Shawnese, and I last winter appointed them to meet me this month to receive the answer of the Virginians. All men must allow that if the Indians find their council-fire disturbed and their superintendent insulted, they will take a dreadful revenge. It is therefore the duty of all people to prevent this, and to satisfy any who may have been injured, and that their suspicions and the allegations they have collected against me are false, and inconsistent with my character and office. I recommend this to you as highly necessary at this time, as my regard for the interest of the country and self-preservation has obliged me to fortify my house, and keep men armed for my defense, till these idle and malicous reports are removed."

The committee, to whom this letter was addressed, observed very truly, that they had an open enemy before their faces, and treacherous friends at their back, but they resolved that the conduct of Col. Johnson was alarming, arbitrary and unwarrantable, inasmuch as he was stopping and searching travellers upon the king's highway, and they added that they would "defend their freedom with their lives and fortunes."

On the 25th of May, 1775, the Indian council convened at Guy Park, but the Mohawks alone were in attendance. A delegation from the Committee of

Safety was also present, and contradicted the report which had been freely circulated among the Indians, that there was an intention to seize the superintendent.

Dissatisfied with the council which had been held at his house, yet professing to be desirous to promote peace between the Indians and the inhabitants, Guy Johnson had called another council to meet in the western part of the county. Under pretense of meeting the Indians in this council, he removed his whole family and retinue to Cosby's Manor, a little above the German Flats. Here he was waited upon by another delegation from the committee, and in answer to a communication they addressed to him, among other things he observed: "I am glad to find my calling a congress on the frontier gives satisfaction. This was principally my design, *though I cannot sufficiently express my surprise at those who have either through malice or ignorance misconstrued my intentions, and supposed me capable of setting the Indians on the peaceable inhabitants of this county.* The interest our family has in this county and my own is considerable, and they have been its best benefactors; and malicious charges, therefore, to their prejudice are highly injurious, and ought to be totally suppressed;" and he concluded by stating, "I am very sorry that such idle and injurious reports meet with any encouragement. I rely on you, gentlemen, to exert yourselves in discontinuing them, and am happy in this opportunity of assuring the people of a county I regard, that they have nothing to apprehend from my endeavors, but I shall always be glad to promote their true interest."

The Provincial Congress of New York addressed a letter to Col. Johnson on the same subject, and in his reply, written from Fort Stanwix, he says: "I trust I shall always manifest more humanity than to promote the destruction of the innocent inhabitants of a colony to which I have been always warmly attached; a declaration that must appear perfectly suitable to the character of a man of honor and principle." Among the documents obtained by the historical agent of this State, are copies of three letters, taken from drafts and originals in the State Paper Office at London, and which throw much light upon the question of the agency of the government in the employment of the Indians.

One of these is a letter from Guy Johnson to Lord Dartmouth, the Secretary, dated at Montreal, 12th October, 1775, and after reading the letters of the superintendent to the Committee of Tryon County, and to the Provincial Congress, we might exclaim, with Hamlet, "look here on this picture, and on this." After enumerating his difficulties and embarrassments, and repeating to his lordship the reports, that it was determined to seize upon his person at Guy Park, and that he had convened an Indian council there in May, he adds: "*And having then received secret instructions from General Gage respecting the measures I had to take*, I left home the last of that month, and by the help of a body of white men and Indians arrived with great difficulty at Ontario, where in a little time I assembled 1455 Indians, and adjusted matters with them in such a manner that they agreed to defend the communication *and assist his majesty's troops in their operations.* The beginning of July I set out for this place with a chosen body of them, and rangers to the number of 220, not being able to get any craft or even provisions for more, and arrived here the 17th of that month, and soon after convened a second body of the northern confederacy, to the amount of 1700 and upwards, who entered into the same arrangement, notwithstanding they had declined coming in some time before on Gov. Carleton's requisition, their minds having been corrupted by New England emissaries."

And thus, at the very time he was writing the letters to the committees, and protesting that he had no intentions of engaging the Indians in the contest, he had in his possession the secret instructions of Gen. Gage, under which he was acting, and in pursuance of which he arranged with more than three thousand warriors to take up the hatchet.

The other two letters to which I have alluded, were from Lord Dartmouth to Col. Johnson, and they settle the question as to the active agency of the English government in the employment of the Indians. The first letter is dated 5th July, 1775, and is as follows: "I have received your letter of the 17th of March, No. 7, and have laid it before the king. The present state of affairs in his majesty's colonies, in which an unnatural rebellion has broke out that threatened to overturn the constitution, precludes all immediate consideration in the domestic concerns of the Indians under your protection. Nor is it to be expected that any measures which the king may think fit to take, for redressing the injuries they complain of respecting their lands, can, in the present moment, be attended with any effect. It will be proper, however, that you should assure them in the strongest terms of his majesty's firm resolution to protect them and preserve them in all their rights, and it is more than ever necessary that you should exert the utmost vigilance to discover whether any artifices are used to engage them in the support of the rebellious proceedings of his majesty's subjects, to counteract such treachery, and to keep them in such a state of affection and attachment to the king, *as that his majesty may rely upon their assistance in any case in which it may be necessary to require it.*"

On the 24th of July Lord Dartmouth wrote the second letter, nineteen days after writing the first, and during which time the news of the battle of Bunker Hill had reached London.

"Sir, I have already in my letter to you of the 5th inst. hinted that the time might possibly come when the King, relying upon the attachment of his faithful allies, the Six Nations of Indians, might be under the necessity of calling upon them for their aid and assistance in the present state of America. The unnatural rebellion now raging there calls for every effort to suppress it, and the intelligence his majesty has received of the rebels having excited the Indians to take a part, and of their having actually engaged a body of them in arms to support their rebellion, justifies the resolution his majesty has taken of requiring the assistance of his faithful adherents, the Six Nations.

"*It is, therefore, his majesty's pleasure, that you do*

lose no time in taking such steps as may induce them to take up the hatchet against his majesty's rebellious subjects in America, and to engage them in his majesty's service, upon such plan as shall be suggested to you by General Gage, to whom this letter is sent, accompanied with a large assortment of goods for presents to them, upon this important occasion.

"Whether the engaging the Six Nations to take up arms in defense of his majesty's government, is most likely to be effected by separate negotiations with the chiefs, or in a general council assembled for the purpose, must be left to your judgment, but at all events, as it is a service of very great importance, you will not fail to exert every effort that may tend to accomplish it, and to use the utmost diligence and activity in the execution of the views I have now the honor to transmit to you. I am, &c.,

DARTMOUTH."

These letters settle the question as to the direct agency of the English government in the employment of the Indians. The directions are peremptory in their language, and admit of no discretion. It was the command of George the Third, that the Indians should be employed, and the Secretary lays the command upon the Indian Superintendent. With how much faithfulness and zeal that Superintendent executed the command, is known to all who have looked into the history of the war, as it was carried on upon the borders.

But it is alleged, in justification, that the rebels had instigated the Indians to take up the hatchet in their behalf. A few of the Stockbridge tribe did early join the continental army; but they were few in number and comparatively a civilized people. I have searched the records of the Committee of Safety, and of the Provincial Congress of New York, but have not been able to find a letter or a speech or even a secret resolve in favor of the employment of the Indians, but there are letters, and speeches, and resolves innumerable in favor of a strict neutrality.

At the council of Guy Park in May, 1775, the gentlemen who attended on the part of the Committee of Safety of Tryon County stated in their speech, that they desired peace with the Indians, and in the reply, the Indians said, "Brothers, we are very glad to hear you speak and hear you confirm the old friendship of our forefathers, which we intend to abide by and thank you for the same."

At the same time, the magistrates and committees of Schenectady and Albany, in a reply to a speech of the principal Mohawk chief, made in behalf of his tribe, said:

"Brothers, we are extremely well satisfied to hear that you have no inclination or purpose to interfere in the dispute between Old England and America, for you must not understand that it is with Boston alone, it is between Old England and all her colonies. The people here are oppressed by Old England, and she sends over troops among us, to destroy us. This is the reason our people are all in alarm to defend themselves. They intend no hostilities against you. Do you continue peaceable, and you need apprehend no danger. It is a dispute wherein you have nothing to do. Do not you disturb any of our people, and depend upon it they will leave you in peace."

In a communication to Guy Johnson, under the same date, May 23d, the Albany committee say—"We are not ignorant of the importance of your office as Superintendent, and have been perfectly easy, with respect to any suspicions of the Indians taking a part in the present dispute between Great Britain and her colonies, knowing them to be a people of too much sagacity to engage with the whole continent in a controversy that they can profit nothing by."

On the 2d of September, 1775, a conference was was had at Albany, between the committees and a few of the Six Nations, and at which commissioners on the part of the Continental Congress were present. In their reply to the speech of the Indians, the committee among other things say:

"Brothers, attend! In your speech you further observed, that you had long since taken a resolution to take no active part in the present contest for liberty. We do not offer to censure you for your conduct, but admire your wisdom, praise your pacific disposition, and hope that you will have fortitude to maintain and persevere in it."

On the 10th day of June, 1775, the delegates from New York in the Continental Congress, Philip Livingston, Francis Lewis, James Duane, William Floyd, and John Alsop, addressed a letter from Philadelphia to the Provincial Congress of New York, in which they say: "We shall not fail to attend to what you suggest concerning the Indians. This is an object to our colony of the highest moment, and we hope in due time it will be considered by Congress. We think the Indians will not be disposed to engage in this unhappy quarrel, unless deceived and deluded by misrepresentation, and this with vigilance and care on our part can be prevented. As one step towards it which we much applaud, are the assurances you have given the Superintendent of his safety."

The proof could be multiplied, if necessary, by many such extracts from the letters, speeches and proceedings of the various public bodies, which were called into existence by the exigencies of the times. The English government understood the mode of Indian warfare, and could not have failed to foresee, that their employment would make the war one almost of extermination upon the borders. That the tomahawk, the scalping-knife, and the fire-brand would do their fearful work, not alone on the field of battle, where armed men meet, but also among the women and children in the homes of the unarmed and defenseless.

Such reflections must have forced themselves upon the attention of the English Secretary, when he penned his letter of the 19th of July, 1775, and he felt called upon to give some excuse for the course which his king and government had determined to pursue.

I have already spoken of the departure of the Indians with General Johnson in the summer of 1775. Few of the Mohawks ever returned to dwell in their homes upon the banks of that river which bears their name. The graves of their ancestors were abandoned. Their council-fires were extinguished. That they should remain attached to the English government is by no means strange, for they had been their allies in war, and dependents in peace, and the chain of friendship had been brightened by constant use for more than an hundred years. They returned however as enemies, and with the other confederated tribes laid waste the frontier settlements of New York and Pennsylvania. Year after year they swept over the valleys of the Schoharie, the Mohawk, and the Susquehanna, until there was scarcely a spot remaining, where the destroyer had not left the impression of his footsteps. It is impossible now to say what would have been the fate of the Six Nations, had they remained neutral in the revolutionary contest. There can be little doubt, however, that their final removal from the land they had so long inhabited would have been delayed. If their employment by the English government was disastrous to the inhabitants of the frontier, it was equally so to the Indians themselves. A considerable portion of the Oneidas refused to take up the hatchet against the Americans. When hostilities commenced on the part of the other tribes, the bond of union which had for so long a time bound together the Six Nations was severed, never more to be reunited. The great council-fire which had burned so long at Onondaga went out, never again to be rekindled. The fame and the power of that distinguished confederacy which had been known and felt over the whole of North America, were thereafter to be numbered with the things that were. Their country was overrun by invading armies; their villages were destroyed; and their cultivated fields were laid waste. During the long years of the war, many a warrior fell in battle; others died from want and its consequent diseases. Their pleasant homes, alike with those of the pale faces, were made desolate.

With the restoration of peace, the tide of emigration set in upon their country with resistless force; and, like the other aborigines, they have gradually faded away before its advance.

Some found a home in Canada under the protection of that government which had prevailed upon them to take up the hatchet, and there their descendants are still found.

A few yet remain upon the soil of their fathers, but they are imperfect representatives of that proud and warlike people, who, by their prowess and skill, earned from the early colonist the appellation of the Romans of North America.

Note N.

LIFE AND SERVICES OF GENERAL JAMES CLINTON.

Lecture on the Life and Military Services of General James Clinton. Read before the New York Historical Society, Feb. 1839. *By* William W. Campbell.

It was beautifully and truly said by Montgomery, that it is difficult to convey to others an accurate impression of an impassioned speaker; that it is like "gathering up dew-drops, which appear indeed jewels and pearls in the grass, but run to water in the hand. The essence and the elements remain, but the grace, the sparkle, and the form are gone." He who has attempted the task will have realized the force and the truth of the poet's observation, and will have felt regret and disappointment when he perceives that his description is comparatively tame and spiritless, of events, and scenes, and efforts which charmed him as a beholder, and produced impressions which are glowing and fresh in his memory. But if the speaker possessed the power of conveying to this audience correct impressions of eloquent men, he would not be called upon to exercise that power in discharging the duty which he has assumed this evening. The individual, whose biography he proposes briefly to sketch, was a plain, blunt soldier, born upon the frontiers, and who spent no inconsiderable portion of a long life amid the toils and perils of border wars—a true patriot, who, if not first, was prominent among the men who sustained the heat and the burden of the revolutionary contest in this state. I mean General James Clinton. A brief sketch of his family, and especially of his father, Colonel Charles Clinton, may not be uninteresting. The name of Clinton has been prominent for the last hundred years, both in the colonial and State history of New York. For nearly forty years of that period, individuals of that name have held the high and responsible trust of governor, besides filling many other offices of a military, legislative, and judicial character. The different branches of the family were originally from England. The first of the name who was distinguished here was the colonial governor, George Clinton, who was the youngest son of Francis, sixth Earl of Lincoln, and who was governor of the province of New York from 1743 to 1753. He returned to England, and was afterwards appointed governor of Greenwich Hospital. He was the father of Sir Henry Clinton, who was in command of the English army during a part of the Revolution.

General James Clinton was a descendant of William Clinton, who was an adherent to the cause of royalty in the civil wars of England, and an officer in the army of Charles I. After the death of that monarch he went to the continent, where he remained a long time in exile. He afterwards passed over to Scotland, where he married a lady of the family of Kennedy. From Scotland he removed to Ireland, where he died, leaving one son. This son, James Clinton, on arriving at manhood, made an unsuccessful effort to recover his patrimonial estates in England. While in England he married a Miss Smith, a daughter of a captain in the army of Cromwell, and with his wife returned and settled in Ireland.

Charles Clinton, the son of this marriage, and the father of Gen. James Clinton, was born in the county of Longford, in Ireland, in 1690. In 1729 he determined to emigrate to America. Being a man of influence, he prevailed upon a large number of his neighbors and friends to remove with him. He sailed from Dublin in a vessel called the George and Anne, in May, 1729, and, by a receipt preserved among his papers, it seems that he paid for the passages of ninety-four persons.

They were unfortunate in the selection of a vessel. The captain was a violent and unprincipled villain. They were poorly supplied with stores, and, the voyage proving long, they suffered from disease and famine. A large number of passengers died, including a son and daughter of Mr. Clinton. They were finally landed upon the coast of Massachusetts, the captain refusing to go to New York or to Pennsylvania, the latter having been his original place of destination. Charles Clinton remained in Massachusetts until 1731, when he removed to the province of New York, and settled at a place called Little Britain, in a region designated as the precincts of the Highlands, afterwards a part of Ulster, and now a part of Orange County. Though within a few miles of the Hudson River, and within sixty or seventy miles of the city of New York, the residence of Mr. Clinton was on the frontier of civilization. The virgin wilderness was around him. In the language of some of the inhabitants of Ulster County after this period, in a petition to the colonial legislature asking for protection, they say that they are bounded on the west by the desert—a desert where, instead of the roaming Arab, the wild Indian erected his cabin, and "made his home and his grave." The inhabitants of that district were compelled to fortify their houses in order to guard against inroads of the savages. In the subsequent Indian and French wars Charles Clinton took an active and efficient part. In 1758 we find him in command of a regiment of provincial troops, stationed in the valley of the Mohawk, and in the summer of that year he joined the main army under General Bradstreet, on his way to Canada, and was present with him at the capture of Fort Frontenac. Colonel Charles Clinton was a good mathematical scholar, and frequently acted as surveyor of lands, an employment of considerable importance and emolument in a new country. He was also a judge of the court of common pleas of Ulster County. He sustained a pure and elevated character, was neat in his person and dignified in his manners, and exerted a great influence in the district of country where he lived.

In a letter to his son James, who was in the army,

dated June, 1759, he says: "My advice to you is, to be diligent in your duty to God, your king and country, and avoid bad company as much as in your province lies; forbear learning habits of vice, for they grow too easily upon men in a public station, and are not easily broke off. Profane habits make men contemptible and mean. That God may grant you grace to live in his fear, and to discharge your duty with a good conscience, is the sincere desire of your affectionate father, Charles Clinton." Among his papers carefully preserved and written upon parchment, I found the following certificate. It was his Christian passport, which he carried with him when he embarked for the New World:

"Whereas the bearer, Mr. Charles Clinton, and his wife Elizabeth, lived within the bounds of this Protestant dissenting congregation from their infancy, and now design for America; this is to certify, that all along they behaved themselves soberly and inoffensively, and are fit to be received into any Christian congregation where Providence may cast their lot. Also, that said Charles Clinton was a member of our session, and discharged the office of ruling elder very acceptably; this, with advice of session, given at Corbay, in the county of Longford, Ireland. Joseph Bond, minister."

I need scarcely add that Charles Clinton took an active part in the advancement of the cause of religion and good morals. He sometimes also courted the muses, and I find in the commonplace-book of De Witt Clinton the following stanzas, with this caption:

Lines written by my grandfather, Charles Clinton, and spoken over the grave of a dear departed sister, who had often nursed and taken care of him in his younger days.

"Oh, canst thou know, thou dear departed shade,
The mighty sorrows that my soul invade;
Whilst o'er thy mouldering frame I mourning stand,
And view thy grave far from thy native land.
With thee my tender years were early trained;
Oft have thy friendly arms my weight sustained;
And when with childish fears or pains oppressed,
You with soft music lulled my soul to rest."

He concludes his last will, made in 1771, and a short time before his decease, with the following directions: "It is my will I be buried in the grave-yard on my own farm, beside my daughter Catharine; and it is my will, the said grave-yard be made four rods square, and open free road to it at all times when it shall be necessary; and I nominate and appoint my said three sons, Charles, James and George, executors of this my last will, to see the same executed accordingly; and I order that my said executors procure a suitable stone to lay over my grave, whereon I would have the time of my death, my age, and coat of arms cut. I hope they will indulge me in this last piece of vanity." He died on the 19th of November, 1773, at his own residence, in the 83d year of his age, and in the full view of that Revolution in which his sons were to act such distinguished parts. In his last moments he conjured them to stand by the liberties of America.

His wife, Elizabeth Denniston, to whom he was married in Ireland, was an accomplished and intelligent woman. Her correspondence with her husband, as far as it has fallen under my observation, exhibits her in an interesting and commanding light. She appears to have been well acquainted with the military operations of the times, and to have shared largely in the patriotic ardor of her husband and her sons. She died at the residence of her son James, on the 25th of December, 1779, in the 75th year of her age.

They left four sons, Alexander, Charles, James and George. The two former were physicians of considerable eminence. Charles was a surgeon in the British navy at the capture of the Havana. Of George Clinton, it will not of course be expected that I should speak at length. He was the youngest son. He was a soldier and a statesman. He was engaged in the French war and in the Revolution; he was a member of the Provincial Assembly just before the Revolution, and in that body was a fearless advocate of his country's liberty. He was the first governor of the State of New York, and for twenty-one years was continued in that high and responsible office, and exerted, perhaps, a larger influence than any other man over the then future destinies of the Empire State. He closed his eventful life while filling the chair of Vice President of the United States.

James Clinton, the third son, and the father of De Witt Clinton, was born on the 9th of August, 1736, at the family residence in Little Britain. It has truly been said of him, that he was a warrior from his youth upward. Born upon the frontiers, with a hardy and vigorous constitution; accustomed to alarms and Indian incursions, he became in early life attached to the profession of arms. As early as 1757 he was commissioned an ensign, and in the following year he was commissioned first lieutenant by James Delancey, lieutenant governor of this, then, province, and empowered to enlist troops; and in 1759, being then twenty-three years of age, he attained the rank of captain in the provincial army. In 1758 a considerable army, under General Bradstreet, passed up the Mohawk valley, and thence to Lake Ontario, and, by a well-directed attack, captured Fort Frontenac, from the French. Colonel Charles Clinton was at this time in command of Fort Herkimer, near the German Flats, in the Mohawk valley, and, as I have heretofore mentioned, joined General Bradstreet with his regiment. James Clinton was also in this expedition, and he commanded a company, his brother George being lieutenant. At the attack upon Fort Frontenac he exhibited an intrepidity of character which gained him great credit. He and his brother were instrumental in capturing one of the French vessels. The capture of this fort was one of the brilliant exploits of the French war.

Colonel Charles Clinton states in his journal, that the "destruction of this place, (meaning Fort Frontenac,) and of the shipping, artillery and stores, is one of the greatest blows the French have met with in America, considering the consequences of it, as it was the store out of which all the forts to the southward were supplied; and the shipping destroyed there, they employed in that service." The expedition was conducted with secrecy, and the French were taken unprepared. The fort contained but a small garrison, and was carried the second day after the commencement of the siege. Similar expeditions were common in that war. Armies plunged into the wilderness and forced their way up streams and over morasses with great labor and difficulty. The province of New York was the principal battle-ground. Fortresses were erected on the whole then northern frontier, extending from Lake George through the valley of the Mohawk, and along the shores of Lake Ontario to the vicinity of the great cataract itself. The Englishman and the Anglo-American fought side by side against France and her dependencies, and it seemed at times as if the fate of nations three thousand miles removed, was to be decided by the hot contests of their armies amid the green forests of this western world.

It is to be hoped that the persevering and able author of the life of the great captain of the Six Nations will follow out his original plan, and give to the world a full and accurate narrative of the thrilling scenes and romantic incidents of these early border wars.

From 1758 to 1763, James Clinton continued in the provincial army, now stationed upon the frontier posts engaged in the border skirmishes, and now enlisting new recruits under orders from the colonial governors, Sir Charles Handy, James Delancey, and Cadwallader Colden. In the latter year, 1763, he raised and commanded a corps of two hundred men, who were designated as *guards of the frontier*. He continued in the army until the close of the French war, and seems to have enjoyed, in a large degree, the confidence of the government and of his fellow-soldiers.

After the close of the war he retired to his farm at Little Britain, and married Mary De Witt, a daughter of Egbert De Witt, a young lady of great respectability, whose ancestors were from Holland. He had four sons by this marriage: Alexander, who was private secretary to his uncle George; Charles, who was a lawyer in Orange County; De Witt, the third son, born in March, 1769; and George, who was also a lawyer and a member of Congress, all of whom are now deceased.

James Clinton, however, in time of peace, could not entirely forsake the tented field. He entered with zeal into the militia organization, and was a lieutenant colonel of a regiment in Orange County. At the commencement of the Revolutionary war he entered warmly into the continental service. His brother George, as has been related, had been for many years a representative in the colonial assembly from his native county, and had, from the first, advocated his country's cause with that fearlessness and energy of character for which he was distinguished.

The two brothers were not unmindful of the dying injunctions of their patriotic sire, and hand in hand, at the first moment of outbreak, they entered the arena and joined their pledges of faith and support to the colonial cause.

In 1775 James Clinton was appointed colonel of the third regiment of New York troops, raised by the order of the Continental Congress; and in 1776 he was promoted to the rank of brigadier general. In the summer of this year he was employed in the expedition against Canada, under General Montgomery, and was before the walls of Quebec at the time of the fall of that brave and gallant general. In the summer of 1777, that gloomy period when almost the whole force of the British armies in America was concentrated upon the State of New York, General Clinton was stationed at Fort Montgomery, upon the Hudson River, and, together with his brother the governor, made a firm though unsuccessful resistance to the advance of the enemy, under Sir Henry Clinton.

The attack upon this fort, and also upon Fort Clinton, separated only by a creek, was made on the 6th of October, 1777, by an army of three thousand men. Some outposts had been carried during the day.

"As the night was approaching," says Sir Henry Clinton in his official dispatch, "I determined to seize the first favorable instant. A brisk attack on the Montgomery side; the galleys with their oars approaching, firing, and even striking the fort; the men-of-war that moment appearing, crowding all sail to support us; the extreme ardor of the troops; in short, all determined me to order the attack." The attack was continued until eight o'clock in the evening, when the enemy carried the forts by storm, and at the point of the bayonet. General Clinton, in the midst of the darkness and confusion, though wounded, succeeded in making his escape. These forts were intended to guard the navigation of the river, and to prevent the ascent of the enemy's ships, and were said not to have been well protected on the land side. Be this as it may, they were not sufficiently garrisoned. As early as March, General Clinton wrote to General McDougal, saying, "I understand the committee are uneasy at the want of stores in this fort, but I think they have more reason to be uneasy that we are not reinforced with more troops, as we have not a sufficiency to do the usual duty of the garrison on each side of the creek." It is presumed that they were better supplied with troops at the time of the attack, but there was still a deficiency. The time of service of many of the troops had expired, and they were with difficulty prevailed upon to remain. The campaign of the north also required the flower of the army. The conduct of George Clinton and James Clinton, in this defense, received the approbation of Congress.

During the greater part of 1778 General Clinton was stationed at West Point, and for a portion of that year was engaged in throwing a chain across the Hudson to prevent the ascent of the river by the enemy's ships. The summer of that year has been rendered memorable upon the then frontiers, by reason of the massacres of Wyoming and Cherry Valley, under armies of Indians and Tories, led on by the Butlers and Brant. On the 16th of November, 1778, and just after the massacre at Cherry Valley, which occurred on the 11th of that month, General Washington wrote to General Hand, acknowledging the receipt of his letter containing the information of the destruction of that place, and adds: "It is in the highest degree distressing to have our frontiers so continually harassed by this collection of banditti under Brant and Butler." He then inquires whether offensive operations could not be carried on against them at that season of the year, and if not then, when and how? This letter was probably referred to General Clinton, as it has been preserved among his papers; and it contains the first intimation which I have seen of that expedition against the Six Nations in the following year, known as Sullivan's expedition, in which General Clinton was called to act a distinguished part.

It was determined to "carry the war into Africa." In other words, it was resolved to overrun the whole Indian country, and thus, if possible, put an end to the constant and harassing inroads of the enemy upon the frontier settlements. For this purpose extensive preparations were made, and after some difficulty in obtaining a commander, the expedition was intrusted to General Sullivan. It was decided that the army should move early in the spring of 1779. General Sullivan was to cross to Easton, in Pennsylvania, and into the valley of the Susquehanna, while General Clinton was to pass up the Mohawk valley, and either unite with Sullivan in the Indian country, or else cross over from the Mohawk River to Lake Otsego, and proceed thence down the eastern branch of the Susquehanna. The latter route was finally determined upon, though General Washington preferred the former, as did General Clinton. The latter gave as his reasons, that the army could move up the Mohawk valley and enter the Indian country with more ease and less delay, and that a movement in that direction would be more decisive and fatal to the Indians. The whole expedition was, however, under the control of General Sullivan, who preferred the other route, and it was adopted.

On the 1st of June, 1779, General Clinton's detachment, consisting of about two thousand troops, moved from Albany and proceeded up the Mohawk valley as far as Canajoharie. Here they pitched their camp, and with great labor carried over their boats and stores to the head of Lake Otsego, a distance of nearly twenty miles.

While encamped at Canajoharie, two spies were arrested, and a court-martial ordered to try them. Their names were Hare and Newberry. They were both natives of that section of country, and had been with the parties of Indians and Tories who had laid waste the settlements. Newberry was a sergeant in one of the organized companies of Tories, and was engaged in the massacre at Cherry Valley, where he killed a daughter of a Mr. Mitchell under circumstances of cruelty almost unparalleled.

A party of Indians had plundered the house, and murdered his wife and children. After they left, Mitchell returned to the house and found one child, a little girl about eleven or twelve years of age, who was still alive. He carried her to the door, and while engaged in endeavoring to restore her to consciousness, he saw another party approaching. He again retreated, and from his hiding-place saw Newberry, with a blow of his hatchet, extinguish the little spark of life that remained in his child. Retributive justice often follows close on the heels of crime. At this court-martial for the trial of Newberry, Mitchell was called as a witness.

If I possessed the wand of the great magician, I might draw aside the curtain and present to your view this court-martial scene. I might show to you the rough soldier brushing away a tear, and the pale cheek and quivering lip of the guilty Newberry, as the witness related the simple and affecting story of his sufferings, of the destruction of all his earthly hopes, of that massacre which had widowed him, and sent him forth upon the world homeless and childless.

Both Hare and Newberry were found guilty and hung as spies, and their execution, says General Clinton, gave great satisfaction to the inhabitants. Their bodies were given to their friends for interment, and were placed in coffins, which were laid upon the ground-floor of a house near the place of execution. While the bodies were lying in that situation, it was alleged that a large black snake ran hissing from the wall of the house, and, passing around or over the body of Newberry, glided away and disappeared in the opposite wall. The tradition was current a few years since, and I have myself heard the statement from the lips of the living actors of that period. The story is also alluded to by De Witt Clinton, in his journal which he kept when exploring the canal route in 1810. The report of this, as was supposed, appearance of his satanic majesty himself, to convey away the soul of Sergeant Newberry, produced a strong impression upon the minds of many of the unlettered and superstitous Germans of the Mohawk valley.

I cannot forbear, in this place, to pay a passing tribute to some of these Germans, whose advice General Clinton was requested to take, who were educated men, and who supported the American cause with great zeal and courage.

Among them was the Rev. Dr. Gross, the clergyman at Canajoharie, and Christopher P. Yates and John Frey, both lawyers, and residents in that vicincity. After the war, the Rev. Dr. Gross was chosen one of the professors of Columbia College, and I cannot present to you so correct and beautiful an outline of his character as is drawn by De Witt Clinton, in his address before the alumni of that college, which has never been printed, and which was the last of his literary efforts.

"The Rev. Dr. Gross," says Governor Clinton, "a native of Germany, and who had received a finished education in her celebrated schools, was a professor of the German language and geography, and afterwards a professor of moral philosophy. He had emigrated to this country before the Revolution and settled near the banks of the Mohawk, in a frontier country, peculiarly exposed to irruptions from Canada and the hostile Indians. When war commenced, he took the side of America, and, enthroned in the hearts of his countrymen, and distinguished for the courage which marks the German character, he rallied the desponding, animated the wavering, confirmed the doubtful, and encouraged the brave to more than ordinary exertion. With the Bible in one hand and the sword in the other, he stood forth in the united character of patriot and Christian, vindicating the liberties of mankind, and amidst the most appalling dangers, ana the most awful vicissitudes, like the Red Cross Knight of the Fairy Queen,

> 'Right faithful true he was, in deed and word.'"

Such was the Rev. Dr. Gross, at the time of which we have been speaking.

Another of the Germans of the Mohawk valley was Christopher P. Yates, an early and ardent friend of the Revolution. He was a lawyer by profession, and some of the resolutions drawn up by him, and adopted by the committees of safety, were patriotic in sentiment and fearless in tone, and would have done no discredit to any provincial assembly, or even to the Continental Congress itself.

Another of these Germans was Major John Frey, a brother-in-law of Christopher P. Yates, and the last chairman of the Tryon County committee. He was one of the most prominent and active of the revolutionary patriots of the Mohawk valley ; and I trust I shall be excused, by an indulgent auditory, for sketching the interview which it was my good fortune to have with him several years since.

It was in the winter of 1830, that I presented myself at the mansion of Major Frey, and desired an interview for the purpose of conferring with him, and of obtaining such manuscripts as he might have preserved.

Age and infirmity then sat heavily upon him. In the language of the good old Oneida chief, Skenando, he was like an aged pine, through whose branches had whistled the winds of an hundred winters. Like Skenando, also, the generation which had acted with him had gone and left him.

My own ancestors had sat in committee with him, and had shared in the toils, and in the fearful and bloody contests of the border. I never shall forget the appearance of this gray-haired sire as I entered his room, and was kindly introduced to him by his son, as a descendant of one of his co-laborers in the Revolution. His son explained to him at the same time, briefly, the object of my visit. He was entirely blind, and nearly deaf, so much so that it required a loud voice to rouse him. As soon as he understood his son fully, like a patriarch of old, he rose up, and extending his trembling hand, requested that I would draw near to him that he might touch me. His fervent language was, "God bless you, my son, and prosper you in your undertaking. Your grandfather and myself fought side by side in the Revolution. I have somewhere several papers which may assist you. They are yours—keep them." In a neglected spot in the garret, from a mass of unimportant and moth-eaten papers, I selected several documents of great interest, and which were of much service in throwing light upon the history of the valley, especially many of the proceedings of the Committee of Safety during the early part of the war.

A few years after this interview, the good old patriot was called to his rest, but the impression will pass away from my memory only with the decay of the faculty itself.

But I am wandering too much from my subject. On the 1st of July, General Clinton broke up his camp at Canajoharie, and crossed over to Lake Otsego, where his boats and stores had previously been carried, and, launching his boats, passed down to the outlet, and again encamped upon the spot where now is built the beautiful village of Cooperstown, the Templeton of the Pioneers. Two hundred and eight batteaux, and a large amount of provisions and military stores, had been carried across from the Mohawk River. Here, under date of 13th of July, General Clinton writes to Mrs. Clinton, saying that she probably expects that the army is in the midst of the Indian country, but that he is still waiting orders to move; that he is impatient for them, but that his situation is by no means unpleasant; that he can catch perch in in the lake and trout in the streams, and hunt the deer upon the mountains. Lake Otsego is a beautiful little lake, about nine miles long, and varies in breadth from one to three miles. Its elevation is about twelve hundred feet above tide water, and it is almost embosomed by hills; the water is deep and clear. The scenery from many points is highly picturesque and wild.

"Tall rocks and tufted knolls, their face
Could on the dark blue mirror trace."

At this period, save in one or two places, no mark of civilization was visible. And though

"Each boatman bending to his oar,
With measured sweep the burthen bore,"

they could not but gaze at times with delight upon the natural beauties which surrounded them.

The outlet of this lake is narrow. General Clinton

having passed his boats through, caused a dam to be thrown across; the lake was raised several feet; a party was sent forward to clear the river of drift-wood; when ready to move, the dam was broken up, and the boats glided swiftly down with the current.

On the 22d of August, this division arrived at Tioga, and joined the main army under General Sullivan.

On the 26th of August, the whole army moved from Tioga up the river of that name, and on the 29th fell in with the enemy at Newtown. Here a spirited engagement took place, in which the enemy was routed; this was the only battle. When it was first announced that an army was marching into their country, the Indians laughed at their supposed folly, believing it impossible for a regular army to traverse the wilderness and drive them from their fastnesses.

On the 14th of September the army arrived at the Genesee River; and the rich alluvial bottom lands, which now constitute the garden of this State, had even then been extensively cultivated by the Indians. Scarcely a tree was to be seen over the whole extent. Modern curiosity and enterprise had not then rendered familiar the mighty valleys and prairies of the West; and officers and soldiers gazed alike with surprise and admiration upon the rich prospect before them. The army, as it emerged from the woods, and as company after company filed off and formed upon the plain, presented an animated and imposing spectacle.

The whole country of the Onondagas, the Cayugas and Senecas was overrun by this expedition. Vast quantities of grain were destroyed; all the Indian villages were laid waste; and it was fondly hoped that the Indians, driven back, and having lost their provisions and stores, would be prevented from making further inroads into the border settlements. This was not considered merely as a retaliatory measure. The western part of New York was the granary from whence the Indians and Tories drew their supplies. Cut off from these, it was thought they would be driven back into Canada, and that a stop would be put to further incursions.

Such, however, unfortunately for the frontier settlements, was not the effect. In the following summer these incursions were renewed; and they were continued throughout the war. For nearly eight years the inhabitants were kept in almost constant alarm, and were the victims of this barbarous warfare until they became a peeled and scattered people. The whole valley of the Mohawk, including the valley of Schoharie, and all the settlements to the south upon the head-waters of the Susquehanna, were entirely destroyed. There was not a spot which had escaped the ravages of the enemy.

"It was the computation," says the author of the Life of Brant, "two years before the close of the war, that one third of the population had gone over to the enemy, and that one third had been driven from the country or slain in battle, and by private assassination. And yet among the inhabitants of the other remaining third, in June, 1783, it was stated at a public meeting held at Fort Plain, that there were three hundred widows and two thousand orphan children." In great justice and truth he has added, "that no other section or district of country in the United States, of like extent, suffered in any comparable degree as much from the war of the Revolution as did that of the Mohawk. It was the most frequently invaded and overrun, and that too by an enemy far more barbarous than the native barbarians of the forest."

In the early part of 1780, the year following the expedition against the Six Nations, General Clinton was stationed upon the Hudson River. In October, of that year, and after the discovery of the treason of Arnold, General Washington wrote to General Clinton, then at West Point, as follows:

"As it is necessary there should be an officer in whom the State has confidence to take the general direction of affairs at Albany and on the frontier, I have fixed upon you for this purpose, and request you will proceed to Albany without delay, and assume the command. You will be particularly attentive to the post of Fort Schuyler, and do everything in your power to have it supplied with a good stock of provisions and stores, and you will take every other precaution the means at your command will permit, for the security of the frontier, giving the most early advice of any incursions of the enemy."

General Clinton repaired to Albany, and took the direction of affairs in the northern department, according to the instructions of the commander-in-chief. That post had been one of great responsibility during the whole of the war, and at the time of General Clinton's appointment it had not lost its importance.

The spring of 1781 found the American army, and especially that portion of it stationed at the north and west, almost destitute of provisions. This arose in part from some defective arrangement in the commissary department, and in part from the fact, that the whole Mohawk valley had been laid waste, which was one of the best sources of supplies in the earlier part of the war. General Clinton communicated intelligence of the destitute condition of the army to General Washington, early in the spring of that year, and, under date of May 4th, the commander-in-chief replied, saying, "he had received and read his letter, and transmitted it to Congress to aid in enforcing his own suggestions. That measures must be taken to procure provisions, and where persuasion, entreaty and requisition fail, coercion must be used, rather than the garrison of Fort Schuyler shall fall, and the frontier be again desolated and laid waste. I am persuaded the State will make a great effort to afford a supply of flour for the troops in that quarter; and I confess I see no other alternative under our present circumstances."

Coercion was used in order to procure supplies of provisions, and coercion saved the American army from dismemberment during the summer of 1781.

In a letter of a subsequent date, General Washington says, "whenever any quantity arrives you may depend upon having a full proportion of it, being determined to share our last morsel with you, and support your posts, if possible, at all hazards and extremities."

The situation of the army at the north was deplorable indeed. The different detachments were stationed not where they were needed for defense, but where they could procure supplies of provisions. The enemy, taking advantage of the trials and sufferings of the soldiers, made great efforts to produce disaffection and desertion in their ranks. Emissaries were sent among them, and the Tories, especially, were active in their efforts. In this they were but too successful, and General Clinton, in a letter dated in May, says, that unless the army is relieved, so prevalent is the spirit of desertion, every post must be abandoned and the country depopulated.

Under this impression, General Clinton determined upon taking decisive measures, which should strike terror into the hearts of the disaffected and Tories, and by executing summary punishment, to prevent, at least, their active interference in causing the desertion of the soldiers.

The following letter to Captain Du Bois, under date of June 1st, 1781, will more fully convey his views:

"Sir: I have received your letter of yesterday. From good information, I am well convinced that parties of the enemy are out on the recruiting service, and that they are protected, harbored, and subsisted, by the disaffected people on the frontiers. I am informed by a letter this morning received from the commanding officer at Johnstown, that several Tories have been apprehended at that place for encouraging our soldiers to desert, and for subsisting them in their habitations until they can have an opportunity to join the enemy. I therefore desire, that as soon as you can be thoroughly convinced of any disaffected persons in your quarter being guilty of either seducing any of our soldiers to desert, or subsisting or harboring them when deserted, you will not be at the pains of taking them prisoners, but kill them on the spot. If, also, you should find any of them to harbor parties from the enemy, by which means any of our good frontier inhabitants do in person get killed, you will also retaliate vengeance on them, *life for life.*

"I have issued and forwarded these orders to the different posts, which you may promulge, and not secrete, that the Tories may know their fate for their future misbehavior.

"I soon expect better supplies of men and provisions."

These measures, it is believed, had a salutary effect.

General Clinton continued in command at Albany until August, 1781, when he embarked the troops immediately under his command, for the purpose of joining the commander-in-chief, and was succeeded in the command of the northern army by General Stark.

In the winter or spring of 1782, some promotions were made by the Continental Congress, by which a junior officer took precedence over General Clinton. The veteran soldier could not brook what he deemed a great injury. He solicited and obtained leave to withdraw from the active duties of the camp. In a letter dated April 10, 1782, General Clinton says:

"At an early period of the war I entered into the

service of my country, and I have continued in it during all the vicissitudes of fortune, and am conscious that I have exerted my best endeavors to serve it with fidelity. I have never sought emolument or promotion, and as the different commands I have held were unsolicited, I might have reasonably expected, if my services were no longer wanted, to have been indulged at least with a decent dismission."

He did not retire from the army entirely, but joined again the commander-in-chief, and was present at the evacuation of New York, where he took leave of General Washington, and retired to his farm at Little Britain. The war was happily terminated, and peace again reigned along the borders.

Then followed what has been well denominated the night of the confederation. In the midst of war, and while pressed by foes from without, the inefficiency of the articles of confederation were not so fully realized. But now darkness shrouded the future, or if that future portended aught, it portended a broken and dismembered confederacy.

The convention which assembled at Philadelphia in May, 1787, for the purpose of forming a federal constitution, arose like the day-star upon this benighted land. The convention of New York, called to ratify this constitution presented by the convention of Philadelphia, assembled at Poughkeepsie in June, 1788, and it embraced men, in themselves a host, and the mention of whose names should excite emotions of patriotism and of pride in the bosom of every New Yorker. There were John Jay, Alexander Hamilton, George Clinton, John Lansing, Robert R. Livingston,

James Clinton, Melancthon Smith, James Duane, Samuel Jones, with others of less note, but well known in those times for their sterling patriotism. Among the number were Christopher P. Yates and John Frey, to whom I have heretofore alluded, and who represented in convention the then county of Montgomery.

George Clinton and General James Clinton were delegates from Ulster County. George Clinton was unanimously chosen president of the convention. The debates were continued for six weeks, with all the talent and address of the distinguished speakers whose names I have mentioned.

On the side of the constitution were John Jay, Alexander Hamilton and Robert R. Livingston, and opposed to its unconditional adoption were George Clinton, Melancthon Smith and John Lansing. General James Clinton united with his brother George, and to the last they both persisted in their opposition, even when many of those who at first acted with them had joined the other party, and were in favor of an unconditional adoption of the constitution.

George Clinton stated, that in times of trouble and difficulty men were always in danger of passing to extremes; that while he admitted the confederation to be weak and inefficient, and entirely inadequate for the purposes of union, he at the same time feared that the new constitution, proposed to be adopted, would give too much power to the federal government. The sturdy democrat foresaw that powers were conferred upon the executive of the Union by that constitution which could be used, with almost irresistible force, for good or for evil; and had his life been spared to have witnessed its operation until the close of the first half century of its existence, he would have learned that his prophesy, to some extent at least, had become history. It was under the views above stated that both the Clintons voted in convention against the unconditional adoption of the present federal constitution. They were in favor of a modification, or of only a qualified adoption.

When the constitution was adopted and became the supreme law of the land, they both supported and cherished it with their usual decision and energy of character.

General James Clinton was afterwads called to fill several imporant stations. He was elected a member of the State Senate, a member of the convention to revise the constitution, and was appointed a commissioner to run the boundary line between New York and Pennsylvania. While engaged in this latter service he was treated with marked attention by the Indians in the western part of New York, in consequence of his having been, as they considered, a brave soldier. They recollected him as having been engaged in Sullivan's expedition, and described his dress and the horse which he rode in the battle of Newtown; and they offered to bestow upon him a tract of land, and desired his permission to apply to the legislature for liberty to make a conveyance to him. Their offer was declined, but it was a flattering compliment, coming as it did from those who had been enemies, and whose country had been laid waste partly by his instrumentality.

With the exceptions above mentioned, the residue of General Clinton's life, after the war, was spent in peaceful retirement upon his estate at Little Britian.

He died at his residence in 1812, just at the commencement of another war. He had seen his country under all the vicissitudes of good and evil fortune.

The pen of his illustrious son has recorded his epitaph, and thus beautifully sums up his character:

"His life was principally devoted to the military service of his country, and he had filled with fidelity and honor several distinguished civil offices.

"He was an officer in the revolutionary war, and the war preceding, and at the close of the former was a major general in the army of the United States. He was a good man and a sincere patriot, performing in the most exemplary manner all the duties of life, and he died, as he had lived, without fear and without reproach."

NOTE O.

CENTENNIAL ADDRESS,

Delivered at Cherry Valley, Otsego County, N. Y., July 4th, 1840, by William W. Campbell.

THE announcement that the great poet, novelist, and historian of Scotland was no more, produced a thrilling emotion throughout the civilized world. Gifted pens in both hemispheres paid noble tributes to his memory, and the beautiful idea was conceived of grouping together and presenting at a single glance the most prominent characters, both fictitious and historical, which had been created and adorned by the genius of the immortal SCOTT. While he lay in state in the proud halls of Abbotsford, there passed in long procession the monarch with his retinue, displaying the pomp and pageantry of the Middle Ages—the belted knight clad in steel, marching with a warrior's step, and accompanied by his lady love—old men and maidens—noble and ignoble, the Jew, the Christian, and the Pagan—each in their turn, as they moved past, casting a last look upon the mortal remains of him whose name, as long as letters endure, can never perish from the earth. But as they come up in review before our own minds, do we not intuitively select some of the most humble and lowly as objects of imitation and of love. Forgetting the proud array of titles and of names, we call up with earnest and admiring feelings the artless simplicity and heroic fortitude of that noble specimen of female character, the Jeanie Deans in the Heart of Mid-Lothian.

My fellow citizens, we are assembled this day at the close of the first century since the settlement of Cherry Valley. We are here on the anniversary of our nation's birthday to mark down the closing hours of that century, and, ere they are all numbered, to sketch out and place on record the scenes, and actions, and events, and characters to which it has given birth in our little valley. It has become my duty, as it is my pleasure, to make up that record which may aid in fixing this day as a landmark for the guidance and direction of those who may come after us. If in the brief review of the century which is just passing away I shall present no gorgeous spectacle—no long train of titled lords and warrior knights, I may be able to sketch characters which shall commend themselves by their intelligence, their morals, their courage, and their undying patriotism. Plain and humble though they may have been, and confined within a narrow sphere of action, they were eminent in their respective stations—they discharged with ability the duties which devolved upon them, and have passed away and left their impress upon this the place of their and your habitation.

Most of the first settlers of this valley, though originally from Scotland, emigrated to North America from Ireland. Some of them came in what was called the Londonderry emigration. A portion of this body of emigrants landed in the spring of 1719, at Casco Bay, near the present city of Porland, in Maine. Like most of the New England colonists, they sought a home and a place to worship God. Immediately upon landing from their vessel, under the open heaven, and upon the sea-shore, they commenced the worship of their Creator. The sands of a new continent were beneath their feet. The waves of the Atlantic were dashing around them. The sky of the new world was over them.

"The perfect world by Adam trod,
Was the first temple built by God;
His fiat laid the corner-stone,
And heaved its pillars one by one."

In this temple our fathers first worshipped God in this western land. Standing on the shore of the ocean, with their little bark riding near them, they raised their voices and sung the 137th psalm of the sweet singer of Israel. As they looked back upon the homes of their youth—upon the friends and kindred left behind—upon the blessings and comforts of civil ization, well might they sing: "*By the waters of Babylon, there we sat down, yea, we wept, when we remembered Zion. We hanged our harps upon the willows in the midst thereof.*"

But they looked forward with hope and constancy, and as they remembered their covenant vows, and their determination to observe and maintain their religious duties, they also united and sung, in the sublime language of the Psalmist: "*If I forget thee, O Jerusalem, let my right hand forget her cunning. If I do not remember thee, let my tongue cleave to the roof of my mouth; if I prefer not Jerusalem above my chief joy.*"

On application made by this colony to the Supreme Judicial Court of Massachusetts, a tract of land was granted them, to which they removed in the summer of the same year. The settlement was named after the place from whence they sailed, and still retains the name of Londonderry, now in the southern part of New Hampshire. The colonists immediately organized a society, settled a minister, and commenced laying broad and deep the foundations of religion and of civil order. Many of the early settlers of Cherry Valley removed from this Londonderry colony in 1741–2; the first actual settlement having been made by Mr. Lindesay, one of the patentees, in 1740.

The patent of Cherry Valley was granted in 1738, by George Clark, then lieutenant governor of the province of New York, with consent of the council, to John Lindesay, Jacob Roseboom, and others. The patentees probably re-leased a portion of the land to Governor Clark, as we find tiers of lots still owned by his lineal descendants in this county.

It has been cause of speculation and inquiry, why the patentees sought a patent of land so remote as this place then was, lying, as it did, beyond unoccupied lands more eligibly situated and of greater value. It has been said that Mr. Lindesay, the principal patentee, was pleased with the wild and romantic features of the country, which were not unlike his native Scotland. We can easily imagine that at that early day, ere the woodman's axe had broken into the forest, the scene which our little valley presented was one of quiet and picturesque beauty. Here was the purling brook, the cascade, the rock and dell, the the beautiful forest tree, the blossoming cherry, and the wild mountain flower. The tall and graceful elm rose conspicuous in the valley, while the dark foliage of the rock maple and the evergreen marked the elevation of the surrounding hills. From the summit of those hills the eye took in at a glance a large part of the valley of the Mohawk, and, stretching on beyond, were seen the Sacondaga mountains on the north, and far away in the northeast the Green Mountains of Vermont. A few German families were scatterod along the banks of the Mohawk, but on leaving that river the emigrant or settler found himself at once in the midst of the virgin forest. The whole country called by us the great west, the vast valley of the Mississippi, was almost a *terra incognita*, an unknown land. An occasional adventurer had made his way into the interior, and had engaged in traffick with the aboriginal inhabitants, who claimed as owners, and roamed over the wide valleys and prairies. A few others, less hardy and enterprising, had passed along the shores of the great lakes, and, like Moses upon Mount Pisgah, caught a distant view of the promised land. A few French from Canada had intermarried with the native population, and introduced some slight features of civilization among the red men of the forest. With these exceptions, the whole country west of Cherry Valley, reaching on to the Pacific Ocean, was one unbroken wilderness.

Attracted more perhaps by the beauty of the scenery than by the fertility of the soil, here Mr. Lindesay took up his abode in the summer of 1740. An Indian foot-path afforded him communication with the Mohawk River. The winter which followed was one of great severity. Long ere spring revisited the valley his provisions were exhausted. The snow had fallen to a great depth, and had entirely interrupted his intercourse with the settlements of the Mohawk. The fierce winds howled around his frail dwelling. The gigantic forest trees glistened with the frosts of winter. The beauty of the summer scene had faded away. He realized in their greatest extent the dangers and trials of a borderer. A lingering death for himself and family by starvation was before him. At this critical period an Indian arrived from the Mohawk River on snow-shoes. This Indian returned and procured provisions, which he carried to Mr. Lindesay upon his back, and thus saved the lives of the first family which settled in this valley.

About the time of his first settlement, Mr. Lindesay conferred with the Rev. Samuel Dunlop, a native of Ireland, and a graduate of Trinity College, Dublin, upon the subject of adding to the settlement through his influence with his countrymen at home and in this country. Mr. Dunlop went to Ireland and returned in 1742. He was married in Ireland, and his young wife came with him to pitch their tents in the wilderness. At the same time Mr. Dickson and Mr. Galt, and families, arrived in company with Mr. Dunlop from Ireland, and Mr. Ramsey and James Campbell with their families, in the same year arrived from Londonderry in New Hampshire. Mr. Dickson and Mr. Galt purchased farms in the south part of the patent; Mr. Ramsey in the western part, and James Campbell purchased a farm north of the village, now owned by his grandson James S. Campbell, Esq. Mr. Dunlop purchased the farm formerly owned and occupied by Dr. Joseph White, and now owned and occupied by his son-in-law Jacob Livingston, Esq.

It may here be observed, that one of the first movements of this little colony was the organization of a church, under the pastoral charge of Mr. Dunlop, and the erection of a rude edifice of logs, in which they assembled to worship the God of their fathers. In his own house Mr. Dunlop opened a classical school, and there educated some young men from the German families on the Mohawk, who afterward, and especially during the Revolution, acted conspicuous parts. Among the number were Col. Henry and Major John Frey. It is worthy of especial remembrance that in this valley the first regular society was organized for religious worship in the English language, and the first classical school established in central or western New York. I have not been able to find an account of any other church or school at that early day, between this place and the immediate vicinity of the Hudson River, though there may have been classical schools at Schenectady. The church organized under the patronage of Sir William Johnson, at Johnstown, was not founded until about 1765.

The conduct of our fathers in the establishment of churches and schools, is the best evidence of the spirit with which the foundations of this settlement were laid. Virtue and knowledge, the two great pillars of republican institutions, were in the very commencement the object of their pursuit. They sought to plant here, in the centre of the wilderness, the seeds of Christianity and civilization. Their aim was noble—their enterprise was worthy, and deserved success. Their numbers were small—their means were limited. But their hearts were undaunted—their courage did not forsake them—their minds had been made up for the undertaking—they resolved to be, and they were, successful.

Settlements were not then, as now, thrown forward almost with the rapidity of the earth's own motion, so that a frontier hamlet of to-day becomes a city with a densely peopled country around it to-morrow. On the contrary, the encroachments upon the wilderness, and upon the home of the red man, previous to the Revolution, were made slowly and with great caution. The white population advanced along the banks of the rivers and the margins of the tributary streams. Occasionally, as was the case with this settlement, a few families, more adventurous, might plunge further into what was then termed the *desert*, and relying for protection on the God of hosts and their own right arm, plant there the foundations of the white man's home. But the increase of these frontier settlements was very slow. In 1752, twelve years after the first settlement of Cherry Valley, there were but *eight* families in the place. In 1765, they had increased to forty families. The number in 1775, and at the commencement of the war, I do not know, but probably it did not exceed sixty families.

In 1744, Mr. John Wells removed to Cherry Valley. He purchased of Mr. Lindesay the farm occupied by him, and called Lindesay's Bush, being the same farm now owned and occupied by Mr. Joseph Phelon. Mr. Wells was a man of fine character, and was highly respected in the settlement. He was appointed the first justice of the peace. His son Robert intermarried with a daughter of the Rev. Mr. Dunlop, and of this marriage, among other children, was John Wells, one of the most distinguished and able lawyers whom the State of New York has produced. His history, I trust, is familiar to all who hear me. You have heard of the destruction of his whole family, of his subsequent labors, his comparative obscurity in his profession, until an opportunity was afforded for a display of his talents and genius, in his defense of the celebrated James Cheatham, editor of the American Citizen; when, as it were, with a single bound, he rose from that comparative obscurity to professional eminence. That distinguished lawyer always cherished a warm affection for this the place of his birth, and it was his intention, had his life been spared for a few years longer, to have purchased the property of his ancestors, and to have retired from his profession, and spent here the closing years of his life amid the scenes of his boyhood.

From 1740 down to 1775, (as has already been stated,) the population of Cherry Valley increased slowly. That period had been one of considerable excitement, alarm and trial.

The long and bloody wars between England and France had been carried forward. The battle-field was transferred from Europe to America, and the contest for national supremacy was maintained with renewed vigor amid the forest homes of our fathers, and upon their inland seas. Most of the Indian tribes at the north, allured away by the French Jesuits, and by the liberal presents of the so-styled Grand Monarch of France, took up the hatchet against the English and Americans. The frontier inhabitants were kept under almost constant apprehension, and though the settlement of Cherry Valley escaped destruction, yet the inhabitants were called into service, and exchanged the peaceable pursuits of agriculture for the excitements and dangers of the camp, and were engaged in distant and hazardous expeditions. When the war of the Revolution commenced, Cherry Valley was still a frontier settlement. A few inhabitants were settled in the present town of Springfield; a few in Middlefield, then called Newtown Martin. Along the banks of the Susquehanna, and in the valley of Unadilla and Otego creeks, a few settlers were found, and the brave and hardy family of Harpers had gone out from Cherry Valley and planted a little colony at Harpersfield; but Cherry Valley was considered the centre and gathering-place of all these settlers.

When the period arrived that the united colonies of North America were compelled to take up arms to maintain their rights, the announcement produced necessarily a deep emotion through the frontier settlements.

War at all times is to be deprecated, and, if possible, avoided. In the case of our Revolution, war became justifiable on our part. The great principles of civil and religious liberty, for which our ancestors contended in the old world, and which they sought to plant here in the new, were invaded. The crisis had arrived when their rights must be surrendered, or the question must be tried by a long and bloody civil war. The minds of men were early made up for the contest. In this section of country, the perils and trials of the inhabitants were probably greater than in any other section of the Union. The Six Nations of Indians, who early joined the English, were the most powerful and warlike of the aboriginal inhabitants. Yet, in defiance of danger, and undismayed by threats of vengeance, the inhabitants of Tryon County rallied together when the indications of the gathering storm were seen only in the distance.

If you will consider what was then the situation of that county, sparsely populated, and separated from the Hudson River and the Eastern States by a powerful tribe of Indians, and a large body of men attached to the English cause, organized and commanded by influential and experienced men, and will then look at the early proceedings of their committee of safety, you will find exhibited a fearlessness and determination of spirit almost unparalleled even in that day of self-sacrificing and heroic devotion to country. Read the proceedings of the Palatine committee, as early as 27th August, 1774, two years before the Declaration of Independence, when they asserted fearlessly their rights, and bound themselves together to abide by all the regulations of the first Continental Congress. Read the resolutions of the same committee, passed May 21st, 1775, when, in answer to the threats of Guy Johnson, then Indian superintendent, they resolved, "that as we abhor a state of slavery, we do join and unite together under all the ties of religion, honor, justice, and a love of freedom, never to become slaves, and to defend our freedom with our lives and fortunes."

When the time, the place, and the circumstances are considered under which that committee met and passed the resolutions referred to, I think you will conclude with me that they are unparalleled. In their tone and sentiment they would have done credit to any provincial assembly, or even to the Continental Congress itself. The original draft of these resolutions I found many years since in a neglected spot in the garret of the house of Major John Frey, and I have deposited the manuscript among the archives of the New York Historical Society, that it may remain as a memorial of the noble spirit of Tryon County. It is in the handwriting of Christopher P. Yates, who was an eminent and able patriot. But if he had done nothing besides being the author and advocate of these resolutions, his name and his memory should be warmly cherished in this section of country where you dwell.

Here, in Cherry Valley, the leading citizens early embraced the colonial cause. In May, 1775, the common article of association was circulated, in which the signers pledged themselves to support the Continental Congress. It is unnecessary here, and indeed I have not time to detail the progress of the war, during the first years of its continuance. A fort was erected which occupied a portion of the present burial ground, and which was garrisoned by a regiment of continental troops under the command of Col. Alden. Alarms and rumors were the order of the day. This region of country seems early to have been marked out for destruction, and the settlement of Cherry Valley, after repeated alarms, was destined to share the common fate of the frontier hamlets of New York.

The 11th of November, 1778, has been rendered memorable by the sacrifices and sufferings, and death of many of the early settlers of this valley. On the morning of that day no bright sun gilded the mountain tops with his beams, nor was the eye gladdened with the view of the rich tints of autumn. Clouds and mists were round about the homes of our fathers, as if veiling the horrid scenes which on that day were to be enacted. The gun from the fort early in the morning announced that the enemy was near. The scouts had been surprised and taken, and the yell of the Indian, and the report of his rifle, heralded his approach to the garrison. The scattered inhabitants, most of them, unarmed, strove to gain places of actual or fancied security, but generally in vain. Some reached the fort and were saved, others were pursued and slain by the wayside, and the tomahawk and scalping-knife drank the blood of others at their own fireside, and even while kneeling in prayer before their Maker. Others were retained as hostages or prisoners, to be borne away through the wilderness to take up their abode with savages, and to suffer a tedious and dreadful captivity. I have endeavored, in the history which I have heretofore presented to my fellow citizens, of the border wars of this State, to give a picture of this valley on the night succeeding the day of the massacre. The place chosen for encampment of the enemy was about two miles south of the village, and near the site of the dwelling-house of James Dickson. The prisoners were gathered around the watch-fires, drenched with the rain and sleet, and shivering with cold, with no protection from the storm. Thick darkness covered the valley, except when some gust of wind kindled a flame for a moment amid the dying embers, and thus marked the spots where once had been their homes. The mangled corpses of relatives and neighbors lay unburied around the ashes of their dwellings. Their own fate was hid from them. They knew not whether a long captivity awaited them, or whether on the morrow they should be offered up as sacrifices to appease the wrath or gratify the passions of their enemies. I can imagine no state of suspense more awful. Mercy, however, in a measure triumphed, and a portion of the prisoners were released, and the rest were carried into captivity, and enabled to return after the lapse of many years. Between thirty and forty of the inhabitants were killed on the 11th of November. It is unnecessary at this time to give their names.

On the following day their corpses were gathered together, and under the protection of the garrison were deposited in a common grave. It would have been very gratifying if, on this occasion, we could have laid the corner-stone of a monument to mark the place of their burial, and which, while it commemorated the death of those who perished on the 11th of November, 1778, might have endured also as a memorial of the anniversary which we this day celebrate.

This destruction of the settlement closed the Revolutionary drama at Cherry Valley. The small fort was abandoned in the following summer, and the troops joined General James Clinton's detachment, when on his way to join Gen. Sullivan, in the famous expedition against the Six Nations in 1779. This whole region of country was swept over by an ever active and vindictive enemy. At the close of the Revolution, and when peace was once more restored, the remnant of the inhabitants returned to their former homes, but war, and disease, and poverty had done their fearful work, and many a once familiar face was never again seen round the domestic hearth. In 1784 a few log houses were built by the inhabitants who had returned, and in the same year the immortal Washington honored our little valley with a visit. He came up from the Mohawk River for the purpose of visiting this place, and also examining the outlet of Lake Otsego, where, in 1779, Gen. James Clinton threw a dam across the Susquehanna, preparatory to his descent of that river.

It has already been stated that the first inhabitants of Cherry Valley were mostly religious people. Like the Puritans of New England they were watchful and jealous of any infraction of Christian duties. Many of my hearers will have read the letter addressed by the committee of safety of Cherry Valley to the general committee of Tryon County. It was as follows:

" *Cherry Valley, June 9th,* 1775.

" Sirs,

" We received yours of yesterday relative to the meeting of the committee on Sunday, which *surprised* us not a little, inasmuch as it seems not to be on any alarming circumstance, which, if it was, we should readily attend. But as that does not appear to us to be the case, we think it very improper; for unles the necessity of the committee sitting superexceed the duties to be performed in attending the worship of God, we think it ought to be put off till another day; and therefore we conclude not to give our attendance at this time, unless you adjourn the sitting of the committee till Monday morning, and in that case we will give our attendance as early as you please. But otherwise we cannot allow ourselves to be cut short of attending on the public worship, except the case be so necessitous as to exceed sacrifice. We conclude with wishing success to the common cause, and subscribe ourselves the free-born sons of liberty.

John Moore,
Samuel Clyde,
Samuel Campbell."

I have introduced this letter for the purpose of calling attention more particularly to a meeting of the inhabitants in 1785, after the storm of war had passed over, and when quiet and peace once more rested upon the borders. Neither war, nor exile, nor poverty had caused them to forget their Christian duties, or the importance of religious societies.

On the 5th of April, 1785, a public meeting of the citizens was held, the objects of which will be best explained by the record made at the time. It is as follows:

"We, the *ancient* inhabitants of Cherry Valley, in the county of Montgomery, and State of New York, having returned from *exile*, find ourselves destitute of our church officers, viz: deacons and elders. In consequence of our difficulties, and other congregations in similar circumstances, our Legislature thought proper to pass a law for the relief of these, viz: 'An act to incorporate all religious societies,' passed April 6th, 1784. In compliance of said act we proceeded follows:

"ADVERTISEMENT.

"At a meeting of a respectable number of the old inhabitants of Cherry Valley, it was agreed upon that an advertisement should be set up, to give notice to all the former inhabitants that are returned to their respective habitations, to meet at the *meeting-house yard* on Tuesday, the fifth day of April next, at ten o'clock, before noon, then and there to choose trustees, who shall be a body corporate for the purpose of taking care of the temporalities of their respective Presbyterian congregation, agreeable to an act of the Legislature of the State of New York, passed April sixth, one thousand seven hundred and eighty-four.

SAMUEL CLYDE,
Justice of the Peace.

Cherry Valley, March 19*th*, 1785."

"*Cherry Valley, April* 5*th*, 1785.

"1st. The congregation being met agreeable to the above advertisement, proceeded as follows, viz: The congregation having no minister, nor elders, or deacons, at present, by reason of death and removal of such in the late war, we, the people at large, did nominate and elect the following two members of the congregation to be the returning officers and judges of the qualification of the electors of said meeting:

Col. Samuel Campbell,
William Dickson.

"2d. Proceeded as follows at the said meeting, and have nominated Col. Samuel Clyde, John Campbell, Jr., and James Wilson, to be the trustees for said congregation. The trustees appointed James Cannon as clerk for said board."

"*Cherry Valley, April* 5*th*, 1785.

"At a meeting of the inhabitants of Cherry Valley this day, the undermentioned were elected trustees for the Presbyterian congregation:

Samuel Clyde, Esq.
John Campbell, Jr.
James Wilson.

"*Electors' Names.*—Robert Shankland, William Thompson, Samuel Ferguson, James Moore, Jr., John Campbell, Jr., Hugh Mitchell, William Gault, James Cannon, Samuel Campbell, Jr., Samuel Clyde, Esq., Samuel Campbell, William Dickson, James Dickson, Daniel McCollum, John McKillip, Israel

Wilson, Luther Rich, James Wilson, Thomas Whitaker, Benjamin Dickson, John Dunlop."

"*Cherry Valley, April 5th,* 1785.

"To all whom it doth or may concern, Greeting: We, Samuel Campbell and William Dickson, returning officers, by virtue of the law of this State, entitled an act to enable all the religious denominations in this State to appoint trustees, who shall be a body corporate for the purpose of taking care of the temporalities of their respective congregations, and for other purposes therein mentioned; passed the sixth day of April, one thousand seven hundred and eighty-four, of the Presbyterian congregation of Cherry Valley, in the county of Montgomery, do hereby certify that Samuel Clyde, John Campbell Jr., and James Wilson, were duly and legally elected trustees of said congregation, *and that the said trustees and their successors shall forever hereafter be a body corporate, and be called, distinguished, and known by the name and title of Trustees of the Presbyterian Church in Cherry Valley, in the County of Montgomery.*

"Given under our hands and seals this fifth day of April, one thousand seven hundred and eighty-five.

SAMUEL CAMPBELL. [L.S.]
WILLIAM DICKSON. [L.S.]"

Measures were soon after taken for building a church edifice, but it was not completed until some years after. The plan adopted seems to have been to sell pew ground, and with the proceeds to erect the building, each purchaser of pew ground stipulating to construct his own pew thereon, according to a uniform plan, after the building should be enclosed. The purchaser of pew ground was to pay partly in money, and partly in produce at the market price. Many of my hearers will recollect the old church, with its square, high-back pews, which occupied a part of the burying-ground, or *meeting-house yard*, as it is styled in the foregoing proceedings, and which was taken down about twelve or thirteen years ago, when the present Presbyterian church edifice was erected.

The meeting of the inhabitants of Cherry Valley on the 5th of April, 1785, is deserving of particular attention. The remnant of the *ancient* inhabitants, as they styled themselves, had returned to their former homes. They had returned, they say, from *exile*. The long and bloody war through which they had passed, had thinned their ranks and whitened the heads, and furrowed the cheeks of the survivors. They had once more a home, but it was again a forest home.

The wild beast had made its lair amid the ruins of their former dwellings. The briar, the thistle and the sapling grew rank upon their garden spots. In the autumn of 1784 a few log huts had been built, but in the spring of 1785, when this meeting was called, there was no building in the settlement where the inhabitants could assemble together. They met, therefore, like their fathers, under the open heavens.

The place where they gathered together was hallowed ground. It had been set apart for the burial of their dead. The graves of their kindred and friends were round about them. It was the place which had been consecrated by their patriotism, for there stood their little fort.

On that same spot the inhabitants assembled together and organized anew, on the 5th day of April, 1785, that Presbyterian society which has continued to this day.

The first regular pastor was settled in 1796, and he was our reverend and distinguished guest,* who has this day honored our little valley with his presence, and who, nearly half a century ago, commenced here his sacred ministrations, and preached here the gospel to our fathers. Long may his valuable life be spared to the church, and to the literary institution over which he has long presided with so much ability and success.

From 1785 down to the present time, our valley has not been signalized by any remarkable changes. The increase of population has been gradual though constant. It has not increased in this town and county as in that vast country west, which has since that period sprung into being, and is now teeming with millions of people. Our own little valley has contributed to swell that western tide, and she numbers there many engaged in the various pursuits of life, and among the learned professions many who received here their academical or professional education.

Of the first settlers, the late Col. Samuel Campbell was the last survivor. Of his character I shall not speak at length, but I may be permitted to say that

* Rev. Dr. Nott, President of Union College.

he was a true patriot and an excellent citizen. He served in the French war, and was with Sir William Johnson at Fort Edward in 1757, at the time of the massacre at Fort William Henry. During the stormy period of the Revolution he was an active and efficient friend of his country, and at its close found himself stripped of most of his property. Again he commenced his laborious life, and lived to see a large and prosperous family around him. He was but three years old when he came with his father to this town in 1741. He closed his eventful life in September, 1824, at the age of 86.

While he was the last of the first settlers, his aged consort, who died a few years since, at the age of 92, may be said to have been the last survivor of the female actors in the Revolutionary drama of our valley.

She was born near the Giant's Causeway in Ireland, and when about ten years of age she removed with her father, Matthew Cannon, to this country. Her settlement, her marriage, her heroic fortitude and attachment to her country, her long and severe Indian captivity, are circumstances upon which I need not dwell; her friends and her descendants cherish her memory with ardent affection.

Col. Samuel Clyde was an able and efficient coworker in the Revolutionary struggle. He was a stern and inflexible patriot, and exerted a large influence in this district of country. He was appointed the first justice of the peace after the war. He, too, in in his Revolutionary toils, was aided and supported by his courageous and patriotic wife.

John Moore was another sterling man. While nature had been sparing in her physical gifts, she had endowed him with a strong and vigorous intellect, which had been well cultivated, considering the circumstances in which he was placed.

Of the Rev. Samuel Dunlop I have already spoken. He was an educated man, and for nearly forty years ministered to the early settlers.

At the time of the massacre his family were slain. He alone with one daughter escaped. Under the protection of an Indian chief he stood and beheld the destruction of his earthly hopes, his home, and the homes of his friends, melt away with the flames.

> "Calm, opposite, the Christian father rose;
> Pale on his venerable brow its rays
> Of martyr light the conflagration throws;
> One hand upon his lovely child he lays.
> * * * * *
> He for his bleeding country prays to Heaven—
> Prays that the men of blood themselves may be forgiven."

He survived the massacre but a short time. The misfortunes of that day carried down his grey hairs with sorrow to the grave.

Of the brave and determined Captain Robert M'Kean, what shall we say; of him who knew no danger and feared no man; who challenged to the combat the great chieftain and captain of the Six Nations, Jospeh Brant Thayendanagea? What shall we say of the eccentric though fearless Robert Shankland, who defended his house single-handed, with the exception of his son,* a lad of 14, against a consid-

---

* The late Thomas Shankland, of Cooperstown.

erable body of Indians, and who abandoned it only when it was about to be consumed over him by the flames? Where are they all, with the Gaults and the Dicksons, and the Ramseys and the Wilsons, who first planted here the seeds of civilization? These are questions of a solemn nature, which crowd themselves upon our minds upon occasions like the present. The century has rolled away and left its impress for good or for evil. Of the early settlers not one survives. Their children and their children's children occupy the places of some, and the voices of strangers are heard in the dwellings of others. They have all been gathered to their resting-places, and the ashes of most of them sleep quietly in yonder grave-yard. The clods of the valley are upon them, to be removed only at the general resurrection.

"The breezy call of incense-breathing morn,
The swallow twittering from her straw-built shed,
The cock's shrill clarion and the echoing horn,
No more shall rouse them from their lowly bed."

In the last ten years, what ravages has death made in our little valley! I miss, amid the scenes of my childhood, many of the familiar faces of those who once greeted my return to the home of my fathers. They are also numbered with the great host of the departed, and their places are fast filling with those who knew them not. Among the leading men we might mention the elder and younger Drs. White, both eminent physicians; Col. James Cannon; Isaac Seelye, Esq., and James O. Morse, Esq., both able lawyers; Jesse Johnson, Erastus Johnson, William C.

Dickson, William Story, Alfred Crafts, with many others who but a day since were living, and whose faces it seems as if I ought now to see before me.

James O. Morse, Esq. always took a deep interest in the history of this place, and in the character of its early inhabitants. He was born in Marlboro', in the county of Middlesex, Massachusetts, in 1788, and removed with his parents, when five years of age, to the county of Oneida, in this State, and when that county was almost a wilderness. Familiar as he was with the biographies of most of the frontier inhabitants who had in any way distinguished themselves, his conversation in relation to such subjects was peculiarly interesting and instructive. Many years ago he spoke to me of this anniversary, and had his life been spared he would have taken a deep interest in the proceedings of this day.

Allow me to mention another name connected directly with the first settlement of Cherry Valley; I mean Deacon John Gault. Humble was his sphere of life. Poverty, and many of the ills which flesh is heir to, sickness and decrepitude, were his portion on the earth. But with a Christian spirit which rose above them all, he drank with cheerfulness the cup given him to drink in life, and looked forward with peace and joy to that better world where sorrow and sighing are no more; where the wicked cease from troubling, and the weary are at rest. Who has not observed his cheerful and contented countenance, as he entered the sanctuary on a Sabbath morn, leaning on his staff, his only aid while plodding along over the tedious miles which intervened between his residence and that sanctuary? Who has not listened to his truly eloquent and appropriate prayers? If he was a Christian, he was also a patriot. This day he would have delighted to honor. But he, too, our old and familiar friend, has been gathered to his fathers in peace. His virtues should be imitated, for they were great, and it is but fitting that on this occasion this passing tribute should be paid to his memory.

We miss also many others who commenced with us the race of life. A part of them still live, and are pursuing their various occupations either in our own wide-spread country, or in distant lands. Many of them also have gone the way of all the living. Some died at home in the presence of their friends, and sleep now quietly beside those who gave them being. Others have been cut off in the prime of life, and have fallen far away from their kindred; and one,* endeared to many of us by her talents, her piety, and her moral courage, has recently departed, and her remains repose in the cemetery of the Nestorian Christians, within the sacred precincts of the first Christian Church planted by the Magi of Persia, and within the confines of that city in Central Asia, where the far-famed Zoroaster, in ages gone by, first lit up the fires of philosophy.

We might add many other names to the list. As we run over the catalogue of departed relatives and friends, we are forcibly reminded how frail and brittle is the cord which binds us to life. In the morning we see

* Mrs. Grant, adopted daughter of Dr. William Campbell, of Cherry Valley, and late missionary at Oroomiah, Persia.

our friends around us, and in health, and ere the sun goes down, the golden bowl is broken at the cistern, the dust returns to the dust from whence it was taken, and the spirit unto God who gave it.

Of this large assembly now before me, in all human probability not one will open his eyes upon the morning of the 4th of July, 1940. Long ere that, even the inscriptions upon our tombstones may be obliterated, and our descendants may look in vain for the green hillocks which mark our resting-places.

But as those who gave us being, labored and toiled for our best interests, so our duty is to transmit to those who shall come after us, the inheritance which we have received, of a free government, religious liberty, and all the blessings of civilization. To discharge that duty successfully, we should, as far as it is in our power, labor to advance the cause of virtue and education, and in this respect to follow in the footsteps of our fathers.

The age in which we live, is an age of bustle, toil and enterprise. But it is by no means a merely useful or a superficial age. The great principles of civil liberty, of the rights of conscience, and of freedom of opinion, were never better understood, or more practically enforced.

It is an age, too, when much is required of us all. Yes, of us, a part and parcel of that great Anglo-Saxon race, which now bids fair to carry our own native language and its literature over a great part of the world. Over all the North American continent—along the shores of the Pacific, in the West Indies, in Great Britain, over the eastern coast of Africa, at the

Cape of Good Hope, throughout many of the islands of the Pacific, and along the southern part of Asia, the language which we speak is fast spreading itself, and bids fair to become in these regions the only language. Like Aaron's rod it is swallowing up the rest.

What changes have been produced during the last hundred years! Society has been revolutionized throughout the greater part of the civilized world. The political elements of all Europe have been violently agitated, and though the forms of government have not been materially altered, the freedom of the citizen has been in many instances greatly enlarged. In our own country, the changes, as we run over them with a rapid glance, appear to have been magical. Our own Empire State, which in 1740 was an English colony, and numbering little more than one hundred thousand souls, now tells her children by millions. The scattered English colonies of North America, then feeble, and with some million and a half of people, stretching for thousands of miles along the sea-board, and looking up to England for support and protection, as infant children to a mother, now present the proud spectacle of a united nation, standing in the front rank, with her canvass whitening every sea, with vast resources, with gigantic internal improvements in the separate States, and with nearly twenty millions of freemen reposing in security beneath the folds of her star-spangled banner.

Could we be permitted to draw aside the curtain which veils futurity and look into coming years—could we cause to pass before us, as a moving panorama, our country as it will present itself a hundred years hence, what an interesting view should we behold! For myself, I can but believe that we shall continue a united people, that the strong ties of interest which have hitherto bound us together, will continue unbroken, and be strengthened by the continually increasing facilities of communication between the distant parts of our widely extended country. In that event this nation, judging from the past, will in all probability occupy the greater part of all North America; will number at least fifty millions of inhabitants, and stand in the van of the civilized nations of the earth.

We are here a small community, and our influence and our efforts may not be widely felt; but while we live, we can labor in our various circles to promote peace and harmony among the different States of our Union, and, dying, we can leave the injunction to our children. We can urge upon them to look back upon their common descent, to consider their common inheritance, and to look forward to a common destiny.

And standing here, and looking back upon the century which has just ended, and upon its history, which is certain; and looking forward to the century before us, whose history is uncertain; may I not in the name of this assembly invoke and enjoin the rising generation, our children, and our children's children, to preserve unimpaired the institutions which we commit to them, and to maintain unbroken our glorious Union?

To them I would say, as you enter into possession of this goodly land; as you walk forth and look upon the hill and upon the valley, upon the river rolling in power, and upon the brook that sparkles at your feet; as you listen to the sighing of the breeze as it moves gently through the forest, and to the music of the feathered songsters, as they warble forth their notes of praise—when the breath of the morning fans you, and you inhale the scented air as it comes to you over the green meadow and the opening flower—remember that these blessings, though in some degree common to all mankind, are no less the special gift to you from your Creator, and that for the same blessings your fathers returned thanks to the great Giver of them all.

As you enter upon the glorious inheritance of civil and religious liberty, upon the blessings and enjoyments of Christianity and civilization, and behold the proud monuments of your country's greatness, may you remember that in by-gone times your ancestors toiled and sacrificed their property and their lives in the purchase of that inheritance, and that they thus consecrated it by their tears, their prayers, and their blood!

We commit then that inheritance to your keeping. It is your as well as our birthright. And may he who at the close of another hundred years shall be permitted to stand up and deliver over to his fellow-citizens the record of that century, be enabled to say, as we can this day, Blessed be the land of our birth, and blessed be the memory, and honored be the names of those who have entrusted that inheritance to us!

Index